ISRAEL MY INHERITANCE

Persecuted Messianic Jews Cry Out for Justice and Reform

ISRAEL MY INHERITANCE

Persecuted Messianic Jews Cry Out for Justice and Reform

RAYMOND ROBERT FISCHER

CREATION HOUSE

Israel My Inheritance by Raymond Robert Fischer
Published by Creation House Books
A Charisma Media Company
600 Rinehart Road
Lake Mary, Florida 32746
www.charismamedia.com

Design Director: Bill Johnson
Cover design by David Coddington

Visit the author's website: www.olimpublications.com

Library of Congress Control Number: 2011921018
International Standard Book Number: 978-1-61638-451-7

First Edition

11 12 13 14 15 — 987654321

Printed in the United States of America

Contents

For I will take you from among the nations, gather you out of all countries, and bring you into your own land. Then I will sprinkle clean water on you, and you shall be clean; I will cleanse you from all your filthiness and from all your idols. I will give you a new heart and put a new spirit within you; I will take the heart of stone out of your flesh and give you a heart of flesh. I will put My Spirit within you and cause you to walk in My statutes, and you will keep My judgments and do them. Then you shall dwell in the land that I gave to your fathers; you shall be My people, and I will be your God.

[EZEKIEL 36:24–28, NKJV]

Dedication

For the heart-wrenching sorrow and profound disappointment they were unjustly forced to endure, I dedicate this book to the incalculable very great number of ethnically Jewish sons and daughters of our fathers Abraham, Isaac, and Yakov who faithfully answered the biblical call to take up their inheritance in the Land of Israel only to be rejected, without due process, by the government they sought to embrace, solely because of their religious worldview that Yeshua is the Holy One, the promised Messiah, their Lord and their God.

It is with enduring love, deepest gratitude, and profound respect that I further dedicate this book to my Gentile brother and sister, Ken and Margie Crowell, who opened the door and lit the flame that called us home to the Land. It was Ken who gave me the "carrot" of employment, and Margie who encouraged me to make Aliyah and explained the profound, multi-faceted meaning of this new and life-changing opportunity and commitment.

ACKNOWLEDGMENTS

MY PROFOUND THANKS to those very special dear ones without whose dedication and faithful support this book could not have come forth. To Advocate Michael Decker and his assistant John Moraga for their tireless and meticulous efforts to ensure the accuracy and realism of the legal issues and courtroom drama;

...to Robert Crysler, copy editor and teacher, who tirelessly and skillfully applied his great talent to each of its several successive drafts;

...to Dr. William Eldridge, my dear friend and respected fellow author whose many suggestions kept my polemics in check and this writing on course.

Finally, to Donna Jean Goade Fischer, my darling, greatly loved wife of fifty-one years, who never tired of responding to my unceasing calls for her always incisive "first take" on what I had just written. For her untiring patience, encouragement, sensitivity and loving care, and most of all, for the great love and the many dreams we have shared and seen miraculously fulfilled by His grace during these glorious eighteen years we have shared together here in the Land of Israel—our inheritance.

FOREWORD

DR. BOB FISCHER's examination of the plight of Messianic Jews in Israel is commendable. *Israel My Inheritance* is a work that sheds much needed light on the dilemma of the little known persecution of the Messianic community. Using the fictitious journey of Hannah, a Holocaust survivor, as a historically accurate backdrop, Dr. Fischer exposes the lack of transparency of the Ministry of the Interior and various discriminatory acts against certain religious communities that the Ministry of the Interior deems to be a threat to the nation of Israel.

Under the ambiguous authority of the Ministry of the Interior, Messianic Jews have been unjustly denied entry, citizenship, and at times their basic freedom of religion. The ministry often defaults on its "discretion" when it makes controversial decisions against Messianic Jews. Israel's only substantive law that regulates a person exercising his religion is the prohibition against proselytizing minors and financially inducing conversions. This caveat is often abused and used as an umbrella regulation to prevent people from entering the country and to deny them government services.

Israel faces a lack of judicial precedent when presented with legal battles concerning citizenship. There is no law against a person's private conviction, but the Law of Return (as interpreted by the Israeli Supreme Court) does not recognize those Messianic Jews who have inarguable Jewish ethnicity as being Jewish on the sole basis of their subscription to the gospel and denies them the opportunity to acquire citizenship. In fact, this law does not recognize anybody as Jewish if they have changed their religion: Hindus, Buddhists, Taoists, Muslims, Baha'i, etc. However, this provision has only been selectively enforced against Messianic Jews when they have applied for citizenship.

Dr. Fischer explores these issues in *Israel My Inheritance*. The legal battles only seem to perpetuate, and the discrimination only seems to spread throughout Israel. *Israel My Inheritance* is a bold initial effort to bring attention to this little known practice of religious discrimination. May Providence provide other works like this.

—Michael Decker
Senior Legal Activist, Jerusalem Institute of Justice
Jerusalem, Israel

Preface
Author's Note

I AM A JEW, the first son of a Jewish mother and father whose entirely Jewish ethnicity can be traced for several generations.

My mother's parents were religiously observant Jews; my father's parents, like my father after them, were forced to suppress their Jewishness owing to strong anti-Semitic employment policies and practices that greatly threatened their respective means of livelihood.

On the eighth day of my life, I was circumcised in a rabbinical Jewish ceremony at the insistence of my maternal grandmother, whose memory I adore for having thus kept the flame of my Jewish heritage alive for me during all the days of my life.

Both of my parents expressed their belief in the basic understandings of Judaism; they led me to my own personal understanding and acceptance of this foundation of my faith. Even so, I grew up in a Gentile Christian–dominated society where I very early yearned to learn more about the Lord God of Israel.

While I investigated various Christian churches and studied Judeo-Christian theology, doctrine, history, and tradition in a postgraduate Christian setting, I have never been "ordained." Moreover, I have never been a member of a "Christian church." In short, I have never "changed my religion," nor am I a "member of another religion."

Let me hasten to add that my lifelong seeking of truth has led me to fully accept and embrace another Jew, Yeshua, as the Jewish Messiah promised in the Tenach (Old Testament), the one who was worshiped during the early first century in the Upper Room on Mount Zion, exclusively, at first, by other Jews.

These first Jewish "believers" were known as "the Way." Several decades later, their understandings, doctrine, and practices became the foundation of the Gentile Christian church and all subsequent expressions of Christianity.

Western Christianity has its roots in the Roman Catholic Church planted by the apostle Paul circa A.D. 62–68. The Eastern church, as I have proposed in my earlier work *The Door Where It Began* (2005), began much earlier, in the Galilee, and quickly spread throughout the Decapolis and then further east, long before the fourth century when Emperor Constantine founded the Byzantine Church in what now is modern-day Turkey.

Sadly, both the Western and Eastern expressions of "Christianity" were quickly Hellenized and otherwise variously polluted by those pagan understandings and practices of the widespread, mostly Gentile people groups to whom these originally Jewish understandings were first introduced. It should therefore not be surprising that today there are more than nineteen thousand denominations within the worldwide church, and the occasional call for unity among them has long remained a highly elusive hope.

Having said this, let me be very clear about where I am "coming from" in my personal understandings as I have endeavored to share them in my various writings. In my book *The Ways of the Way* (2009) I included a detailed study of the theology, writings, and worship practices of the first Jewish believers in Yeshua. My purpose was to provide detailed guidance for both Jewish and Gentile believers of today who seek to emulate these first Jewish believers by establishing full and/or home congregations based upon the Way's early model.

In seeking to worship the Jewish Messiah, Yeshua, as He was first worshiped by Jews, I am by no means coming against the church. It was, after all, through the good offices of Christian education that I learned about the teachings of my distinctly Jewish Messiah. Without the church who kept the gospel of Yeshua alive for us all, I would most likely still be seeking the truth, which today is the light of my life.

Moreover, neither do I in any way mean to offend or come against any of my fellow Jews who do not share my own very deep Messianic convictions and faith. On a personal level, I have come to greatly love my totally committed mainline Orthodox Jewish brothers and sisters with whom my wife, Donna, and I have lived closely and in many ways shared our lives during these past eighteen years. After all, they, like we, are among God's chosen people, which would explain why we have found them the most loving, kind, faithful, and caring dear ones we have encountered during our already long and well-traveled lives.

While I do not embrace some of the teachings of the rabbis, principally those that directly conflict with Holy Scripture, I do embrace all Jews, irrespective of the several varied belief systems that they represent, as my respected and dearly loved brothers and sisters who, like me, were blessed to be born as blood descendants of Abraham, Isaac, and Jacob. We all worship the same God, the Lord God of Israel. We are all co-inheritors of the Holy Land of Israel.

However, let me be perfectly clear. I do have a serious problem with some of the understandings and practices of a very small (7 percent) fundamentalist minority of "ultra-Orthodox" or Haredi. They have managed to advance their own narrow agenda through political maneuvers that do not reflect the mainstream opinion in Israel and conflict with the core values of democracy. For example, they have used this position of ill-gained political power to produce an amendment to the Law of Return, which would entirely banish Messianic Jews from Israel, solely on the basis of our religious worldview. Moreover, they have long waged a continuing war of harassment and persecution against those Messianic Jews who are already citizens.

It is my most profound prayer and greatest hope that one day all ethnically rooted Jews in Israel and those who seek to take up their biblical inheritance here will be allowed to do so in peace and with loving acceptance.

Prologue

The Word of God

From the Torah

> For you are a holy people to the Lord your God; the Lord your God has chosen you to be a people for Himself, a special treasure above all the peoples on the face of the earth. The Lord did not set His love on you nor choose you because you were more in number than any other people, for you were the least of all peoples; but because the Lord loves you, and because He would keep the oath which He swore to your fathers, the Lord has brought you out with a mighty hand, and redeemed you from the house of bondage, from the hand of Pharaoh king of Egypt.
>
> —Deuteronomy 7:6–8

The Laws of Men

From the rabbis

> Israel hath sinned—Even though the people have sinned, they are still "Israel." Israel is the name of honor for the people when faithful to God. Thus, people say, "A myrtle, though it stands among reeds, is still a myrtle, and it is so called."
>
> —Talmud, Tractate Sanhedrin Folio 44a

> According to the Talmud, even if a convert (to Judaism) later regrets having undergone conversion and reverts back to his or her former religion, he or she remains halakhically Jewish (Yevamot 47b). In this respect, the status of such a convert is no different from that of a renegade Jew-by-birth who, according to the Talmud, "despite having sinned, is still one of Israel" (Sanhedrin 44a).[1]

> In the world of Hebrew jurisprudence there is no force capable of changing a Jew...into a gentile. Even if the Jew were to desire this, and even if every Christian priest in the world were to baptize such Jew into Christianity, he would remain a Jew. Moreover, if a convert to Judaism

wishes to deny his Judaism, he will not be able to do so and return to his previous faith. He is and will always remain a Jew, and there is no way in the world to take this away from him.[2]

—RABBIS BRALI, TZARFATI, AND BASS
JUSTICES OF THE HIGHEST ISRAELI RABBINICAL COURT

From the Government of Israel

THE STATE OF ISRAEL will be open for Jewish immigration and for the Ingathering of the Exiles; it will foster the development of the country for the benefit of all its inhabitants; it will be based on freedom, justice and peace as envisaged by the prophets of Israel; it will ensure complete equality of social and political rights to all its inhabitants irrespective of religion, race or sex; it will guarantee freedom of religion, conscience, language, education and culture; it will safeguard the Holy Places of all religions; and it will be faithful to the principles of the Charter of the United Nations.[3]

—FROM THE DECLARATION OF THE ESTABLISHMENT
OF THE STATE OF ISRAEL, MAY 14, 1948

From the United Nations Universal Declaration of Human Rights

Everyone has the right to freedom of thought, conscience and religion; this right includes freedom to change his religion or belief, and freedom, either alone or in community with others and in public or private, to manifest his religion or belief in teaching, practice, worship, and observance.[4]

From the Law of Return (5710–1950) and as amended (5730–1970)

Every Jew has the right to come to this country as an oleh [new immigrant]...

An oleh's [immigrant's] visa shall be granted to every Jew who has expressed his desire to settle in Israel, unless the Minister of Immigration is satisfied that the applicant is engaged in an activity directed against the Jewish people; or is likely to endanger public health or the security of the State.

...The rights of a Jew under this Law...are also vested in a child and a grandchild of a Jew, the spouse of a Jew, the spouse of a child of a Jew and the spouse of a grandchild of a Jew, except for a person who has been a Jew and has voluntarily changed his religion.

...For the purposes of this Law, "Jew" means a person who was born of a Jewish mother or has become converted to Judaism and who is not a member of another religion.[5]

Introduction

David Ben-Gurion and the other founding fathers of the modern-day State of Israel could not have made it clearer. The long-held dream of a homeland for all Jews had at last become a reality. Never mind that the nascent Jewish nation was surrounded even then by powerful and determined enemies who sought its immediate annihilation and the death of all Jews; the dream of Israel had come thus far, and those who would become its first Jewish citizens, richly blessed by their God, would miraculously consummate its birth.

Even so, there wasn't time to memorialize the particulars of how the new state would be governed. The angry hoards set upon its destruction attacked relentlessly from all sides, even before the ink was dry on its "Declaration of Establishment."

While David Ben-Gurion and the others proclaimed their intention to eventually write and ratify a constitution on the Western model, thus establishing a government of the people, by the people, and for the people with a system of checks and balances and the guarantee of basic human rights, these matters were necessarily deferred until the enemies of the new state were defeated, the borders were secured and blessed, and peace had been restored to the region.

One need only minimally search the pages and channels of today's world media to learn the sad truth: none of these three seemingly ever evasive goals have yet been achieved. Instead, during the ensuing sixty-two years since Ben-Gurion declared its founding, the State of Israel has been marred by nine costly wars perpetrated by its Arab neighbors who remain resolved to kill all Jews and wipe Israel from the face of the earth. Moreover, the entire world is still quibbling about the specifics of Israel's final borders, and even more devastating, the hope for regional peace has been replaced by the globally held expectation that a devastating regional war appears imminent. Thus, it isn't difficult to indefinitely defer the nearly forgotten vision; the creation and ratification of a foundational constitution has been denigrated into a far distant and faded dream.

From the outset, the enormous vacuum created by the absence of such a constitution and democratic form of government that would naturally follow was quickly filled by an ad hoc cobbling together of disconnected administrative elements that have evolved into what is today the State of Israel's highly dysfunctional coalition form of government.

Three branches of government with an often startling imbalance of power leave a population with an ambiguous understanding of its functionality.

The Executive Branch is headed by a prime minister who, as the head of the political party that managed to achieve that closest to a majority of "mandates" (seats in the Knesset) during a national election, is charged by a titular, otherwise powerless, president to form a governing coalition. This governing coalition is comprised of selected politicians taken from a priority listing of potential members of the Knesset of his own party and those likewise appointed proportionately by other less successful minority parties. The result of this process is a governing legislature created and dominated by self-interest political horse trading with seemingly little or no priority given to the national interest.

From the very outset, a variously named ultra-Orthodox religious, minority political party succeeded in aligning itself with the much larger, near majority party so as to superimpose its own agenda on the direction of the new government in exchange for its participation therein. Such has been the political reality from the days of the state's formation with only two very short interruptions when a religious party's participation was not sought or required to form a majority in the Knesset.

The second branch of the Israeli governmental system, the Legislature, is comprised of a fixed number of 120 members of the Knesset, the appointment of which is based directly upon the relative electoral success of the political parties who gained a minimum of 2 percent of the total votes cast in a national election. These members of the Knesset, like the prime minister, are not chosen directly by the general population but rather are appointed from a party list based mostly upon seniority and/or other political considerations. During the most recent election, in February 2009, an astounding thirty-four political parties fielded lists of candidates. Of these, only twelve parties gained more than 2 percent of the total votes cast and thus were entitled to appoint members to the Knesset from their respective political lists. Interestingly, even though the centrist party, Kadima, received one more "mandate" (seat in the Knesset) than right-wing Likud, the president (Shimon Peres) called upon

Benjamin Netanyahu (Likud) to form a coalition since he felt that Netanyahu would be best able to cobble together a majority among the twelve successful parties who had "mandates" to trade—something akin to the ultimate ownership of the houses and hotels in the board game of Monopoly. In the end, the only way Netanyahu was able to succeed in forming a government was to include Shas (ultra-Orthodox), and, as will later be explained in some detail, the political price demanded by Shas for inclusion of its eleven "mandates" was politically very high indeed.

Unlike Israel's Executive Branch or Legislature, her Judiciary's basic laws are not "reinforced."[1] While the Executive Branch and the Legislature require a majority in the Knesset to make amendments to their basic laws, Judiciary basic laws can be usurped without a majority. This inevitably creates an imbalance of power in the Israeli government. Therefore, if decisions of the Supreme Court (the High Court) and its related orders are not to the liking of the Central Government's Ministry to which they are directed, then, historically, such ministries have seen fit to legislatively change/alter or even simply ignore such orders of the court.

Israel is generally known to be the only "democracy" in the Middle East.[2] However, there is plenty of room for improvement when this Israeli form of government is viewed against the Jeffersonian model. The guarantee of basic, inalienable human rights, such as freedom of religion, speech, assembly, etc., lies at the very heart of any government that would dare to describe itself as founded on democratic principles. While such rights have been enacted by the Knesset, some of these rights have only been legislated via several basic laws that continue to await the great day when they will be incorporated into what remains the writing and ratification of a perpetually elusive constitution. In the meantime, such basic human rights have routinely been selectively unenforced by the central government, along with associated orders of the Judiciary, whenever it has been inconvenient and/or politically inexpedient for the concerned ministry or ministries to honor them.

Such has been the historical treatment by the Ministry of the Interior when dealing with otherwise qualified, ethnically Jewish applicants who have sought to become citizens of the State of Israel as provided for by the Israel Law of Return, those whose only disqualifying "offense" has been to embrace Yeshua (Jesus) as their Messiah.

Again, from the founding of the state, except for two brief periods, the Minister of Interior has been appointed from an ultra-Orthodox party, which has maneuvered itself into this position of each successive government and then used this high office to wantonly and inviolably impose its own highly prejudicial religious understandings and judgments upon the entire citizenry. In short, those Jews who have described themselves as religiously Hindi, Buddhist, atheist, or as adherents to any other understanding, except those who have dared to embrace Yeshua as Messiah, have routinely been accepted as citizens, while those who have embraced Yeshua have been routinely rejected.

Moreover, the tiny minority (less than 1/10 of 1 percent) or some five thousand such Messianic (born-again) Jews in Israel have become the perpetual, unconscionable targets for persecution by the Ministry of the Interior working in concert with the Shomrei Israel[3] (Guardians of Israel), a huge "anti-missionary" organization dedicated to denying the privacy, to harassing, and to revoking the basic government services, such as passports, etc., and even in the extreme, the very citizenship of the citizens who have fallen into their sights. Michael Decker,[4] an Israeli attorney whose practice is focused in a large part on protecting the rights of such Messianic Jewish citizens, writes:

> The Law of Return, in its current wording, grants every Jew the right to immigrate to Israel. Moreover, the Law of Return also grants the family members of Jews the right to immigrate to Israel, even if they themselves are not Jewish. As a result, a situation has been created whereby, as of today, there are many citizens in Israel who are related to Jews, yet hold to different religious beliefs. There are also citizens who are devoid of any religion whatsoever. What's more, among mixed families who immigrated into Israel, there are many people who have grown up with a mixed religious worldview. Nonetheless, the uniting factor is that all of the above mentioned are Israeli citizens.
>
> Lately, a troubling situation has arisen. Certain faithful citizens of the nation of Israel have been receiving letters whereby they have been summoned into the offices of the Ministry of the Interior in order to review their civil status. What was the transgression of those who received these strange letters from the Ministry of the Interior? Have they betrayed the nation? Do they represent a security threat? Have they ever visited an enemy State of Israel? No. Their only transgression was in relation to matters of personal conscience and their religious worldview. More specifically, they belong to minority religious groups in the nation of Israel such as Evangelical Christians, Messianic Jews, and others.
>
> The aforementioned letter of inquiry is not an indictment wherein

> the nation is accusing these people of any offenses. Even for the worst offense, a defendant has the right to receive a proper letter of indictment by which he can properly defend himself and present counter-claims.
>
> In this letter of inquiry, there is no mention that the person receiving the letter has the basic right to be represented by a lawyer. Neither is there any warning that this person's citizenship may be revoked. It is simply stated that this person is being summoned before the Ministry of the Interior in order "to inquire about his/her status."
>
> In many cases, these innocent citizens have appeared before a registration clerk, who then interrogates them about their religious worldviews and thereafter demands that they sign a document, of which they are not even given a copy. These citizens subsequently find themselves in a helpless situation, whereby the Ministry of the Interior will not grant them many basic services, such as the registration of their children in the population registry, the renewal of their passports, the issuing of new identification cards, and in some cases, the Ministry of the Interior even goes so far as to revoke their citizenship and deport them from Israel.[5]

This currently ongoing veritable "witch hunt" being perpetrated by the government of Israel upon its own citizenry is not simply a modern-day phenomenon, nor did it begin with the founding of the state in 1948. Rather, the roots of this deep-seated religious discrimination extend all the way back to the early first century when the first Jewish believers in Yeshua assembled in the Upper Room on Mount Zion to worship their risen Lord.

There were three main religious sects operating at that pinnacle moment in history: the Sadducees, the Pharisees, and the Essenes. The Sadducees attended to the affairs of the temple, and when the temple was destroyed in A.D. 70, the Sadducees essentially vanished along with it.

The Pharisees relocated at first to Yavne where, under the leadership of Rabbi Akiva and others, they emerged as the redactors of the Mishna and later the Talmud, which, along with other commentaries, are known today as the "Oral Law" and otherwise as the "Laws of Men." These were the progenitors of what has emerged as modern-day rabbinical Judaism, which, in the extreme, has been the source of the militantly anti-Yeshua/anti-Messianic Jewish group that stands in such great opposition to born-again Jews in Israel today.

The book you hold in your hands traces the nonfictional history of religious discrimination and persecution imposed upon Jewish believers in Yeshua from their emergence on Mount Zion in the first century up to modern times. Such anti-Messianic Jewish invective and abusive actions have not been undertaken solely by the Pharisees and, over the ensuing centuries, by their rabbinical religious offspring. Both their respective civil governments and the Christian church have from time to time come against the Messianic Jews in concert with the rabbis and/or for reasons entirely their own. Several representative instances of this often-strenuous opposition are pointed to in the following text.

The unique genre I have chosen for this work begs further explanation. This writing began entirely as a work of nonfiction. But this approach was quickly discarded as unnecessarily polemic. Next, the work took the form of a traditional historical novel. However, this genre was also quickly discarded since the essential historical facts were easily lost and often difficult to separate from their compelling fictional background, thus defeating its underlying purpose. Hence, I have categorized this work as "narrative nonfiction."

Stylistically, nonfiction segments, most often identified as "Hear O Israel" are interjected at various points between segments of the underlying historically accurate fictional backdrop entitled "Hannah's Story" that traces a Holocaust survivor and her family from 1938 Munich to contemporary Israel.

In addition to Hannah Meyers Silberman and her family, the characters Andrew (Drew) Sterling and his wife, Carla, who first appeared in my earlier work *The Door Where It Began*, are reintroduced.

While the story of Hannah Meyers Silberman is populated with fictional characters, the events of their lives are in fact mostly nonfictional and solidly historical. Thus, to help the reader better separate fact from its historical backdrop, I have carefully documented such nonfiction elements with endnote citations.

Finally, I have had a deeply compelling purpose for writing this book. During my eighteen years as a citizen of Israel I have become totally convinced that the extreme religious prejudice of a tiny ultra-Orthodox controlling minority has become deeply entrenched and is eating away at the very fabric and heart of this nation. Moreover, I am fully persuaded that without sweeping electoral reform, this political self-destruction will eventually lead to the State of Israel's tragic undoing and ultimate demise.

Stated differently, the long-standing and continuing religious discrimination and persecution against Israeli Messianic Jews by a tiny minority that has an un-proportional influence is not the underlying problem that demands immediate attention; it is rather the very form and system of the government that permitted the birth of this discrimination and persecution and unwaveringly allows it to continue.

Moreover, I am persuaded that the urgent need for immediate and sweeping electoral reform must be predicated upon creating and adapting a long-suppressed constitution—the rock-solid, foundational law mandating three clearly equal branches of government replete with genuine checks and balances. The creation of such a constitution and the sweeping electoral reform that will follow is of at least equal concern to this nation as the radical Islamic armies that now stand on its every border, poised to attack without notice.

Israel has a mighty, expertly led military that, with God's help, will once again emerge victorious on any given field of battle.

The governmental system of Israel, however, without sweeping electoral reform and a glorious constitution that establishes and guarantees basic human rights for all its citizenry, will most certainly eventually fall into the pit of its own organizational inadequacies, innate corruption, and immoral and excessive political practices.

Chapter 1
Hear O Israel
The Martyrdom of Stephen
(Circa A.D. 35)

Stephen awoke to the cacophony of multiple cocks crowing to greet the new morning as the rising sun peeked over the distant hills of Judea, illuminating the myriad crowded dwellings on Mount Zion that lay just to the east of Herod's temple in the heart of Jerusalem. He yawned deeply and blinked his dark brown eyes into hurried wakefulness so as not to lose a precious moment. Then, arising quickly from the simple straw-filled mat that comprised the only furnishings of his tiny, nondescript hovel situated nearby to what was even then known as the Upper Room, he fell to his knees and continued the solemn prayer he had been praying even as he slept:

> My dear heavenly Father, You rejected the tent of Joseph,
> And You did not choose the tribe of Ephraim,
> But rather You chose the tribe of Judah,
> Mount Zion which You loved.
> And You built Your sanctuary like the heights,
> Like the earth which You have established forever.
> You also chose David, Your servant,
> And took him from the sheepfolds;
> From following the ewes that had young, You brought him
> To shepherd Jacob his people,
> And Israel his inheritance.
> So he shepherded them according to the integrity of his heart,
> And guided them by the skillfulness of his hands.[1]

> And then Father, out of Your unfathomable love, You chose Yeshua, Your only begotten Son, to dwell among us as both God and man. Father, You allowed even me, Your most unworthy servant, to behold Him with my own eyes, to hear Him with my own ears, to walk by His side and to joyfully accept His promise of eternal life.
>
> Holy Father, then You chose those who were to build the foundation

of His body here on earth: James, Peter, John, the other apostles, and all the rest of the inner circle.

Then, wonder of wonders, Lord, despite my great unworthiness, You chose me, Your humble servant, to serve Your body as one of seven *mebaqqerim* [deacons].

You called upon us seven, as well as our sister deaconesses whom You have appointed, to shepherd, disciple, anoint, and baptize those many thousands of our brothers and sisters of Judah who have been called by You to their own salvation through Yeshua, and to thus enter into His body here on earth.

O Lord God of Israel, when Your precious Son, Yeshua, was here with us, He was bitterly opposed by many of our fellow Jews. And now, even these same greatly misled brother Jews, the Cyrenians, Alexandrians, and those from Cilicia and Asia, have been coming against me, persecuting me with threats of death simply because I have been boldly spreading forth the wonderful pure gospel of Yeshua. Father, I am told that the lies about me they have spread forth to the likes of the scribes and elders have now reached the ears of the Sanhedrin, who sit in judgment of all Jews.

Protect me, O Lord, according to Your will, for I seek only to serve You and to glorify Your holy name.

And so it was that God's holy and often unfathomable will became manifest later that very morning as Stephen, on his knees, as was his practice, continued in his constant daily prayer in the courtyards of the temple.

Stephen, a physically well-developed, dark-tanned Jewish man in his early thirties did not struggle or resist, not even for a moment, for he knew by the power of the Holy Spirit who dwelt within him that the two raucous, burly men who pulled him violently to his feet, without even a word of warning or explanation, were guided by the font of all evil, Satan himself. Deep within him Stephen understood, and he was already fully girded for the physical horror that lay just ahead.

A short time later, as he stood before the Sanhedrin, who were to judge him, even as the false charges of blasphemy were set before him, both his accusers and his judges had to shield their faces from the bright, supernaturally generated glow of righteousness that emanated from Stephen's face as if it were the face of an angel.

Even so, he who presided over the council cried out accusingly, "We have heard him speak blasphemous words against Moses and God. Are these things so?"

Stephen responded with an incisive, matter-of-fact summary of his own history and that of his people, from the time Abraham was called to cross over and take possession of the Land to this very moment when he stood before them.

He spoke of Joseph's travail in Egypt and then of his ultimate glory through the power of the Holy Spirit brought forth by his obedience and faithfulness.

He spoke of Moses, chosen, guided, and upheld by God to lead His people out of captivity in Egypt into the Land of their inheritance.

He spoke of God's very presence with His people: first in a tabernacle in the wilderness, then in a wondrous temple, and finally of the coming of the Messiah who had been promised to His people as spoken of by Moses: "The Lord your God will raise up for you a Prophet like me from your brethren. Him you shall hear."

Then, no longer able to contain the consuming anguish he had long endured, a deep, torturing anguish driven by his fellow Jews' widespread rejection of Yeshua as the promised Messiah, the One he knew so intimately and treasured so totally, Stephen cried out from the depths of his soul:

> You stiff-necked and uncircumcised in heart and ears! You always resist the Holy Spirit; as your fathers did, so do you. Which of the prophets did your fathers not persecute? And they killed those who foretold the coming of the Just One, of whom you now have become the betrayers and murderers, who have received the law by the direction of angels and have not kept it.[2]

The response from his judges was as immediate as it was predictable. When they heard these things, they were cut to the heart and they gnashed with their teeth. But Stephen, totally at peace and full of the Holy Spirit, gazed into heaven and saw the glory of God the Father with Yeshua standing at His right hand. Seemingly oblivious to the physical horror that was about to befall him, innocently and deeply longing to share the glory of heaven he now beheld, he cried out, "Look! I see the heavens opened and the Son of Man standing at the right hand of God!"

However, blood was in the air, and none would listen. Instead, they cried out with a loud voice, stopped their ears to shield themselves from the truth, the very truth they had been led by Satan to believe was blasphemy, and they took Stephen to a place of execution outside the city.

It has been well said that in every group a leader will emerge, and those who were about to stone Stephen symbolically removed their tunics and laid them at the feet of the one who was to be their leader, a young Pharisee named Sha'ul of Tarsus.

One can only speculate whether Sha'ul was the one who cast the first stone that tore into Stephen's flesh, but Luke tells us in the account of this execution that "Sha'ul was consenting to his death." Moreover, Luke goes on to describe Sha'ul's reign of terror perpetrated against those of the Way who had dared to embrace Yeshua: "As for Sha'ul, he made havoc of the church, entering every house, and dragging off men and women, committing them to prison."[3] It was this very same Sha'ul who later, along the road to Damascus where he was going to arrest those among his fellow Jews who had accepted Yeshua, was encountered by Yeshua, physically blinded, eternally redeemed, and eventually made an apostle to the Gentiles by Yeshua Himself.

As for Stephen, the stones fell torturously upon his body until, finally, he called upon his Master: "Lord Yeshua, receive my spirit." Then he knelt down, and filled with God's awesome love and spirit of unconditional forgiveness, he cried out in a loud voice, "Lord, do not charge them with this sin." And when he had said this, he fell asleep.

I have long pondered what might have motivated Sha'ul to embark upon his pre-salvational, murderous campaign against his fellow Jews. As a member of the tiny minority of "born-again" ethnic Jews who have boldly and joyfully taken up our God-given inheritance, after eighteen years as a citizen of the State of Israel, I have concluded that there were multiple reasons that most likely set him on this path.

Sha'ul was first a self-declared Pharisee, a leader of the sect that would evolve into "rabbinical Judaism," the only major expression of traditional Judaism that has survived into modern times. During His walk among us, Yeshua had several direct, strongly critical encounters with the Pharisees of that day with respect to their theological understandings. Yeshua's central issue here, I believe, was the Pharisees' continuing denial of the possibility that the Godhead could be divided and therefore that the promised Messiah could be an equal member thereof with the Father and the Holy Spirit.

Certainly, before his salvation, Sha'ul was motivated and driven by Satan to do all things possible to interfere with the salvational calling of the Way, led by James, Peter, and the rest who were already bringing countless Jewish souls into the body of Yeshua throughout Israel. Luke informs us that three thousand were saved on the Day of Pentecost alone and that others were entering the body each day. From a purely spiritual perspective Satan lost a soul at the very moment a Jew accepted God's truth rather than his own unrelenting lies, and this was something to be overcome.

However, I believe there was another, albeit, parallel, secular motivation that drove Sha'ul in his terrible pursuit of believing Jews. This very same issue continues even today to fuel the deep fear and seemingly boundless opposition of rabbinical Judaism toward their fellow Jews who, otherwise remaining totally "Jewish," have been led to understand that Yeshua is their promised Messiah. Let me explain my thinking on this point.

While there have been several estimates, all highly conjectural, regarding the number of Jews in the world toward the end of the first century A.D., Adolf von Harnack (1851–1930), a well respected German theologian and prominent church historian, reckons that there were 1,000,000 Jews in Syria during the sixties and some 700,000 in what then was still called Israel. To these he adds, what seems to be arbitrarily, another 1,500,000 in "other places," thus estimating that there were in the first century some 3,200,000 Jews in the world.[4] These comprised a plausibly sized minority (2 percent) of the world's then total estimated population of 170,000,000.[5]

Whatever the actual Jewish population may have been at that vital foundational time in the history of my people, they nevertheless were even then a tiny minority with each of its members at least materially and statistically precious. What I am getting to here is that at this time there were two simultaneously emerging Jewish sects, rabbinical Judaism and "the Way" (the first Jewish believers in Yeshua) who were, even then, irreconcilably separated by greatly divergent theological understandings as they mutually struggled to expand their respective influence and body of adherents.

In the very beginning of the Way, following Pentecost, the relatively tiny Upper Room was woefully inadequate in size to accommodate these very first followers of Yeshua. Accordingly, apparently not realizing the implications of doing so, and at the very first considering those of the Way to be simply brother Jews with a different take on messianism, the Pharisees warmly welcomed these brethren into their already existing synagogues where seemingly, at least for a time, they worshiped the Lord God of Israel together.

Sadly, however, this incipient bonding of the two divergent sects quickly began to unravel. On one day alone, three thousand Jewish "bodies" embraced Yeshua and joined the Way; others followed them each day. Considering an assumed total Jewish population of Israel at that time as seven hundred thousand, this rapid growth of the Way posed a considerable problem for their rabbinical brothers. Before the temple was destroyed in 70, and with it the essentially self-implosion of the Sadducees, there were two sources from which this migration to the Way could come. Now, suddenly, there was only one, and the growing numbers involved began to take a painful toll on the newly constituted sect of rabbinical Judaism, which by then had relocated to Yavne, where both their theological agenda and their membership likely became early central concerns. These concerns soon came to a head, and, at least from the perspective of rabbinical Judaism, the battle lines were drawn. As I wrote in my earlier work *The Ways of the Way*:

> Thus, in A.D. 90, some twenty years after the Sanhedrin had moved to Yavne, they finally got around to officially venting their growing hostility toward those whom they called *minim* ("foreigners, sectarians, or apostates"). These were, quite pointedly, for the most part Jews who had embraced Yeshua and in the process of doing so had, according to the Jewish law promulgated by the Pharisee-dominated Sanhedrin, forgone their Jewish ethnicity and heritage in the process.
>
> Toward this end, "Samuel the Lesser," a member of the Sanhedrin, was commissioned to add a nineteenth "blessing" to the Amidah, the central prayer of Jewish liturgy, which came to be called the Birkat haMinim ("blessings for the foreigners"). In its original form, this nineteenth blessing, which was read communally three times each day in every Pharisaic synagogue, cried out from the lips of each congregation:
>
>> *For the renegades let there be no hope, and may the arrogant kingdom soon be rooted out in our days, and the Netzarim [Nazarenes] and the Minim [other sectarian Jews who were then inciting warfare with the Romans] perish as in a moment and be blotted out from the Book of Life and with the righteous may they not be inscribed. Blessed are You, Lord, who humbles the arrogant.*

This "benediction," which was obviously rather a pointed curse on the Nazarenes of the Way, achieved its intended purpose of casting them out of the Pharisaic synagogues since any born-again Jews who attended would be expected to recite a curse upon themselves. Certainly, Yeshua had given them fair warning of the vitriolic opposition that was rising up against them.

> *They will put you out of the synagogues; yes, the time is coming that whoever kills you will think that he offers God service. And these things they will do to you because they have not known the Father nor Me. But these things I have told you, that when the time comes, you may remember that I told you of them.*
>
> —John 16:2[6]

I have begun this writing with an account of the martyrdom of Stephen because, occurring as it did only four years after Yeshua's resurrection, this violent episode in our history codifies the deeply saddening, continuing conflict that has existed between the Jewish followers of Yeshua and their rabbinical brethren from the very beginning.

Other representative episodes in this saga of my born-again Jewish brethren that occurred during the ensuing centuries up to the present time are interspersed throughout the text. My purpose here is to convincingly demonstrate that nothing has significantly changed in this historical conflict between Pharisee-founded rabbinical Judaism and the Messianic Judaism of today that began in the Upper Room as the Way.

Today, in the State of Israel, there is a tiny minority of fewer than five thousand believing Jews, scattered in some one hundred twenty mostly small home congregations, who have been forced to endure continued, often physical, violence at the hands of some of the most radical of their ultra-Orthodox Jewish brethren. They are still regularly cursed in the modern state's synagogues while being aggressively discriminated against by the religiously controlled government that seeks to find a legitimate way to take away their citizenship and expel them from the Land of their biblical inheritance.

While the characters who populate the chapters that follow are mostly fictional, I have done my best to ensure that their interspersed stories present an accurate, biblical, and historical recounting of the believers in Yeshua's journey from the place of Stephen's martyrdom to the Israel of today, the Israel of my inheritance.

Chapter 2
Hannah's Story
Munich
(April 1938)

HANNAH RUTH MEYERS and her beloved Michael Silberman snuggled together on the swing seat of the large, pristine-white gazebo, the central feature of the exquisite and spacious garden set behind the Meyers' massive and elegant four-story private residence at Maria Theresia Strasse 27. It was here, in the very heart of Bogenhausen, the most prestigious neighborhood in the city, they had been born, grown up, and long dreamt of their sweet and lovely future together.

The reflection of the late spring full moon added even more luster to Hannah's already perpetually dancing, very large, dark brown eyes, which were the most compelling feature of her exquisitely beautiful, naturally tanned, classic Semitic face.

Michael was tall, strong bodied, and no less handsome in his own right. He easily reached the nearest branch of many blossom-laden lilac bushes from which he plucked a stem of the heavily fragranced, royal purple floret clusters.

"For you, my darling," he spoke, breaking a mutually self-imposed silence with what to him was a characteristic special softness. How deeply he had grown to adore this exquisite young woman, he reflected, as he placed the impromptu floral offering in her hands, this lovely, precious one whom he had known since their births only one week apart nearly eighteen years ago.

"These are heavenly," Hannah replied appreciatively as she held the stem of clusters to her face taking in their rich fragrance. She leaned toward him and gave him a soft kiss on the cheek.

"That won't do!" he protested as she quickly came into his arms. They kissed deeply until finally they could bear it no more, and she gently pushed him away.

"Dear God!" he protested resignedly, as he struggled to regain control of his deep longing. "How much longer must we wait? It seems we have been waiting all of our lives."

"It isn't like we've never had this conversation before," Hannah replied tenderly, "but we are who we are. You are the son of Ernst Silberman, owner and president of Bankhaus Silberman, and I am the daughter of Hans Meyers, the executive vice president of the same said bank. We just happen to be the only offspring of two of the wealthiest, most generous, and most respected families in all of Germany. We must do what is expected of us."

"OK! OK!" he interrupted. "You need say no more, but Hannah, it will be years before we can marry and get on with our lives. We will only start university in September, and that gives us at least another four years!"

"Forget the 'at least' part!" she exclaimed. "I'm already working on Papa to set the date of our wedding for June 18, 1942, and he is about ready to announce this to the world!"

"Yes! Yes!" he replied with some passion. "I know the rest! I will study banking and finance so that I can immediately take the next step toward my destined place as the next bank president in waiting, and you will major in sociology to better prepare yourself for a life of philanthropy consisting of giving away large parts of our mutual family fortunes to our fellow Jews who are beginning to immigrate in droves to what the Romans named and the British still call 'Palestine.'"

"You are quite right, Michael!" she replied teasingly. "So isn't all of this worth waiting for? Isn't the honor of our families worth preserving? Aren't sacrifice and preparation the right thing for us now?"

He sighed deeply. "Of course they are," he agreed with more than just a hint of reluctance.

Even as their children waited impatiently for the unfolding of their future, their fathers, Ernst Silberman and Hans Meyers, relaxed together as they enjoyed the special, trusting intimacy known only to lifelong friends. Ernst passed Hans another half-liter bottle of Weinstephan helles beer, the fourth so far of the evening, then took another for himself from an ornate silver ice chest that sat between two luxurious mahogany leather reclining chairs in Ernst's private study.

It was here where it was their long-established custom to spend every other Friday evening together after sharing a sumptuous Erev (the evening before) Shabbat dinner prepared by their respective kitchen staffs. They had alternated such elaborate Shabbat dinners as this between their two nearby mansions for the past twenty years, ever since they had assumed the top management reigns of the Bankhaus Silberman from their own respective retiring fathers.

Ernst and Hans were second-generation bankers, each very, very wealthy in his own right, models of philanthropy and widely known and respected throughout the country and in banking circles throughout much of Europe, and even beyond.

The two of them were far more than simply ultra-successful business associates and intimate personal friends. They were more like inseparable twin brothers, their respective immediate families being more like one rather than two. So it had been with the previous generation of Meyers and Silbermans, and so they took for granted it would be with the next.

It had always been Ernst's and Hans's foregone conclusion that Hannah and Michael would marry right after they completed their university education, and that one day Michael would succeed to Ernst's position as president of Bankhaus Silberman.

"And now for the highlight of the evening," Ernst announced, as he took two rare gourmet Cohiba Cuban cigars from a nearby pearl-inlaid mahogany box, passed one to Hans, and kept the other for himself.

"Let me do the honors," Hans offered, not waiting for a reply, striking a long wooden match, and then reaching to light Ernst's cigar and then his own.

"Tell me," Ernst took up a conversation that had begun earlier in the day but had been cut short by more immediate bank business, "have you taken any of my thoughts about the changing political situation a bit more seriously than the last time we shared our views on the subject?"

"Come on, Ernst!" Hans pretended to complain. "Don't you realize this is all you talk about these days? I don't mean to throw caution to the wind, Ernst, but you seem to have grown obsessed with this fellow Hitler and his band of idiots. I really think you are taking all of this much too seriously—at least for now."

"Hans!" Ernst challenged. "How can you ignore the implications of the German takeover of Austria just last month and the concentration camps he's opening all over the country? Pay attention, man! They have been operating such a camp for the past five years right down the road from us in Dachau."

"Perhaps these are simply new prisons to house his growing army of political enemies," Hans countered. "I really don't see how this has any clear or immediate effect upon the bank or upon us personally. The fact is that our economy is taking off like it hasn't done in several generations. This Hitler fellow may be just what our country needs to finally get over the still lingering economic tragedy of the so-called 'Great War to end all wars.'"

"I'll tell you the truth, Hans," Ernst continued with a depth of seriousness that made his voice noticeably tremble, "I'm convinced that the takeover of Austria is only the beginning of an utterly insane movement led by the devil himself. Why can't you see that our so-called Fuhrer has some sick, misguided ambition that will inevitably lead our beloved Germany and the world into another terrible war? Once more, if you've bothered to read his *Mein Kampf*, you can't have missed how he refers to us Jews as 'parasites, liars, dirty, crafty, sly, wily, clever, without any true culture, spongers, middlemen, maggots, eternal blood suckers, repulsive, unscrupulous, monsters, foreign, menace, bloodthirsty, avaricious, and the mortal enemy of Aryan humanity…' Just maybe he is building the concentration camps for more than only his immediate political enemies."

Hans took a long drag on his exquisitely expensive cigar and exhaled a series of smoke rings as he framed his response to Ernst's outburst. "I'll tell you something, my friend—something I have not yet even shared with Flora and Hannah, or for that matter, until this moment that I even intended to share with you, my closest friend and confidant, at least not just yet."

Hans paused for a few moments before he continued, making every effort to hold back tears that were beginning to flow down the large round cheeks of his corpulent face. "Two weeks ago I opened sizable personal accounts, one at Union Bank of Switzerland, the other at Credit Suisse. Should the situation deteriorate to the point where these are needed, then and only then will I share access information to these funds with my dear ones. I don't want to do this now—to alarm them unnecessarily."

"I don't mean to pry," Ernst probed, "but have you provided sufficiently for them in the event that they may no longer be able to return to Germany?"

"Do not worry about this, Ernst," Hans replied with deep sadness. "Should it become necessary, I have deposited a sufficient amount for all of them, including our future son-in-law, your dear Michael, and, God willing, the children they will bring forth, to lead long and very full lives."

Munich: November 1938

The Silberman and Meyers families once again sat together at the Silbermans' massive dark oak dining room table as they waited quietly for Ernst, who held forth from the place of honor at its head, to begin their deeply serious discussions of the evening, continuing discussions that had been forced by the horrendous events of recent days.

Both families were "traditional" Jews in the matter of their observance, but Shabbat was Shabbat, a time that is sacred and set aside for all but a small minority of ultra-secular Jews. For those gathered here it was the one time each week when the men wore kippahs (skull caps).

It was thus that Ernst raised the family's lovely silver chalice filled with expensive Kiddush (sweet red) wine and blessed its contents, chanting, *"Baruch Atah Adoni Elohanu, Melech haOlam, Boray Puree haGefen, Amen."* (Blessed are You, O Lord our God, King of the Universe, who creates the fruit of the vine.)

Having done this, he then took a sip from the chalice, which was then passed in turn to Hans, then Michael, and then to the women according to their age, first to his beloved wife, Ritha, then to Flora Meyers, and finally to Hannah.

When the chalice had been returned to him, Ernst next took the home-baked Challah (traditional Shabbat loaf) and likewise blessed it, chanting, *"Baruch Atah Adoni Elohanu Melech haOlam haMotze Lechem Meen haEretz, Amen."* (Blessed are You, O Lord our God, King of the Universe who brings bread forth from the earth.)

Then he tore off a piece and passed the loaf across the table to Hans, who likewise took a piece for himself and then passed it around the table where each of the others in turn tore off and retained a piece. When all had been so served, following Ernst's lead, they ate of the traditional Challah together.

Then, by silent mutual consent, they deferred what would be at the very least a deeply distressing sharing until after they had concluded their sacred traditional Erev Shabbat meal together. Instead, their table conversation had been merely perfunctory in order that they might keep their individual and collective peace to the extent that this was possible in the face of the disaster each of them knew well had already begun to tear apart the very fabric of their lives and assault the great promise of their futures.

When they were finished eating, Ernst cleared his throat and then lifted his Bavarian hand-cut lead crystal chalice filled with the finest Auslese dessert wine. As he began to frame the words and tone of his traditional end-of-meal toast, he paused as he looked into the trusting and dependent eyes of all those seated around his table, those who were the most precious and dearest to him in the world: Ritha, the still greatly fetching stereotypical middle-age Jewish matron who very much remained the deeply loved bride of his youth. He struggled to suppress a sudden rush of guilt and regret as he realized how oblivious and utterly vulnerable Ritha remained to the realities of the world that lay just beyond the fairy-tale place he had constructed for her with the well-insulated walls of his affluence. It was within this now grown paper-thin facade of false security wherein she innocently dwelled. He felt himself shudder as he now came face-to-face with the horrendous reality that she was, as were all of his dear ones, terribly ill prepared as these walls of their now crumbling safe haven were closing in upon them from all directions.

Ernst managed to shake off this moment of despair as he turned next to Michael, his beloved son who sat alongside his striking mother. He felt a rush of righteous fatherly pride as he recalled the frequent comments of many friends and colleagues who had boasted that this, his only son, now in the flower of his youth, possessed all of the better qualities of his parents: intellectual brilliance, his mother's physical good looks, and his father's gentle, warm, and loving disposition. More importantly, Ernst reflected, everyone who knew them could see the obvious deep love and commitment between Michael and Hannah as he delighted in the thought that one day soon she would become his daughter-in-law.

Ernst next looked toward those dear ones seated on the opposite side of the table. First there was Hans, whose ever-expanding corpulence had dictated ever-continuing adjustments to his expensive hand-tailored wardrobe. Ernst loved this man deeply. As long as he could remember, Hans had been his "brother," an intimate member of his family. But, Ernst agonized how from time to time he had privately and rightfully questioned Hans' judgment concerning what to himself were simple, common sense challenges that somehow seemed beyond Hans' ability to process then properly act upon.

"Thank God," Ernst reflected, as he next focused affectionately upon Flora Meyers, who sat beside her husband; those qualities Hans lacked had been given to Flora in abundance. She was strikingly different from Hans, both physically and in most other ways. She had succeeded in maintaining the slim attractiveness of her youth, and from time to time she was mistaken by those who did not know otherwise as Hans' daughter rather than his wife.

Moreover, although her family on both sides was solidly Jewish, Flora was a natural blonde with deep blue eyes, rare characteristics for a German Jewess that the family supposed were owing to some distant unknown, to use the parlance of the day, "Aryan" ancestry.

Last, but by no means least in his affection, Ernst next beheld with loving pride their precious Hannah, younger and even more exquisite, save for her jet black hair, large brown eyes, and classic deep tan Semitic coloring, a near duplicate of her mother.

Although it was unnecessary, since all of his dear ones were already focused upon him and patiently awaiting his expected deeply serious discourse, he nevertheless tapped his dessert knife on his crystal chalice in the formality of gaining their attention; then he began to speak.

"First, my precious family, and each of you are indeed a very real member of my family, I want to thank you for maintaining the sanctity of our Shabbat table, even in the face of such ominous and terrible happenings of the past few days. We have nourished our bodies, and through our prayers we have, I trust, renewed our souls.

"It is now time for us to carefully and objectively review what has happened here in our beloved Germany and to consider precisely how and when we are to deal with these most serious circumstances.

"Please bear with me," Ernst continued, unable to completely mask his own mixed emotions of fear and sorrow beneath his attempted executive poise and authority, "as I once again bring to our minds the major events of which I speak."

"First, you will remember how shocked we all were last April when, as Jews, we were commanded by the government to register our wealth and property. Then, in June, how we were further commanded to register with them the most minute affairs and administrative details of our bank."

"You didn't seem too alarmed at the time!" Hans interrupted. "As I recall, you took it to be some not too unreasonable requirement of establishing a more effective tax base."

"Yes," Ernst confessed, "taken alone these events did not seem overly ominous, but taken in the context we can see now, they were part of a clear pattern. Please, let me continue."

He did so without further comment. "Next, in August, Hitler's thugs totally destroyed the main synagogue in Nuremberg. Some said that the fire was an act of nature, but eyewitnesses later clearly established that this horror was a deliberate act of the Nazis.

"Furthermore," he paused to wipe away his just beginning tears, "there can be no question about what happened last evening throughout Germany, and especially here in our own beloved Munich; neither can there be any doubt about who was responsible! All over our beloved country, bands of these Nazi hoodlums attacked our Jewish homes and businesses, breaking glass wherever they went and defiling the rubble they left in their path with anti-Semitic graffiti. It is no small wonder that our own homes escaped their notice, and, thank God, the physical damage they did to the bank was minimal and has already been completely repaired.

"But," he paused for a moment to regain control of his emotions, "what they did to our three beautiful and historic synagogues can never be repaired or forgotten. All that remains of them is rubble and ashes.

"As if this were not enough," he continued, his abject anger breaking through the now obliterated mask of his attempted self-control, "I heard on good authority earlier today that tomorrow we Jews, collectively, will be fined one billion marks for our supposed responsibility for these deliberate acts that they have so unrighteously perpetrated upon us.

"Dear ones," he struggled to find the best way to present what to him was now an inescapable conclusion. "I could go on and on with other examples of the terrible situation we face, but I think I've already said enough to validate my conclusions on how we, my precious family, must respond.

"From what we've already seen, it has become obvious to me that all Jews are now marked for, at the very least, unprecedented discrimination and suffering if not imprisonment or even, God forbid, eventual annihilation. In the face of this, I see only one possibility. We must leave Germany very soon, before it is too late! I've already made an initial contact toward this end with highly placed friends in the United States Department of State."

There was an absolute interminable silence after Ernst had finished until it was suddenly shattered by Hans. "Ernst!" he shouted. "The historical realities of what you have shared are entirely correct, but your dramatic conclusions are at the very least seriously premature and I believe entirely ill founded! My God, man! We are Germans! Germans do not annihilate Germans!

"We may be going through some difficult times right now, and more difficult times may lie ahead but there is nothing I can see that would justify closing the bank, leaving our homes, and running away like frightened rabbits!

"Surely," Hans continued passionately, "the world will rise up against these current extremist happenings. Hitler will be forced to modify his ways. After all, he is nothing but a cheap politician! Those of his kind have no set values and bend with the wind!"

"I ask you once again; have you read *Mein Kampf*?" Ernst countered. "In this so-called book Hitler divides humans into categories based upon their physical appearance, establishing higher and lower orders, or types of humans. At the top of this scheme is the Germanic man with his fair skin, blond hair, and blue eyes. These Hitler calls Aryans, whom, he asserts, are the supreme form of human, or the master race.

"The rest of humanity, according to Hitler, is racially inferior, especially us Jews. Hans," he now pleaded, even begging his closest friend to be rational, "do you really think that this is only a passing political position? Are they not rather the foundational ravings of a madman who has set out to destroy us?"

"I'm sorry, Ernst," Hans replied. "Go if you must, and take your family with you, but we will remain here. I will guard the bank until you return after a few weeks or even months away. Then, I can assure you, after you return and have properly eaten crow for a while, we can all get back to normal."

When confronted with a wall of shocked silence, Hans continued, trying to make light of the situation. "Look at it this way. My blondie Flora looks more like one of them than she does one of us! Maybe, if life really gets difficult around here, she can pass herself off as an Aryan."

No one laughed or even smiled in response.

Late that same evening Hannah and Michael once again sat in the Meyers' gazebo swing. They were distraught over the events of recent days and their respective fathers' reaction and immediate plans that would seriously impact their own lives and relationship.

Finally, after a long and emotionally charged discussion, they summarized their own absolute, bottom-line conclusions. "Hannah, I will not be separated from you under any circumstances!" Michael pronounced. "If you remain here in Munich with your family, then I will remain here with you!"

"And I, my darling Michael, I will likewise not be separated from you under any circumstances. If you go to America with your family, I will go there with you! We can find a whole new life there for ourselves!"

"Hannah! You know that your father would never permit such a thing! You must remain in his care and under his roof until we marry. It is I who will remain here with you! In the eyes of the law I am already a man. Never mind that my father will object. I am free to decide for myself—I have already done so!"

Munich: Winter 1939

The four of them—Hans, Flora, Hannah, and Michael—sat huddled together on a small well-worn throw rug, the pathetic replacement for the luxurious Persian carpet that ever so recently had covered the entire huge salon of what was now the almost totally unfurnished, once exquisitely appointed Meyers family mansion. They listened intently, with fearful expectation as the Fuhrer was about to speak from the Reichstag to the entire nation and to the world. It was January 30, and the winter chill permeated the thick walls of the now sparsely heated tomb-like edifice that had been looted of nearly all of its lovely and expensive furnishings by the "official" scavenging of minor Nazi functionaries who claimed simply to be implementing the requirements of the "New Order."

When recently the Silberman mansion had likewise been stripped to its walls, floors, roof, and foundation, Michael had moved in with his future wife and her family, who were able to afford him some semblance of what was mostly imagined protection.

Everything was gone, Hans lamented: his treasured private art collection that had earlier been known throughout all of Germany—not a single canvas remained; the handmade Queen Anne Chippendale furniture; the Steinway grand piano—all of these material things he had once held dear; now everything was gone.

Even beyond their two, once luxuriously appointed magnificent family mansions, nothing remained of their previous rich and carefree lives. The bank had been seized by the government, along with all of its assets. Their synagogue had been burned to the ground. In short, they would have been entirely dependent upon the largess of their fellow German brothers, now turned ruthless tormentors, had it not been for the considerable cache of currency, gold, and diamonds Hans had painstakingly hidden in a secret place in their expansive basement. Beyond this, he relished in his earlier wisdom that had led him to transfer a large percentage of his enormous personal liquid assets into two numbered Swiss bank accounts. For a moment, Hans stiffened his back in the self-revelation of his own defiance; then the radio crackled loud enough to snap him back to the sickening reality of the moment.

The four of them trembled in unison as the last strains of Deutschland über alles faded from the barely adequate speakers of the now, prohibited to Jews, tiny receiver Michael had defiantly concealed. They now were instantly sickened by the ravings of the madman who held each of their fates in his hands:

> In the course of my life I have very often been a prophet, and have usually been ridiculed for it. During the time of my struggle for power it was in the first instance the Jewish race which only received my prophecies with laughter when I said that I would one day take over the leadership of the State, and with it that of the whole nation, and that I would then among other things settle the Jewish problem. Their laughter was uproarious, but I think that for some time now they have been laughing on the other side of their face. Today I will once more be a prophet: if the international Jewish financiers in and outside Europe should succeed in plunging the nations once more into a world war, then the result will not be the Bolshevization of the earth, and thus the victory of Jewry, but the annihilation of the Jewish race in Europe![1]

They sat in shocked, utter silence for several moments after the outrageous broadcast with its all too clear threat. It was Hans who finally spoke, his voice barely audible as he fought to hold back his own deep despair.

"Our beloved Ernst was entirely correct," he painfully confessed, his heart obviously broken over the depths of his own profound misjudgment and all it implied. "If I had just listened to him we all could be living in safety, basking in the sun with them in Miami, waiting out this horrible tragedy that has only just begun.

"They have already taken away our means of livelihood," Hans continued forlornly. "They have seized virtually everything we own. Now they are even about to cram our empty houses full of the less fortunate of our people from the tenements—then God only knows what they will do with all of us!

"But now it is too late!" Hans lamented as he continued, his voice a sorrowful wail. "There is no way left for us to run away from our beloved Germany! Thanks to my own pride and misjudgment we are left to our own fates."

"Papa," Hannah replied with a hint of encouragement, "there may still be a way for us to get to America, but only if we act very quickly."

"How, Hannah? How?" Hans pleaded, ready to grasp at any straw that might offer their possible survival. "What have you been keeping from me?"

"We thought it might be against your wishes, Papa," Hannah replied. "But even so, Michael and I have been meeting with Papa Ernst's good friend in the American Consulate. He told us about an additional sailing from Germany to America via Cuba. The ship is the *S.S. Saint Louis* from the Hamburg-America Line; it is set to sail for Havana on May 13. They have already booked almost one thousand Jewish passengers from among many others like us who are desperately seeking to escape."

"There may be complications," Michael added. "The passenger list is already oversubscribed, and it is necessary to get exit visas, which are issued at the whim of the Nazi government. Our friend told us that substantial bribes must be paid up front to a number of 'officials,' and there is absolutely no guarantee of success."

"Never mind the money or the odds of our success!" Hans exclaimed. "I am willing to pay whatever it costs to get us all aboard that ship! Any chance to escape, no matter how slim, is better than no chance at all!

"So, you two," he now commanded with suddenly renewed hope, "get on with this immediately! Do whatever is required to make this happen. Money is no object! And may God be with you!"

The Voyage of the S.S. *St. Louis*: May 13–June 17, 1939

Hannah and Michael stood silently, arm in arm on the large stern passenger deck until the sparkling lights of Hamburg had finally twinkled out from their view on the now distant horizon.

"We've done it, my darling Hannah!" Michael exclaimed. "With your father's money, my father's American friends, and the hand of God, we are safe, Hannah! Gloriously safe! We will get married in America, build new lives there until this incredible mess Hitler has made of the world has finally been resolved. Then we will one day return to the land of our birth!"

"Amen, brother!" Hannah replied with playful mock derision. "Your father's contacts, my father's money, yes, but when did you start getting religion? What's this 'hand of God' business you are talking about? Do you really believe that there is a God?"

He replied in the same spirit of playful relief born of the reality of their successful escape. "I was circumcised on the eighth day, and I was bar mitzvahed. There must be a God who made me go through all of that!"

"Call it what you will, Michael—God, careful planning, money, family influence, or just plain good luck—we are free, free to live out our lives together. For this I am deeply thankful."

"Well," he replied, "there is one thing they hadn't quite gotten around to taking, and that is our clothes. So come, my precious one; it is time for us to change for dinner. Your father tells me we've all been invited to dine with the captain at his table."

"I wonder how much that little hors d'oeuvre set him back," Hannah replied as she giggled at her own speculation.

Captain Gustav Schroeder had given the 231 members of his crew stern warnings that these passengers, even though they were Jews, were to be treated just like any of the others. Even so, being a highly sensitive man, he knew that such things as the Nazi flag flying high above his stately ship as well as the huge portrait of the Fuhrer that hung in the social hall could not help but be very disquieting for all 937 of his Jewish passengers, many of whom had already endured considerable persecution.

Once more Captain Schroeder knew a frightening truth to which no one else on board had yet been made privy. Just before his ship had set sail from Hamburg, the Cuban government had changed its immigration laws with Decree 937. This seemingly arbitrary change effectively closed the way by which many of the passengers had hoped to enter their country. The new law required the payment of a large cash bond before any alien could disembark, and then that person also needed to have the prior written approval of both the Cuban secretaries of state and labor.

Most of the passengers on board *St. Louis*, however, had only tourist visas that they had purchased from the Hamburg-America Line. Then, adding to all of this difficulty for his Jewish passengers, Captain Schroeder received a telegram from the shipping line official in Havana, stating that his ship must anchor at the roadstead instead of docking at the line's pier in

Havana harbor. Then the message went on to make it perfectly clear that the refugees on board were being denied entry into Cuba.

Captain Schroeder sighed deeply as he contemplated how he would memorialize the tumultuous events of this fateful day in his personal diary. Before he finally took pen in hand, he straightened the black bow tie of his smartly tailored formal dining uniform in preparation for joining his guests for the sumptuous meal to be served at his table. He then emptied his generous glass of the finest schnapps in a single swallow, took the seat at his desk, and recorded what seemed to him to be the most appropriate account for some unknown posterity:

> There is a somewhat nervous disposition among the passengers. Despite this, everyone seems convinced they will never see Germany again. Touching departure scenes have taken place. Many seem light of heart, having left their homes. Others take it heavily. But beautiful weather, pure sea air, good food, and attentive service will soon provide the usual worry-free atmosphere of long sea voyages. Painful impressions on land disappear quickly at sea and soon seem merely like dreams.[2]

"Wake up, everyone!" Hans shouted loudly enough to instantly rouse all three of his precious cabinmates from their deep sleep.

"It's already four-thirty and time for breakfast. We will soon dock in Havana, and we should have plenty of time to look around the city before we set sail again for Miami."

None of them complained as they took turns in the cabin's small lavatory and hurriedly dressed. It was May 27, and they were all most anxious to set their feet on dry land after more than two weeks at sea.

It had been a generally pleasant crossing, Hannah reflected as she patiently waited for her mother to put the final touches on her makeup before presenting herself once again at Captain Schroeder's table. Hannah chuckled to herself at her perhaps not too farfetched notion that the good captain had taken more than just a casual notice of the quite striking Flora Meyers. Never mind that her dearly loved, grossly overweight father was no physical match for the strikingly handsome, trim captain; Hannah knew that her parents were deeply in love, and she surmised that this somewhat obvious mutual flirtation was really nothing more than harmless fancy.

As the captain's special guests, the four of them stood on the observation deck immediately adjacent to the bridge where they could enjoy the best view of the ship's landing. The sunrise over Havana presented a glorious welcome, and their spirits soared as the S.S. *St. Louis* approached the harbor.

However, little did they, or any of the other nearly one thousand Jewish passengers know that Captain Schroeder had, a few hours earlier, received a telegram from the shipping line's local official in Havana that stated despite all of the shipping line's efforts to the contrary, the *St. Louis* had been directed to anchor at the roadstead, a sheltered offshore anchorage area for ships.

It was Flora who verbalized the first hint that something might be amiss. "Why do you suppose we've stopped here, outside the harbor?" she questioned no one in particular.

"It's nothing, I'm sure," Hans responded encouragingly. "This must be where the customs officials and the pilot board to make certain everything is in order before we proceed to the landing pier."

Since they had originally planned to dock at the line's pier, anchoring at the roadstead had been a concession by the Cuban government, especially since the highest level of government had now confirmed their earlier decision to disallow the *St. Louis* passengers to land on Cuban soil.

Captain Schroeder waited until just after noon before he confirmed Flora's earlier suspicion that something indeed was very much amiss with his plan to land and then allow his passengers to disembark in Havana. Speaking over the ship's public address system, his somewhat faltering voice belied his vain attempt to project confidence and encouragement, as he now informed his universally disquieted passengers.

"Ladies and gentlemen, dear passengers and friends," he began with genuine warmth and concern. "Last Thursday, ten days after we sailed from Germany, the company informed me that the Cuban government had become reticent to grant permission for you to disembark here in Havana. They informed me that this was because of some supposed administrative irregularities with your landing visas. I can assure you that high level and local officials of our company are already making every effort to resolve this problem, and they are hopeful that this unfortunate delay will soon come to an end. You can be sure that I will keep all of you closely informed of any new developments.[3]

"Now," he concluded, "I suggest that we all retire to the lounge for a somewhat late luncheon."

While Captain Schroeder continued to update his passengers through a passenger committee he had hastily organized, he next addressed them collectively, four days later, on May 31, after they had remained under police guard while the ship had remained moored to the roadstead.

"Dear passengers," he said as he got right to the substance of the distressing matter at hand, "despite the great and still continuing efforts on our behalf, the Cuban cabinet made a final decision this morning to deny the majority of you refuge. However, twenty-two of you acquired what they have defined as proper immigration visas before we departed from Hamburg, and they alone will be allowed to disembark.

"Finally," he continued, trying without much success to conceal his own disappointment and anger, "we have been given a strict order to depart Cuban waters within two days, no later than ten o'clock Friday morning.

"As I see it, our next best course of action is to proceed to the United States with the hope that we can negotiate permission to land and disembark at some port in Florida. The company has supported me in this decision, and we are already in close contact with American officials in an effort to gain permission for our landing there. Again, I have high hopes that all of this will come to a good end, and I will continue to keep you closely informed."

Now, two days later, the four of them again stood on the captain's private observation deck, along with a small number of the others who had been selected to dine at his table throughout the long and now turned desperate journey. It was very early on a lovely, clear morning, and the skyline of Miami was a picture-postcard display as the rising sun behind them illuminated the alabaster-appearing city on the distant horizon.

"O Lord," Hans pleaded loudly enough for them all to hear, "I am not a praying man, and I never have been what one would call religious, but I plead with You to have mercy upon us all—to allow us to disembark upon the shores of the land of freedom that lies just ahead—"

BOOM!

The crashing report of a single cannon round fired from a yet unseen source screamed just over their heads, where they stood, close to the bow of the crowded liner, abruptly cutting off Hans' plea for divine intervention.

"Attention, attention!" came the loudly amplified voice from the American Coast Guard cutter that had now pulled just ahead of the *St. Louis* from where it had fired the single warning shot from just abeam on the starboard. "This is the captain of the United States Coast Guard Cutter, CG-244. You have now entered the territorial waters of the United States, and you are hereby ordered to turn back and depart these waters immediately!"

And so it was that when his ship was not allowed to dock in Cuba, Captain Schroeder sailed it to the Florida coast. There he hoped that the United States would admit his forlorn Jewish passengers. Desperately trying to avoid a forced return to Germany and the horrors that they rightfully feared awaited them there, the passengers—more than four hundred of whom were women and children, and many of whom actually had quota numbers to eventually enter the United States—collectively sent a telegram to President Franklin D. Roosevelt asking for his personal help.

They received no reply from the president. However, the State Department sent word that it would not interfere in Cuban affairs, and it therefore refused to allow the passengers to come ashore. Now, when this final plea had been abruptly answered with a shot across the bow and with it an unseemly cruel command to depart, Captain Schroeder knew there was no other choice but to turn back toward Germany.

Even so, as they turned to the east and slowly made their way back to already war-torn Europe, there was to be a new surge of hope in the collective body of those who had been so abruptly and wantonly turned away from the nation that had beckoned to them: Give me your tired, your poor, your huddled masses yearning to breathe free, the wretched refuse of your teeming shore. Send these, the homeless, tempest-tossed, to me: I lift my lamp beside the golden door.

The passengers on the S.S. *St. Louis* had left Germany with joy. Now they were returning there with foreboding and dread. As they steamed toward what then seemed like a potentially tragic ending to their terrible journey, nevertheless, their own on-board passengers committee, with the assistance and full cooperation of Captain Schroeder and his company, pleaded with world leaders to give them asylum so that they could avoid going back to Germany.

The results of these desperate efforts were first announced to those who had become his favorite passengers when Captain Schroeder knocked on the door of the Meyers' stateroom just before dinner on the fourth evening since they had turned back to the east.

"Good evening, Gustav!" Hans greeted the captain in what was an unprecedented visit to their shipboard accommodations. "My two ladies were just making some final touches before joining you for dinner. Please come in."

"I will only be a minute, Hans," the captain replied, smiling with satisfied anticipation at the news he was about to share with Hans and Michael. "I just wanted to let you all know, before I make a general announcement to everyone at dinner, that the Joint Distribution Committee and the other agencies with which we have been negotiating have so far managed to persuade four countries to admit most of you who are seeking asylum in anyplace other than Germany. These are Belgium, Holland, France, and England.

"I am pleased to inform you that you three Meyers and you, Michael, are among the two hundred twenty-four who have been accepted by Holland and, in fact, you have already been further allocated to the city of Lisse, a quaint village just north of Leiden.

"Even more," he continued excitedly, "you will all be long-term guests of the Theo de Goede family, who, I have learned, are devout Christians."

"Praise God!" Hans replied, almost unable to speak as he choked with emotion. "This is indeed wonderful news!"[4]

Chapter 3
Hear O Israel
The Martyrdom of James, Brother of Yeshua
(Jerusalem, circa A.D. 62)[1]

The twelve apostles sat in their usual places around the large hand-carved wooden conference table that was the central feature of the Upper Room on Mount Zion where they, the Council of Twelve, had regularly assembled since the founding of the Way at Pentecost.

Even now each of them struggled to suppress what, to this point, had been their unspoken yet growing disquiet over the unexplained purpose of their sudden summons to this most unusual, unscheduled, apparently urgent meeting by James, their beloved and characteristically unshakable leader.

Peter finally ended their contemplative silence by addressing Matthew. "We are so honored, my brother, that you seemingly dropped everything in your greatly blessed ministry and journeyed home to be with us from the depths of Syria."

"My brothers," the writer of the first Gospel replied as tears began to stream down both sides of his thin face into the thick black curls of his full beard, "I would have traveled from the end of the earth even at the whispered beckoning of our blessed leader."

"Amen!" the others responded in heartfelt unison.

"He is a man, holy above all others who walk among us this day," Peter continued to verbalize their shared adoration of James. "Only he, besides the high priest himself, because of his Nazirite vow and his unequaled righteousness and purity, is allowed to enter into the holy place in the temple.[2] How truly amazing it is that he, the brother of Yeshua who lives only to propagate our people's faith in Him, our blessed Messiah, should be simultaneously called out as the purest of the pure, the only one who may thus enter into the holy of holies."[3]

John, the disciple whom Yeshua so deeply loved, added his own testimony:

> Blessed James, our Lord's brother, has been universally called 'the Just,' from the days of the Lord down to the present time. For many bore the name of James; but this James has been called out and holy from his mother's womb. He drinks no wine or other intoxicating liquor, nor does he eat flesh; no razor comes upon his head; he does not anoint himself with oil, nor make use of the bath. He alone is permitted to enter the holy place: for he does not wear any woolen garment, but fine linen only. He alone, I say, is wont to go into the temple where he can be found kneeling on his knees, begging forgiveness for the people, so that the skin of his knees has become horny like that of a camel's, by reason of his constantly bending them in adoration to God, and begging forgiveness for the people.[4]

As John's emotion-filled voice stilled, Peter summarized their innermost collective adoration of their leader. "Is it any wonder then, that in consequence of his preeminent justice, he is called 'the Just,' and Oblias, which signifies Defense of the People, and Justice, in accordance with what the prophets declare concerning him."[5]

"Amen and amen," they exclaimed together in soul deep adoration.

It was then, at this perfect moment that James entered into their presence. He was adorned in pristine pure white linen raiment, his long, thick black hair touching and blending with the thick, uncombed locks of his massive full beard that extended below his waist. Spontaneously, they stood and one by one exchanged kisses with him on both cheeks, embracing him with their love and admiration of which they had just spoken and solemnly agreed.

When their emotional exchange had run its course and the twelve had all resumed their seats, they turned attentively and expectantly toward their beloved leader, who had taken his place at the head of the table.

His countenance now turned visibly solemn, James began to address those whom he held most dear, making no attempt to mask his deep and growing sense of urgency.

"My dear brothers, some of you like Matthew, had the good sense to remove yourselves from this place twenty-seven years ago when the blood of our beloved Stephen was poured out as that of a martyr at the hands of our fellow Jews. Those of you who did so went with my blessing since our Lord made it clear to me then by remaining here you risked the same fate, thereby cutting off the great and foundational work He had ordained for you to accomplish. In the case of Matthew, he obediently removed himself to Kochaba, in the region of Damascus where in relative security, in the company of many brothers, he completed his great Gospel in 37, after which, over the ensuing years, he refined this foundational work and widely saw that it was distributed throughout the great and growing body of Yeshua that our Gentile brothers have come to call the church.[6]

"Dear ones, you may not all know that our brother Paul received justice at the hands of the procurator Festus, who found no great fault in him, but Festus is now dead and Caesar has replaced him with one called Albinus, who, unfortunately, will not arrive in Judea for yet a number of weeks. Thus, a window of opportunity has opened for rampant persecution of those of the Way who remain here in the city. Ananus, the newly appointed head of the Sanhedrin, has seized upon this opportunity. He has already proven to be a bold man in his temper and very rigid in judging all whom he deems to be offenders of the Torah, which by his thinking includes all of us. To state it simply, my brothers, Ananus is reportedly on a witch hunt to find and destroy all who would dare to uphold the name of Yeshua. I personally am an obvious target for his wrath, but every one of the many of our brothers who still remain anywhere in Judea are most certainly in great jeopardy for their very lives."[7]

James paused for a moment, sipped some water from the clay cup that had been set before him, and glanced from face to face of those dear ones who offered no comment but rather waited in rapt attention for him to continue.

"As if this stringent and direct opposition from our fellow Jews were not enough," James exclaimed passionately, his deep concern now completely unmasked, "dear ones, it would seem that many of our Jewish brothers, led by the zealots, are on the brink of an all out rebellion against Rome. Even so, such a war cannot be won. In my view, even if all Jews were united in this call to rise up against the Romans, which of course we are not, such a rebellion would still be an utter insanity; as if we Jews were a miniscule David facing a gargantuan Goliath but without the benefit of a sling shot, much less the interceding hand of the Lord. Moreover, those who would make war against Rome with absolutely no possibility of success have demanded from me the full cooperation of all followers of the Way—they would actually have us join their army of fools and be led, along with them, into an inevitable and terrible slaughter."

"What would the Lord have us to do?" Peter nearly shouted, unable to restrain himself.

Peter's characteristic impetuous outburst gave rise to a much-needed tension-releasing communal guffaw from his fellow apostles. Even James smiled broadly and seemed somewhat less intense as he continued, "I told Ananus in no uncertain terms that we would not be a party to this insanity. Even so he has continued in his strong opposition to those of us who embrace Yeshua. The fact is, I have heard it on good authority that Ananus is about to assemble the Sanhedrin for the purpose of directly confronting those of us who they can lay their hands on—starting with me."

"Then you must flee from the city at once!" Peter interjected excitedly, this time without evoking a mirthful response from his brethren, who were equally fearful for the safety of their beloved leader as they as one through their body language and brief outbursts made their agreement abundantly clear.

"The Lord would have it otherwise," James cut them off. "He has made it quite clear to me that I am to remain in the city and to stand strong in the midst of those who oppose us. I have called you all here for a clear and urgent purpose. You are to begin here on Mount Zion, then sweep in ever growing circles all throughout Judea until you have personally commanded each and every follower of Yeshua and their families to leave this region at once, or place their very lives in grave jeopardy. As you all likely know, we have already established a community of our Gentile brethren at Pella in the Decapolis. Tell our endangered dear ones that they will be welcomed there with open arms and that provision has already been made for them. If for whatever reason any should not believe they are called to flee to Pella, tell them to flee to the relative safety of the Galilee instead."[8]

James stood fearlessly before the assembled Sanhedrin. It was Passover, and only a few days since he had dismissed the Council of Twelve and sent them upon their urgent mission to evacuate all followers of Yeshua from the imminent danger that he now personally faced. He listened calmly as his accusers cried out to him, "Tell us, O righteous one, what is meant by 'the door of Yeshua'?"

James replied, "This is Yeshua, the Son of God, of one essence with the Father."

Therefore there was great murmuring among those assembled who were now all the more convinced that there was a great danger that all Jews might now be inclined to believe in Yeshua. Therefore they beseeched James, "O righteous one: instruct the people, for they have gone astray and believe in Yeshua, that He is one with God and the Messiah. Therefore, since this is the Feast of Passover and all have gathered on the grounds of the temple, persuade them not to be deceived by a mere man. We implore you, be so good as to do this, for we all acknowledge you to be a righteous and impartial man. Therefore, we beseech you: ascend the parapet of the temple, that you may be easily seen by the people, and that they may hear your just words, to instruct them."

When the Passover arrived, all the tribes had gathered, and the believers in Yeshua were among them. It was then that the arrant liars, not really believing that James shared their beliefs, and seeking to entrap him, caused him to stand on the parapet of the temple. Then, in a loud voice, that all present might hear, they shouted, "Tell us, O righteous one, since we all accept you, what say you of Yeshua who was crucified by Pilate, and after whom the people have gone astray, thinking He is the Messiah and even believing that He is God? Make it clear to us and proclaim the truth!"

The time had come to speak the truth against the false ones, and James did not shrink back in fear before death and deny the truth, but, contrary to their expectations, he lifted up his voice and with an unrestrained spirit and tongue replied, "Why do you question me concerning Yeshua? He is seated in heaven at the right hand of His Father with the heavenly powers, and He will come again on the clouds of heaven, to judge the world with righteousness!" By this testimony, many were convinced, and cried aloud, "Hosanna to the Son of David!" But the blind Pharisees and scribes, seeing the results of James' witness, now regretted that they had allowed him this audience, even though he had given the response they had expected. Therefore, greatly incensed, they called out to the crowd, "Lo! Even the righteous one has gone astray!" Then they ascended the parapet, seized him like wild beasts, and cast him down to the earth. Despite this, the blessed one did not expire. Then they began to stone him. He accepted the stones calmly as a precious treasure and knelt and prayed: "Lord God and Father, forgive them, for they know not what they do."

These were the very words uttered by both the Master on the Cross and the long-suffering martyr Stephen. Thus did James, the brother of the Lord, pray for his heartless murderers. Now some overheard him praying on their behalf, but the ungrateful ones had no respect for his forbearance and continued to rain down stones upon him. One of the descendants of

Rechab, the son of Rachabim, of the priestly caste, cried out, "Cease this! O wretched ones, what are you doing? The righteous one is praying for us, the unjust, who stone him!" Then one of the murderers took a fuller's club, which is used to beat out cloth, and smote James mightily on the head, and the righteous one gave up the spirit.[9]

The Epistle of James is regarded by many to be the oldest book in the New Testament. It was most likely written not long before the martyrdom of its author, who in chapter 5 and verse 1 foretold the destruction of Jerusalem. Interestingly, many of the Jews of that day concluded that the devastating outcome of the first rebellion against Rome, followed soon after by the destruction of the city and the temple by order of Vespasian, were God's requital for the wicked murder of James, the one who had been called by his brother Yeshua to lay the very foundations of what today we have come to call the church.

Chapter 4
Hannah's Story
Lisse, Holland
(1939–1943)

Look everyone!" Michael cried out from the still lingering remnant of his youthful optimism, as the ancient inter-city bus came to a jerking halt in front of the Lisse City Bus Terminal. "We're here!"

"Indeed we are, my dear Michael," Hans replied, the weariness in his voice almost palpable. "Indeed we are. Come, everyone," he groaned, as he dragged his totally spent corpulent frame from the last of the three tiny seats into which he had been crammed on three successively more ancient buses during their exhausting eight-hour, one hundred fifty mile transit from the port at Ostende to Lisse via Antwerp and then Rotterdam.

"There is no one here to meet us!" Flora exclaimed, trying without much success to control her near panic as she instinctively gathered her family closer to herself in a protective circle. "What are we to do?"

"Mutti," Michael, with Hannah cuddled close beside him, spoke with attempted confidence, "there is obviously only one thing we can do, and that is to wait until our host either comes or sends someone else to fetch us.

"Let me tell you," he continued emotionally, speaking to them all as well as to himself, "this isn't a time for us to be worried about transportation. We are so very blessed to have been chosen for this sanctuary. Just think for a moment of the horrors to be faced by those many hundreds of thousands, perhaps even millions of our people who either have or will ultimately fall into the hands of the madman who is set out to kill all Jews!"

"In the meantime," Hannah suggested, trying to change the subject that was unceasingly at the forefront of each of their thoughts "why don't we buy some sandwiches and enjoy them in the lovely park right across from the station. We can watch for anyone who might come to look for us from there."

Thankfully, they didn't have long to wait. Some thirty minutes later, just as they were finishing their pleasant Gouda cheese on black bread sandwiches along with huge portions of crisply prepared pommes frites, washed down by half-liter mugs of local Pils lager beer, there was suddenly no mistaking that their rescuers had arrived. "Theo de Goede, Tulip Farm" was emblazoned on both sides and the rear of the 1936 model Mercedes delivery truck that screeched to a dust-cloud-producing stop in front of the bus terminal and gave clear and much welcomed notice that their new life in Holland had just begun.

The four suddenly revived refugees rushed into the waiting open-armed embrace of Theo and Gerta de Goede as if they had been physically drawn into an instant bonding by some mutually irresistible magnetic force.

"How wonderful it is for us to have you and your lovely children light up our lives!" Gerta exclaimed in perfect High German, after they had concluded their all around spontaneous introductory embraces. "Theo and I never had children of our own, so we look at you all as an answer to our prayers—a gift from God. Praise Him; He has given us a new family!"

"It really is quite amazing," Theo, a light-complexioned, blue-eyed, slightly built, living stereotype of a Hollander in his late sixties, added. "Your Flora and Gerta could be sisters. The same straw-colored hair! The same lovely blue eyes—they even have the same quite Dutch-like facial features!"

Gerta's entire large body shook as she laughingly further commented. "Actually, if we are comparing relative poundage, I also look very much like Hans!"

"How can we begin to thank you for your loving outreach to us?" Hans replied emotionally. "We have only just met, yet it seems like we have known each other, as you say, like family for as long as we can remember."

The sun had just begun to set as the four new residents of Lisse and environs concluded their inspection of the spacious, nicely furnished wooden bungalow situated some one-half kilometer to the east of the de Goedes' very large, simple, yet somehow still elegant two-storied, red-bricked, main residence.

"This is really lovely," Flora exclaimed as she took her place beside Hans on the large, plush sofa set in front of the living room fireplace fashioned from native stone. "We are so blessed to have been given this sanctuary. Perhaps there really is a God in heaven."

"I suppose so," Michael, who had heard his future mother-in-law's observation, interjected, "but I must say that I don't go along with these peoples' puritanical idea of giving me a room in the main house."

Hannah laughed. "As I recall from my studies, their Jesus taught them, 'Lead us not into temptation, but deliver us from evil.'"

"You certainly have been a temptation for me since about the time we turned twelve," Michael joshingly replied, "but there is nothing about you that I find even slightly evil."

"Enough, you two!" Flora scolded playfully. "Come, let's be on our way—we mustn't be late for supper. Michael, bring your things!" she commanded. "Like it or not, you will be staying in the main house, and that will help us all to sleep a bit more soundly."

"This place is so pleasant, so peaceful—it makes me feel so safe," Hannah observed as the four of them made their way along the narrow road leading from their bungalow to the main house.

It was with a sense of near overpowering, unspoken awe, peace, and thanksgiving that they individually and collectively basked in the somehow protective reality of being surrounded on every side by endless fields of now mostly spent variously colored tulip blossoms, the scattered groupings of which punctuated the seemingly limitless deep green carpet created by their foliage into a patchwork quilt of full spectrum loveliness.

"It is very good indeed that we have found this haven," Hans cautioned. "But let us not forget, even for a moment that we are Jews, and Jews have become a despised quarry."

"Vatti!" Hannah objected. "Holland isn't Germany. Surely we're safe from the Nazis in this place."

"America would have been safer," he replied in a way that the others found suddenly chilling.

It was Sunday evening, and like every Sunday evening that would follow during their time with the de Goedes, the Meyers joined their hosts in the main house for a sumptuous Lord's Day dinner.

"Gerta!" Flora sighed with deep satisfaction when they had finished their elaborate whipped cream–laden strawberry shortcake dessert. "Everything was so very delicious—you have made us feel so much at home!"

"You are home, dear ones," Gerta replied, wiping away a tear from her cheek with her linen napkin. "You are our long-lost family, and we already love you very much. Please tell me—have I served you anything you found offensive? Before you came, we studied your Torah dietary restrictions, and I pray that we didn't miss anything."

"You are so very kind and thoughtful," Flora replied. "We do follow the dietary instructions as they were set down by the hand of God, but we do not follow the much greater restrictions that were created by the laws of men, that is, by the rabbis. We are not what are generally known as 'religious' Jews. Most would call us 'traditional.'"

Theo now ventured into the after-dinner conversation. "May I ask, before all this happened, if you regularly attended synagogue services?"

"We always attended synagogue on our annual special feasts, but rarely at other times," Hans quickly replied.

"Not so fast, dear!" Flora corrected. "The fact is, Hannah and I were attending regular Shabbat services much more frequently than you may care to acknowledge." She paused for a moment to regain her self-control, which was beginning to slip away. "That is, we used to attend—before the Nazis destroyed every synagogue in our beloved Munich."

"Now may I ask a question?" Hans ventured rhetorically, emboldened by the drift of the conversation. "How is it that you, a Christian family who worship a different God than we Jews—how is it that you can so sincerely and lovingly adopt us and care for us in such a wonderful, unqualified way?"

"First of all, Hans," Theo responded thoughtfully, "by no means do we Christians and you Jews worship different Gods. We embrace the one true God, just like you—Yahweh, the God of the Jews who handed down the Torah on tablets to Moses on Mount Sinai.

"Our principal difference," Theo continued, "is that we have come to understand that Jesus, the one you call Yeshua, is the promised Messiah, the Son of God, who is one with the Father and the Spirit of God whom we worship as a trinity.

"You Jews held and widely taught this same three-part understanding of the Godhead as long ago as 500 B.C.[1] many centuries before we believe that Yeshua came in the form of a man to sacrifice Himself for the sins of the world."

"Pardon me," Hannah interjected. But doesn't your New Testament also teach something like 'He who does not love does not know God, for God is love' and 'By their fruits you shall know them'?"

"It does, indeed, my dear," Gerta replied with obvious delighted surprise. "If I may ask, where did you learn about the New Testament?"

"I read and studied it quite thoroughly in a comparative religions class," she replied. "But to tell you the truth, I never thought much about the meaning of these words until we met you two precious people. It is quite obvious that you not only believe the words of your Bible, but that you also live by them."

May 10, 1940

As had become their greatly enjoyed new avocation, very early on this beautiful spring morning, right after they had consumed a huge farm worker's breakfast, the entire Meyers family joined their hosts in the massive fields of just flowered tulips in the ongoing, time-critical harvest of new bulbs. They worked quietly yet quickly in groups of two, gently pulling each bulb individually from the rich soil and placing it in appropriately labeled cardboard cartons for further processing, a process that would continue well into the late-night hours.

"This is good work!" Hans proclaimed openly to his beloved Flora as he shielded his eyes from the first direct onslaught of the rising sun and joyfully went about this new and most unaccustomed work for a wealthy and formerly internationally prominent German Jewish banker.

"All of this has also been very good for your health, my dear Hans," she replied lovingly. "Just in case you haven't noticed, you haven't looked this well since I can remember. Despite your voracious appetite for the most fattening Dutch foods, you still have lost at least twenty pounds in the past few months. How very wonderful!"

Suddenly, as Hans was about to reply, the lovely calm of this glorious spring morning was shattered by the distinct sound of multiple distant explosions coming from the south, perhaps even from as far distant as the twenty-five miles between their farm and Rotterdam.

"Oh, no!" Michael, who had been working with Gerta de Goede, cried out in sudden terror. "What was that? What is happening?"

Before anyone could reply to Michael's panic-driven plea, a flight of four Ju-87 Stuka dive bombers provided an answer of their own as they screamed some two thousand feet over their heads, their German markings clearly visible as they roared off in the direction of Rotterdam.

Now, just as suddenly, seemingly every church bell in their nearby normally tranquil country village joined the cacophony that had driven each of them opened-mouthed to their feet.

"Hurry!" Theo commanded. "The Germans have finally begun their invasion! Let's get back to the house and see what we can learn from the radio."

Very late that evening, as they all sat in the de Goedes' spacious living room listening to the increasingly discouraging reports of a growing succession of early German advances into their beloved Holland, Theo finally verbalized what each of them had already silently concluded.

"It will only be a matter of days before our country falls into Nazi hands," he proclaimed sadly, his words of truth burning into each of the Jewish hearts that were present.

"Can anyone tell me what we are to do?" Hans cried out in response to the just stated obvious reality.

"Of course we can!" Gerta replied comfortingly. "Surely you don't think we are surprised by this atrocity. Anyone with any sense at all could see this coming. We have very carefully planned for this eventuality, especially as it applies quite pointedly to you, our precious Jewish family."

"How could you possibly plan to prevent us from falling into their hands?" Hans beckoned, his voice broken, reflecting his own near full-blown panic.

"Quiet down for a moment, Hans," Theo insisted, "and I will tell you. In the first place, you were directed to us almost a year ago by an international committee that surely has not been a priority interest of the Germans.

"No one, absolutely no one, beyond yourselves and Gerta and I have any knowledge that you are Jewish or where you came from. In fact, I seriously doubt that anyone besides the seven of us has any knowledge that you are living here with us.

"What little contact you have had in the last eleven months with the world outside this farm has been made by Flora in her very few shopping excursions to Lisse with Gerta, and, as you can plainly see, Flora looks more Dutch than Gerta herself. Beyond this," he continued with growing conviction, "you have pointedly avoided any contact with the large native Jewish community that is scattered throughout the country, including even those of the very small Jewish group here in Lisse.

"In short," he concluded, "you were not registered as Jews or as anything else here in Lisse after you arrived, and as far as I can tell, we can reasonably say that none of you officially exist. If and when the Nazis come looking for Jews to mistreat, there is no reason whatsoever to assume that they will have any interest in looking here on our farm."

"Still," Hans persisted, "what are we to do if we are challenged by the police to present our identity cards? We can hardly show him the special ones we were issued by the Nazis in 1938 identifying us as German Jews!"

"I can certainly understand your deep concern, my friends," Theo replied, "but I don't have to tell you that there is only one reasonable course of action open to you. There is no place else for you to go, and if there were, there is no way for you to leave this farm without attracting unwanted notice. It would seem to me that we all need to remain here and wait out this war in relative safety. From here on until then, you must do absolutely nothing any more out of the ordinary than tending to our tulips."

After a chilling period of stunned silence, it was Flora who finally responded to Theo's pronouncement. "We could have it a lot worse than hiding out here in the confines of this beautiful farm!" she declared with understanding and acceptance. "I'll tell you, beyond our own safety, what has been eating away at my heart since this morning," she continued in a manner of confession. "What about you, our dear Theo and Gerta? God forbid, what would happen to you if by some chance we are eventually discovered here by the Nazis?"

"Please don't think that we haven't thought of this as well and carefully weighed the consequences," Theo replied resolutely. "Dear ones, as you know, we are Christians; we take our faith and the teachings of our blessed Savior most seriously.

"In the nearly one year since we first met, beginning that first day when you all became our precious adopted family," he continued, "we have made it a point never, in any way to change or even to discuss your religious convictions. You are Jews—and so was our precious Jesus! We have long had a clear understanding that the roots of Christianity are Jewish. Our faith sprang forth from the rich spiritual soil of Israel, not from Rome! The first believers in Jesus were Jews, and it was they who opened up the way for us Gentiles to share in what we hold as the way to eternal life."

As Theo continued, his eyes glowed with the strength of his conviction as the others listened, spellbound by what he was sharing for the first time with them and the obviously very deep faith from which it flowed. "Our Lord, Jesus Christ, laid down His life for all the people of the world that they might be forgiven of their sins and have eternal life. He told us this, my dear adopted family: 'Greater love has no one than this, than to lay down one's life for his friends.'" He paused for a moment to regain control of his great emotions before he concluded. "Gerta and I are quite prepared to lay down our lives for your own."

Theo spent most of the second day after the Nazi invasion had begun in Lisse, making contacts within its small Jewish community in an overt effort to help them in any way he could, which amounted to little more than expressing his own outrage at what seemed at the time to be their quickly developing horrendous situation.

However, Theo had another motive. The contacts he thus established would also serve as a conduit for keeping Gerta, himself, and the precious Jewish family in his care closely informed about the activities, developments, and level of threat that would surely soon be present as the Nazis quickly established their anticipated torturous anti-Semitic web.

It was after supper that evening that he shared the results of his day's activities with his extended family while they were all still seated around the massive oak dining table.

"Dear ones, there may, after all, be another way for you to consider," he began. "I learned today that a considerable number of your Jewish brothers and sisters throughout the country are planning to make their escape from the Nazis by fleeing to France and from there to other places of sanctuary like Spain and England. Some families from Lisse have already left, and others will soon follow.

"In fact," he continued, "one of those whom I met today, Morris Cohen, has been managing the Lisse Branch of the Rabobank for a number of years. I told him about your situation without giving him any personal identifying details, and he was immediately sympathetic and anxious to help. Morris and his family will begin to make their escape to France tomorrow morning. They seem to have planned very well and have contacts in France who will be waiting for their arrival.

"To get to the point, Morris expressed his willingness for you four to join up with them, but to do so you will have to move quickly. Remember, they plan to leave Lisse just before sunrise tomorrow morning. Certainly there are risks," Theo concluded with deep seriousness, "but you must carefully weigh these against the risks of remaining here with us."

"Let me have a word about this, if I may," Flora interjected before Hans had time to frame a response. "We must very much consider your safety, Theo and Gerta! If we were to take advantage of this opportunity and leave now, it would immediately reduce the grave danger to you both posed by our presence."

"Don't even consider this for a moment!" Theo nearly shouted. "Gerta and I are committed to help and protect as many of you dear Jewish people as we are able. This is a decision that only you can make, and you must make it very carefully, without any regard whatsoever to us or for our well-being."

"May we also have a word, Vatti?" Hannah added resolutely, not waiting for her father's permission before she proceeded. "Please consider this. If we remain here for the duration of the war, which may take who knows how many years, without a rabbi to marry us, we may have to linger here together in this unnatural state forever! Vatti, we want to be married now! There is no longer any need for us to wait until we complete our education. As things now stand, we will have no further education and no careers beyond working in the tulip fields. I beg you, Vatti, if you have decided that the family should remain here, then give your blessing to Michael and me to leave with the Cohen family tomorrow morning."

It took only a few moments for Hans to respond to the five who were gathered with him that fateful day. He cleared his throat and then proceeded with his life-impacting pronouncement. "First," he began, "our dear hosts really know nothing about the Cohens; they only met them yesterday. Who can really say how reliable they may or may not be, or what traps may have been laid for them along the way? You can be sure that the Nazis will be covering the border like flies on flypaper. If we were there, we would be the hunted. As long as we remain here, our very presence in their midst will most likely remain unknown, and we will be able to begin our lives again when this tragedy has finally come to an end. Need I say more?" he paused for a moment before he presented his already obvious conclusion. "With our deepest gratitude, we will remain here in the relatively safekeeping of our blessed Christian hosts for as long as they will have us."

"It will be our honor and privilege to have you do so," Theo replied humbly.

"But what about us?" Michael demanded. "You can stay here if you please, but Hannah and I greatly desire to leave for France in the morning. Either there, or in some other place where we will finally be able to join with a community of other Jews so that we can at long last be married under a chuppah and get on with our lives."

Hans responded firmly and with finality, but still his words had a patina of gentle understanding. "Michael," he began, "you are the only son of my dearest friend and more like a son of my own than a future son-in-law. Still, you are a man, and as such you are free to decide these heady things of life this world gone mad has thrust upon us all. If you want to take a chance with the Cohens, then you are certainly free to do so with my blessings. But also hear this. Hannah is still an unmarried young woman, my daughter who remains in my keeping. She will remain my responsibility to protect until she becomes your wife, and thus, however you may chart your own fate, Hannah will remain here with her family."

"Then," Michael, sighing with great sadness, relented without further discussion, "so will I."[2]

May 14, 1940

Hannah watched Gerta with great interest as the two of them, side by side on their knees, looked over a four square meter bed of young tulip cultivars in various stages of development. "There are more than one hundred tulip species," Gerta continued what had been to Hannah a fascinating lesson on tulip cultivation. "Within these many species, there are an almost infinite variety of mostly man-developed cultivars in seemingly every color combination imaginable. Even so, we tulip growers are ever trying to be instrumental in bringing forth new and even more beautiful varieties; it is a passion with us."

"Perhaps, in your case, this is more of an art form," Hannah suggested. "This bed of hundreds of new possibilities is to you what a pallet is to an artist or a pen to a poet. For me this all seems so very exciting!" She continued, "Tell me, Gerta, when will the next cultivars bloom so that we may see what new beauty you have brought forth through the work of your hands?"

"It takes from five to seven years from the time the seeds germinate until the first flowers appear," Gerta explained. "I've planted from the front to the back of this cultivar bed. The first five rows were planted in 1937, three years ago, when all this new savagery in our world had not yet begun. Some of these may blossom as soon as in 1942, but I really don't expect to see many of them until at least 1943."

"What are you planting now, Gerta?" Hannah asked, genuinely fascinated.

"Technically, I am transplanting last season's seedling cultivars from their hot house seed beds into the back five rows of this bed. But we won't see anything from these new plantings until at least 1946. May God grant us all the blessings of His holy peace in that day and even soon before!" she exclaimed.

"It's happened!" Theo announced loudly as he came up behind the two of them without warning, his startling pronouncement rudely snapping them back from the sweet peace wherein they had been joyfully basking together into the sad and terrible reality of the moment. "Our pathetically weak military has just surrendered to the Germans!"

"How could such a thing happen?" Hannah exclaimed in utter disbelief, "and so quickly?"

Theo's reply was a crescendo of anger and despair that emanated from the depths of his soul. "My dear ladies—these monsters virtually destroyed our beautiful Rotterdam in a mere five hours of what they call blitzkrieg—an unmerciful, unceasing, devastating bombardment from the air!" His face now turned bright red from outrage as he continued his outburst. "They killed more than thirty thousand innocent civilians in just five hours! Then they made it clear that they planned to do the same to Amsterdam! Our air force did what they could to resist, but they were like a God-forgotten David standing against an army of modern-day Goliaths led by Satan himself. There was nothing they or anyone else could do. Their strategy worked brilliantly—we had no other real choice but surrender."

Gerta spoke in a near whisper as Hannah rushed into her outstretched arms and the waiting comfort of her loving embrace. "May God help our precious Jews."

"May God help us all," Hannah replied.[3]

April 1942

"I am so sorry, *liebchen*," Gerta shared her own disappointment with Hannah, using the German diminutive meaning "young loved one" as they once again knelt together to more closely examine the first five rows of the tulip cultivar bed. "They all look so healthy and promising, but we will have to wait at least another year to see what lovely new flowers God may have in store for us here."

"It is a bit disappointing," Hannah sighed, "but in a way it seems to me there is an implicit promise in this delay of at least another year. Perhaps it means we are to have another year of blessed sanctuary, here in this island of peace you have made for us, surrounded as it may be on every side with such terror and horror."

"I know," Gerta agreed, putting her arm around the lovely young woman who knelt beside her. "I have grown to hate listening to the reality of what Theo keeps bringing back to us from the city. I can't imagine how things could get much worse for all of your precious Jewish people, now that Adolf Eichmann has rounded up nearly all one hundred sixty thousand of them from all over the country and crowded them like animals into Amsterdam."

"It seems to me that Eichmann's purpose is quite clear," Hannah replied, her poorly suppressed fear nearly palpable. "He has herded them into a giant city pen, like sheared sheep rounded up to be hauled away for slaughter! Can't you see, Gerta, how very much this confirms the rumors Theo has heard in Lisse? Jews from all over Europe are being transported to some mysterious, terrible places in the east where they are being used as slave labor, then slaughtered when they are no longer able to work."

"There, there, *liebchen*," Gerta comforted. "I can't believe that even the Germans are capable of such terrible atrocities. Remember, these are only rumors, and in times like these, rumors become the bread of life upon which the idle feed.

"Speculating upon such rumors can accomplish nothing," Gerta continued, as the two of them now stood in a close, mutually comforting embrace. "You have been safe with us here for nearly three years—the Nazis know nothing of you—that the Meyers of Munich even exist. Eichmann and his henchmen are far too busy in Amsterdam with the one hundred sixty thousand of your dear brothers and sisters they do know about. And so, my little Hannah, let us continue to believe that your father's choice to remain here was correct, and let's get about our lives. What other choice do we have?"

Hannah's wave of terror subsided, and after a few moments, she began to smile. "Yes, Gerta, you are quite right; there is nothing else left for us to do," she pronounced. "So, let's get back to work. It seems to me that we have five new rows of cultivars to transplant."[4]

April 10, 1943

Flora tiptoed into Hannah's room. She and the others had arisen earlier, just after sunrise, to properly prepare the beginnings of a festive day of celebration. This was her lovely daughter's twenty-third birthday, and all of them, especially her beloved Hannah, needed at least one day of joyfulness to break the growing tedium and tension of what was occurring in and around the Theo de Goede Tulip Farm, their island of protection in a sea of hatred and despair.

"Wake up, Hannah!" Flora summoned as she kissed her daughter on the cheek. "Happy birthday!" she spoke a bit louder as Hannah sat up, rubbing the sleep from her eyes. "We have quite a wonderful day planned for you," she announced joyfully. "So out of bed, and let's get on with it!"

When they had all taken their places for breakfast at the giant oak table, Gerta, her large frame about to burst with excitement, stood in her place and spoke excitedly, "Happy birthday, Hannah! We had planned to start your special day with a breakfast fit for a queen, or should I say a Jewish princess. But it seems that our dear God has done us one better. So, if you will all kindly come along with me, I would like to present a very wonderful gift He has provided especially for this occasion."

As the six of them followed Gerta, Hannah suddenly understood the reason for her excitement as they approached the cultivar bed. "Ohhhh! Gerta!" she nearly screamed, as the first distant glimpse of the newly presented to the world lovely flower entered the theater of her perception. "One of them has blossomed at last!"

"Ohhh! Gerta! It's beautiful, exquisite!" Hannah exclaimed as she rushed the short remaining distance to the bed and fell to her knees immediately in front of the perfectly formed, long-stemmed, fluted, brilliantly red and white flower that had opened for the first time with the rising sun that very morning.

"This really is something special!" Theo proclaimed when he had taken his turn to examine God's handiwork manifested there in the rich soil of his dearly loved farm. "Yes indeed! There is no other red and white tulip anywhere nearly as lovely as this!" He had continued with an excitement matching that of the others. "This is one of those rare miracles we experience that makes our work among these lovely flowers so pleasing and rewarding. One day, when we have been able to produce enough bulbs for national recognition, this cultivar will take its place among the loveliest tulips in the world."

"And," Gerta continued, "when it does become famous in the eyes of the world, they will know it by a perfectly chosen and appropriate name." With that she took a label stake that she had been concealing under her full sweater and carefully pushed it into the rich soil immediately in front of the newly flowering cultivar. "From this day forward the world will know this glorious tulip by the name 'Hannah Ruth Meyers.'

"No other name could be more fitting," she continued. "The brilliant red of the flower is symbolic of Hannah's great courage and strength. Its alabaster white speaks fittingly of her remarkable loveliness and virginal purity. I could go on and on, but to summarize what I see in this incredible tulip, its elegance, beauty, strength, and so very much more are a God-painted mirror of our Hannah. May she, and this precious new flower, long survive in this world gone mad."

Amsterdam, Holland: April 10, 1943

Herr Doctor Arthur Seyss-Inquart took great personal pride in what he had already accomplished in his position as *Reichskommisar* of the German civil administration that had been installed in Amsterdam, shortly after Holland had surrendered to the Third Reich. His mission as the principal perpetrator of the annihilation of Dutch Jewry had been remarkably well accomplished, and now, after only three short years, he had won the personal commendation of the Fuhrer himself for having eliminated all but a very few remaining pockets of his Jewish prey who were already scheduled to be rounded up for transport to the east.

Now, as Dr. Seyss-Inquart sat imperially by himself in the plush backseat of his recently assigned Mercedes-Benz 540k Roadster, one of only a handful of duplicates of the magnificent original that had been custom built for Herman Goering himself, he knew that he had risen to the very top of those destined for the greatest responsibility and reward in the ever-expanding Nazi regime.

After the unrelenting quest of SS investigators had located the hitherto secret records of the International Dispersal Committee, how simple it had been for his own personal staff of investigators to locate yet another pocket of vile Jewry that had long lingered, right here, under their noses, Dr. Seyss-Inquart pridefully conjectured.

Caution had been one of the principal rungs in Seyss-Inquart's meteoric rise within the party, and he had not failed to cautiously assure that his currently sought prey would not once again escape their ultimate participation in the "Final Solution." He knew that he had planned well as his driver came to an abrupt stop in front of the principal residence of the de Goede Tulip Farm, and the two passenger trucks filled with SS troops, augmented by ten motorcycle-borne soldiers, quickly fanned out and meticulously surrounded the entire residential area so there could be no reasonable possibility of escape.

"Gerta!" Theo cried out in a vain, anguished warning from the direction of the main residence, where he had been taken in shocked surprise by the small party of SS, led by Seyss-Inquart himself. Now, after the main house had been thoroughly searched with no further results, they turned next toward the nearby bungalow, led by the now handcuffed Theo with Seyss-Inquart's PM Mouser 9mm Lugar held closely to the back of his head.

"Oh my God!" Gerta gasped out of sudden and sheer terror as she turned from where she had been standing with Hans, Flora, Hannah, and Michael for an early evening visit to the exquisite new floral arrival in the cultivar bed. Immediately she recognized the terrible nature of the quickly approaching party and all that it implied.

There was nothing to be done, she surmised, no possible escape. Desperately she struggled to frame a solution. "Good evening," she explained in a credibly normal greeting. "Welcome to our tulip farm. We have something very special to show you!"

"Indeed you do, Frau de Goede!" Seyss-Inquart exclaimed with delight as he correctly concluded the identity of the others who clearly matched the file photographs he had previously studied.

First, he screamed loathingly at Hans: "You, would be Hans Meyers, the long lost, overstuffed Jew banker!"

Then, turning to Michael, who stood by Hannah's side, holding her in the futile protection of his arms, Seyss-Inquart continued with absolute delight: "You would be Michael Silberman, son of yet another famous Munich banker who has so far managed to escape us."

"And you, my dear, would be Hannah Meyers," he continued in mock gentleness toward the most lovely of his cornered prey as he reached out and gently stroked Hannah's face, then, without missing a beat, he violently wrenched her away from Michael and into the arms of two nearby SS who quickly took them both into custody.

Next, filled with the visceral satisfaction of complete success, Seyss-Inquart grabbed Flora by her long, flowing, beautiful blonde hair as he shouted menacingly, "And you would be the most unusual Jewess, Flora Meyers!"

Flora tried to mask her pain, but even so, she screamed loudly as her jubilant captor savagely dragged her by her hair into the waiting grasp of yet another of the SS.

Finally, with the delight of a hunter who had just bagged a rare trophy, Seyss-Inquart once again turned to Gerta. "Tell me, my dear lady, how do you explain the presence of this family of vile Jews, here among your lovely tulips?"

"They had no idea who we were!" Hans clumsily tried to intervene. "We only arrived here yesterday and told them we were seeking work on their farm!"

"Liar!" Seyss-Inquart screamed, brutally striking Hans across his face with his Lugar, knocking him to the ground with his nose and mouth gushing blood. "Do you think we are fools?" their torturer continued. "You have all found sanctuary here since you arrived in Holland nearly four years ago!

"Isn't that so, Frau de Goede?" he continued, turning his vicious attention back to Gerta, who did not reply while she stood defiantly before her captor.

"Never mind, Frau de Goede," Seyss-Inquart continued as he raised his Lugar and pointed it toward her lovely, knowing, yet peacefully accepting pale blue eyes. "We all know that the punishment for hiding Jews is summary execution." With that, he calmly pulled the trigger.

"Noooo!" Theo screamed as he tried to break away from the grasp of the SS who held him and rush to his beloved Gerta's lifeless body as she fell headlong into the cultivar bed, her blood quickly forming a large crimson pool that hideously soaked into the rich finely broken soil as it eerily accentuated the red petals of the single lovely blossom that had come forth only that morning.

Seyss-Inquart was a well-practiced and skilled executioner. It took only another single, well-placed bullet between Theo's horrified eyes to send his lifeless body sprawling next to that of his beloved Gerta, where they would remain together for a time as a gruesome testimony to their knowing and freely given sacrifice.

Westerbork Transit Camp, Holland: July 1943[5]

The four of them peered out of the wire meshed windows of the crowded, heavily guarded SS transport bus as their steel-helmeted driver turned right off the main highway onto a narrow freshly asphalted entry road marked by an innocuous sign: "Welcome to Westerbork Transit Camp, 15 kilometers."

"Yakov, do you know anything of this place, Westerbork?" Hans inquired of Yakov Cohen, the black-clad, orthodox rabbi in his mid-fifties who was seated directly across the aisle. The two of them had struck up an immediate friendship and had enjoyed at least some mutual comfort from their almost unceasing conversation during the nearly two hours since they had departed the Amsterdam central prison.

"All Dutch Jews know a great deal about Westerbork," Yakov replied sadly. "It is quite ironic," he continued, "that this facility was built just before the war by the Dutch themselves as a place to house people just like you and your family, refugee German Jews who had managed to escape the Nazis. God forgive us, we Dutch Jews didn't want to take the risk of polluting our own community with any outside influence, so we urged the government to construct this camp very near the German border."

"We knew nothing of your Dutch Jewry," Hans replied with growing emotion. "We were insulated from all outside contact by a lovely Christian family until we were discovered, and they were slaughtered like animals before our very eyes for their 'crime' of trying to protect us."

"Your story is far from unique," the now ministering rabbi replied in a vain effort to comfort Hans, who had begun to weep. "I've heard of several other such sad situations, like your own, where Christians have been summarily executed for hiding Jews. You can be sure that Ha Shem[6] now holds these righteous ones very close to Himself."

"But what more can you tell me about Westerbork?" Hans abruptly turned away from pursuing their recent horrific experience any further.

"Of course, my friend," Yakov replied tenderly, "it is best not to dwell upon the past, but rather to look for ways to cope with what lies immediately ahead.

"Right after Holland surrendered," Yakov continued, "the Nazis took over Westerbork and expanded it considerably for their own purposes. What we had intended to be a place of long-term isolated refuge, they immediately turned into a *Durchgangslager*, a transit camp. They even constructed a railroad spur that terminates in the very heart of the camp. Now, every Tuesday, a train packed with our people leaves this place headed to a place called Auschwitz, far to the east in Poland."

"We have only heard wild rumors about this Auschwitz," Hans interrupted. "Surely, what we have heard—"

"I don't know what you've heard," Yakov interrupted Hans in turn, "but there have been so many mutually verifying reports that what you've heard, however terrible, is likely to be the truth of what may eventually await us all."

Hans, now shaken by what he had just heard, probed further. "These Tuesday transports you speak of," he asked nervously, "how does the SS select those who are to leave?"

"This is perhaps the most insidious and tragic aspect of our new 'transit home,'" Yakov continued. "The sad truth is that the SS has turned over the matter of transport selection to our own quasi-governmental Jewish Security Service. These are Jews—fellow camp inmates who have been delegated a wide range of administrative authority and control.

"The Nazi camp commandant merely gives the weekly quota as an order; the Jewish "governing" body simply carries it out, in fear of themselves being deported. Imagine the irony, Jews selecting other Jews for what they believe must be almost certain death."

"What criteria does this Jewish 'governing body' use to make their selections?" Hans asked incredulously. "Time spent at Westerbork? Health? Age? Their own survival? How could Jews manage such a thing?"

"Quite frankly, I've been amazed by what I've heard," Yakov replied incredulously. "All of the criteria you mentioned seem to play some role in the weekly selection; however, you've left out what may be the greatest criterion of all. Those of us with money or other material assets seem to survive the longest, as do those of our beautiful young women who are willing to exchange the use of their bodies for yet another week of assured life."

Despite his self-disgust at the thought, Hans felt a new surge of hope as he considered with great satisfaction the imminent life-saving potential of the individual cache of diamonds that by his insistent foresight he and his two dear ones had so far managed to keep hidden in the secret places of their bodies.

"Can you tell me more about the camp itself?" Hans changed the subject, failing to conceal the surge of relief he felt from the possibility that his wealth might once again assure his dear ones and himself of continued survival.

"Of course," Yakov replied, keeping to himself his own mixed feelings of sadness and joy regarding the apparent relative affluence of this lovely and desperate family.

"Westerbork is a very strange place, indeed," he continued. "There is a school for the 'orphans,' that is, for children who came here without their parents. There are even such luxuries as a hairdresser, an orchestra, and a fine restaurant. As a matter of fact, if you have money, you can openly buy goods that are impossible to find anywhere else in Holland.

"There are also workshops," Yakov continued, "music, and a well-equipped hospital, staffed by the best Jewish medical personnel in the country—there is even a maternity ward.

"Now let me tell you the most amazing thing of all—there is even a makeshift synagogue where we are allowed to conduct regular religious services!"

"Why would they allow us such comforts if they intend to eventually transport us to the east for annihilation?" Hans asked incredulously.

"I'm certain, from all I've heard," Yakov replied, "this 'comfort' system was designed by the SS in order to avoid any problems during the transfers to Auschwitz. Despite the growing numbers of highly credible reports to the contrary, many of us who are held in this place actually have been led to believe that the condition of life will be the same in the camps of Poland. The Nazis always seem to leave just a little hope for survival.

"Ahhh," Yakov exclaimed as the bus pulled to an abrupt halt in front of a smiling and waving group of camp inmates who were obviously a welcoming committee of sorts. "This is Monday," he concluded as he rose from his seat. "You must remember that there is also a Boulevard of a Thousand Sighs in this place where the selected ones board the train."

"Tuesday is the day of terror, when the weekly train leaves for the east. Whoever finds their name on the list must pack their meager belongings and get ready to leave here with a bowed head. "Those of us who aren't on the list can be relieved that our future life has been extended for at least one more week.

"This weekly Tuesday train," Yakov concluded, as he boldly stepped from the bus into the next numbered day of his remaining life, "this damnable Tuesday train has precedent over everything else and dominates life here in what has just become your new home!

"Hans, my friend, if we both manage to survive the morning selection, then let's make it a point to continue our conversation tomorrow evening."[7]

"By all means," Hans replied sincerely. "I will look forward to our continued friendship."

The four of them instinctively huddled closely together seeking mutual, albeit nonexistent, protection as, transfixed by the incongruous silence of the horror before them, they witnessed the last of the selected "transport" of more than four hundred of their fellow Westerbork Jews, peacefully and without protest, board the boxcar, the railed conveyance to their inevitable doom.

It was Hannah who first spoke as the grossly overloaded train laboriously began to pull away from the camp's railhead. "It is only a matter of time," she gasped in a near whisper uttered between poorly suppressed sobs, "before we too will take our final journey to the east."

"Hannah!" Hans protested loudly. "I will hear none of this kind of talk! Do you think I've stood idly by doing nothing to protect us all these months?"

He paused for a moment to carefully survey the area around them to make certain that he would not be overheard before he continued. "After we men and women were herded last night into our gender-separate barracks, I accomplished a great deal while you were all sleeping."

"Like what?" Flora asked skeptically.

"Like, first of all," Hans replied defensively, "I sold one of my diamonds for a great deal of Lager Westerbork Gutschein [Camp Westerbork coupons]. We now have enough local currency to last us until we are finally released from this place, and I for one plan to stay here for a very long time—at least until the war is over."

"And just how are we to manage escaping the weekly 'transports' to the east until then, whenever it may be?" Flora continued to probe bitterly.

"It may not be as long as you think!" Hans protested. "Just last night I heard that the Americans had landed in force at Sicily and that the Germans are suffering huge losses on their eastern front and are being beaten back by the Russians. And that's not the best part!" he added. "It is widely being reported that both the Americans and the British are bombing the life out of all the major cities in Germany!

"Listen to me, you three!" he exclaimed passionately. "All we have to do is to wait this thing out here, and we will survive!"

"Hans!" Flora countered with equal passion. "You haven't answered my question. Just exactly how do you plan for us to avoid the weekly 'transport' until then?"

"Money, my dear! Money!" He exclaimed. "From what I have already learned, money can buy anything in Westerbork, and between us we have enough diamonds to practically buy the entire place and everything in it."

"This is almost starting to sound encouraging!" Michael opinioned.

"Of course it is!" Hans quickly picked up on this increasingly rare note of optimism. "The fact is," he continued, "we can actually live better, more normal lives here than many non-Jews are living throughout this country."

"Do you call men and women sleeping in separate barracks 'normal,'

Vatti?" Hannah questioned sarcastically. "When will Michael and I do the very normal thing of becoming husband and wife—maybe even years from now at the end of the war?"

"You won't have to wait quite that long," Hans replied, smiling broadly. "You see, I was saving the best news from my night's work until last." He teasingly waited a few moments before he continued. "I also had a nice chat with Yakov Cohen, you know, the rabbi we met on the bus just yesterday. Well, it seems that he will be in charge of Jewish religious affairs here in the camp, and he sees no reason why he cannot marry you two in a small unofficial ceremony at any time of your choosing. We tentatively agreed on next Sunday!"

"Wonderful! How absolutely wonderful!!" Hannah squealed in sheer delight. "What do you say to Sunday, Michael?"

"Perhaps even sooner!" he replied ecstatically. "But, please tell me, what is an unofficial wedding?"

"It seems that the Germans have officially banned all Jewish marriages everywhere—they see no need for us to procreate," Hans replied resolutely. "What I have arranged is a simple private exchange of vows between the two of you, officiated by Rabbi Cohen and witnessed by Flora and myself. There will be no official civil record of this marriage, not even a Ketubah (religious marriage contract). But, children, you will be married in the eyes of God, and later, after the war, you can make it more official in the eyes of men."

"Pardon me for asking," Hannah ventured, "but what about—well, you know—"

"That's the difficult part of this," Hans understandingly replied. "As you both well know, the men and women here, married or not, must sleep separately. And during the day we are crowded into this place like animals—there is no place, no opportunity."

"No honeymoon!" Michael interceded, as his future father-in-law groped for the right words of explanation.

"Yes, Michael, you are quite correct," Hans replied with deep sadness. There will be no consummation, no honeymoon, only your mutual expression of eternal love and commitment made before God and us two witnesses. I'm afraid this is the best I could do."

Instinctively, the four of them came together in a tight, loving circle of embrace. "Vatti," Hannah spoke from her heart, "one day when this insanity has finally come to an end, Michael and I will present you and Mutti with blessed grandchildren—the fruit of our love for one another and for you both."

"Yes," Michael sighed resignedly before verbalizing his already silent acceptance. "The bride of my heart will be a wonderful and blessed gift for now—the bride of my flesh will have to wait."

From the moment they all came together for the best fare the Westerbork's singular restaurant could provide for a wedding breakfast, Sunday, July 18, 1943, was a glorious day for the four of them, filled with the excitement and joy of the long-delayed union of Hannah and Michael. For each of them it was an indescribably wonderful, albeit momentary, relief from the nagging, ever present fear that had become the tedium of their daily lives, ever since the horror of their captivity had begun amidst the murderously shed blood of their beloved benefactors, Gerta and Theo.

Hans, the father of the bride, beamed with the pride of his great accomplishment as he held forth the bottle of 1939 Laurent-Perrier he had managed to barter for late that morning. "This may not be the wedding that we and the Silbermans had planned for our children," Hans exclaimed, "but let me tell you, it will be the finest that money can buy in this terrible place."

"It must have cost you a fortune," Flora replied, her face lit up with a moment of sheer happiness.

"My dear," he replied with relish, "you'd be surprised how far the proceeds of one small diamond will stretch in the Westerbork marketplace. There will also be a lovely bouquet of white roses for Hannah, an orchid corsage for the lovely mother of the bride, and boutonnieres for the groom and of course for the dashing father of the bride."

"Shouldn't we be very discreet about all of this, Hans?" Flora asked with a sudden return of the chilling fear that had become the companion of her every moment. "We must remember what Rabbi Cohen told us: weddings aren't permitted in this place."

"It isn't like we've invited all of Westerbork to attend, Flora!" he replied with mock severity. "The only people who know about our ceremony this afternoon are the four of us and Rabbi Cohen."

"What about the people who sold you the champagne, to say nothing of the wedding bouquet and the rest of the flowers?"

"They are all Jews, like us," he replied, the reality of his own rising fear almost choking off his words. "I said nothing to them, nothing—and why would they betray us?"

"The Nazis have turned all of us into animals struggling for survival," she replied with newfound wisdom. "There are those of us here who would sell their souls to gain just one more week's reprieve from a transport to the east." Then, in sympathetic response to her husband who had now begun to visibly tremble, she added, "Never mind, Hans. What's done is done, and I am probably being overly cautious—after all, it's my right to be emotional; I'm the mother of the bride!"

For the ceremony, Rabbi Yakov Cohen had selected the small, windowless storeroom behind the men's barracks where he resided in order to avoid any undue attention from even those captive residents who regularly attended his religious services in the large public meeting place that had been provided for this purpose by the camp authorities.

By relocating most of his meager personal belongings and furnishings, the clandestine officiate was thus able to make room for a traditional chuppah (a canopy symbolizing the new home the newlyweds will make together) formed at the top by two laced together tallitim (prayer shawls) held aloft by long wooden poles affixed to each corner at the top and mounted in wooden blocks at the bottom to temporarily secure it to the floor.

"She is so beautiful!" Hans whispered with rightful fatherly pride to Flora, who stood closely by his side as they, holding hands, joyfully witnessed Hannah as she joined Michael under the chuppah.

"Oh yes!" the mother of the bride quickly agreed. "And Michael is such a gorgeous young man—Ernst and Ritha would be so very proud of him today."

Speaking intimately to his miniscule congregation of four, Rabbi Cohen began the ceremony with a brief introduction:

> The Jewish view is that marriage is a fusion of the souls, a partnership for life. God created the first man, Adam, and the first woman, Eve, from one body. Marriage returns us to oneness. Men and women become complete through marriage. Rabbinic tradition teaches that a marriage will only be peaceful if God is a part of the union.
>
> The Hebrew word for man is *eish*, which is spelled *Aleph-Yud-Shin*.

> The Hebrew word for woman is *eisha*, which is spelled *Aleph-Shin-Hay*. The letters *Yud* and *Hay* combine to form the Hebrew name for God. Removing the letters *Yud* and *Hay*, that is, removing God from the words *eish* and *eisha*, leaves only the letters *Aleph* and *Shin*.
>
> *Aleph* and *Shin* spell *esh*, which is the Hebrew word for fire. Thus, Judaism teaches that if God is not made a part of the union between a man and a woman, then the couple will be left only with fire.

"Michael and Hannah," Rabbi Cohen continued, "I am aware that you two have been ordained to marry for virtually all the days of your lives. Thus, your years together, growing up from childhood to the two young adults who now stand before us in the presence of God, have been your time of engagement. Sadly, however, our circumstances are such that there can be no *ketuvah* [written marriage contract], but never mind, the absence of this document in no way diminishes the sacred fact that you will be married in the eyes of God."

Raising his hands, Rabbi Cohen then solemnly recited the seven traditional wedding blessings:

> You are blessed, Lord our God, the sovereign of the world, who created everything for His glory.
>
> You are blessed, Lord our God, the sovereign of the world, the creator of man.
>
> You are blessed, Lord our God, the sovereign of the world, who created man in His image, in the pattern of His own likeness, and provided for the perpetuation of His kind. You are blessed, Lord, the creator of man.
>
> Let the barren city be jubilantly happy and joyful at her joyous reunion with her children. You are blessed, Lord, who makes Zion rejoice with her children.
>
> Let the loving couple be very happy, just as You made Your creation happy in the Garden of Eden, so long ago. You are blessed, Lord, who makes the bridegroom and the bride happy.
>
> You are blessed, Lord our God, the sovereign of the world, who created joy and celebration, bridegroom and bride, rejoicing, jubilation, pleasure and delight, love and brotherhood, peace and friendship. May there soon be heard, Lord our God, in the cities of Judea and in the streets of Jerusalem the sound of joy and the sound of celebration, the voice of a bridegroom and the voice of a bride, the happy shouting of bridegrooms from their weddings and of young men from their feasts

> of song. You are blessed, Lord, who makes the bridegroom and the bride rejoice together.
>
> You are blessed, Lord our God, the sovereign of the world, creator of the fruit of the vine.

"Michael," Rabbi Cohen continued, "do you take Hannah Ruth Meyers to be your wife?"

"I do," Michael replied, his eyes already swelling with joyful emotion.

"Do you promise to love, cherish, and protect her, whether in good fortune or in adversity, and to seek with her a life hallowed by the faith of Israel?"

"I do," Michael replied with strong conviction.

Rabbi Cohen now turned to the bride. "Hannah, do you take Michael Joshua Silberman to be your husband?"

"I do," she replied out of the deep love and mutual commitment born in their early childhood.

"Do you promise to love, cherish, and protect him, whether in good fortune or in adversity, and to seek with him a life hallowed by the faith of Israel?"

"I do," she replied with profound joy.

It seems Hans had not been the only shopper in the family that morning since Michael had managed to find and purchase two matching gold wedding bands from a fellow inmate turned entrepreneur.

Rabbi Cohen now withdrew Hannah's ring from his pocket and handed it to Michael.

"Michael, as you place this ring on Hannah's finger, speak to her these vows: 'With this ring you are consecrated to me as my wife according to the law of God and the faith of Israel.'"

When Michael had repeated these vows and lovingly placed the ring on Hannah's finger, Rabbi Cohen withdrew the other ring from his pocket and presented it to Hannah.

"Hannah" he continued, "as you place this ring on the Michael's finger, speak to him these vows: 'With this ring you are consecrated to me as my husband according to the law of God and the faith of Israel.'"

When Hannah had repeated these vows and placed the ring on Michael's finger, Rabbi Cohen presented them with a partly filled glass of red wine.

When the bride and groom had both partaken, he took the now empty glass from Michael, wrapped it in a piece of white cloth, and then handed it back to him.

"I now, in the presence of God and in the faith of Israel, pronounce that you are husband and wife."

Michael now excitedly placed the wrapped wine glass on the floor and then stomped it soundly, thoroughly shattering it with his heavy, right-shoed foot.

"Mazel tov!" the five of them shouted joyfully.

Michael and Hannah, who had ever so reluctantly parted to spend their wedding night separately in their designated places, greeted one another with a long, close, loving embrace when they met the next morning for breakfast with Hans and Flora.

Then, at long last, as husband and wife, they spent the rest of the day together, hand in hand, sharing their dreams and stealing an occasional kiss when they hoped no one would pay them any notice.

It was very late on this Monday afternoon when a sober-faced, Jewish minor camp official found Hans and Flora sitting quietly together waiting for the evening meal that was soon to be served. After requesting to see their camp identity cards for confirmation, without a word, he handed them individually addressed sealed envelopes.

Ashen faced and with shaking hands, Hans opened this horrifying communication and withdrew its one-page notice. What he read confirmed what he already had dreadfully surmised. The notice began: "You are ordered to report to the Westerbork Rail head at 1530 hours, Tuesday, July 20, for transport to a Labor Camp in the East."

Within the next half hour, more than four hundred other inmates had received identical notices. Hannah, Michael, and Rabbi Cohen were among them.

Chapter 5
Hear O Israel
Rabbi Akiva and the Emergence of Rabbinical Judaism
(The Estate of Kalba Savua, March A.D. 75)[1]

Akiva ben Joseph stood in awe before the huge and exquisite manor house of Kalba Savua located near the place where the Jordan River flowed out from the Kinneret (Sea of Galilee) to make its way south until it reached and, over the ensuing centuries, has continuously replenished what we know today as an Israeli national treasure called the Dead Sea.

This strapping, commandingly personable, strikingly handsome, and obviously intelligent young man of twenty-five had done his best to prepare for this vitally important meeting with the Kalba Savua, the fabulously wealthy master of a magnificent plantation. Even so, he still struggled to fend off his growing feelings of inadequacy as he considered his own meager qualifications to assume the key position as general supervisor of the estate that would make him personally responsible for its many and greatly varied activities and business affairs.

To start with, Akiva lamented, he was not a Jew but rather the first son of a humble pagan family who struggled to survive while working as tenant farmers on their own miniscule assigned portion of this very rich and enormous estate. He was genuinely amazed at his own chutzpah to think that he might somehow be appointed to this high executive position. The fact was, he knew practically nothing of and cared even less about Judaism. What little he did know about this religion of the Jews, he knew by observation and common knowledge, and he knew it was the driving force in the life of the notoriously kind and generous gentleman whom he now dared to seek as his employer.

Certainly Akiva had heard reports of the devastation reaped upon the Jews of Judea and the destruction of their temple only five years earlier, but all of this, the blood that flowed in the streets, and the now-emerging sect that would one day be known as "rabbinical Judaism" meant nothing whatsoever to him at this crucial point in his young life. Even in his wildest imaginations, he had no way of knowing that he was destined to be regarded by all future generations as the greatly beloved and most highly esteemed "father of rabbinical Judaism."

While there was much he did lack, with respect to his present situation, Akiva did enjoy the full confidence, personal friendship and support of one called Hurkanos, a lifelong neighbor and trusted confidant of Kalba Savua. Moreover, he had been assured by Hurkanos, their mutual friend, that he had already highly recommended him to Kalba Savua. With this in mind, he took a deep breath and knocked firmly upon the thick, hand-carved, wooden door of the mansion that would also be the entryway to his amazing new life that lay just ahead.

Whether it was the hand of the God whom Akiva did not then know, or the great impact of Hurkanos' recommendation, or both, Kalba Savua had been instantly impressed with the young man with whom he had now been warmly and intimately conversing for nearly two hours as they sat across from one another in large upholstered leather chairs set in the center of the estate's luxuriously appointed library.

"As you may know, Akiva," Kalba Savua began to share what already seemed like the obvious conclusion of their meeting, "my wife and I were not blessed with any sons, only one daughter, our precious Rachel. I have therefore hired several older men over the years whom I felt might progress to the point where they could take over the huge responsibilities you are now seeking to undertake. Sadly, my judgment proved wrong in each case."

He paused for a few moments before he continued, searching for just the right words. "Akiva," he went on with conviction, "I may have been wrong before, but I am most confident that I am not wrong now. You may be very young and not well experienced, but you are bright, strong, eager to learn, and boundlessly ambitious. Once more you have a way of capturing the confidence and heart of those whom you seek to impress. Need I say more? Akiva, you have won both my confidence and trust. I assume you can relocate to the nearby supervisor's residence, which has stood empty for some time, and that you will be able to begin your new work immediately?"

Akiva's gratitude and sincerity were greatly apparent as he replied without a moment's hesitation, "I am overwhelmed by your great confidence, sir.

You can be certain that I will dedicate my every energy and prove to you that you have not misplaced your trust in me, your humble servant. By all means, I will begin my new work even before the sun sets on this the most memorable day of my life."

With that, Kalba Savua stood, as did Akiva. It was a moment they would both always remember as they embraced and shook hands to seal their mutual commitment.

"Please, Akiva," his new employer invited, "I trust you will join us for the midday meal, which should now be ready to serve."

"I would be greatly honored," Akiva replied, trying to conceal at least some of the joy that now threatened to come forth in an unrestrained outburst.

"Wonderful!" declared his host, fully understanding and admiring his just hired supervisor's self-control as he reached for the dinner bell and shook it energetically.

In the next magic moment that was to define the rest of his days, Akiva was smitten instantly and totally captivated by the beautiful young Jewish woman who entered into their presence in response to her father's call.

"Akiva," this is my precious and greatly treasured only child, Rachel." Kalba Savua introduced his daughter with righteous pride.

"Rachel," he continued, filled with the satisfaction of what he had just arranged, "this is Akiva, who, effective immediately, has become the supervisor of our estate."

Now addressing them both, he added, "You two will be working closely together, along with the members of your staff, on those matters that need to be coordinated on a day-to-day basis. I will only be concerned with very major issues that may arise from time to time."

Akiva was barely able to speak at the incredible good fortune that had come his way in a matter of only one morning. Not only did he suddenly find himself in a social and economic position he had only dreamt of achieving by the end of his days, but here before him stood the living realization of all of his romantic and sensual fantasies since these deep stirrings had first made themselves known within his inner being so long ago. Even so, he fully understood that this lovely object of his great fascination was first and foremost the treasured daughter of his prominent Jewish employer, whose continued chastity had now become a part of his own sacred trust.

"I am so pleased to meet you, Rachel," he managed to speak in something more than a whisper. He cleared his throat, struggling to regain complete control. "It will be so good to be working with you and your staff. I already feel like I have become part of your greatly blessed family."

Rachel, it seems, was equally smitten. "While we have only just met, it seems to me that you may be the brother for whom I have always longed."

In a sudden flash of realization, Kalba Savua knew he had perhaps gone too far. He scowled deeply, then exclaimed, "You must always remember, both of you, we are a family of Jews!"

In keeping with their charter from Kalba Savua, Akiva, and Rachel, at first always in the company of others, met at least once each day. Two things were inarguable concerning their relationship. First, between the two of them, in only a few weeks they had more than met Kalba Savua's expectations. The various activities of the estate that had long been in terrible disrepair were now beginning to thrive as a direct result of Akiva's extraordinary management as it was greatly enhanced by Rachel's own special insights and guidance. Second, not surprisingly, their mutual subtle flirtations, driven by their irrepressible physical attraction demanded what had long been their natural human response. Finally, one evening when they had managed to slip away from all the others, they met alone for the first time in the secluded rose garden behind the mansion. Even then, with their first passionate embrace, they had fallen deeply in love.

Bringing their love to its ultimate fruition in marriage was yet another seemingly insurmountable problem.

"We simply cannot go on this way," Akiva cried out one morning, several weeks after their now frequent stolen private times together had begun. "What must I do to gain your father's acceptance as your husband? God knows, I am willing to do anything!"

"That is exactly my point," Rachel responded, unable to suppress her soul-gripping sadness. "God knows this too; my father will never accept you because you are not a Jew! Nothing can change the nature of your birth or the pagan blood that flows through your veins!"

"What if I were to leave this place for an extended time and go to the rabbinical academy at Yavne to study under their brilliant scholars? However long it might take, I would stay among them, studying night and day until they finally accepted me as one of their own, a fully enfranchised member of their and your faith, no matter my ethnic heritage."

"You would do such a thing for me?" she replied incredulously. "You would give up your wonderful position here? Your future? All of this, no matter how long it might take with the two of us living apart?"

Akiva was now on his knees before her. "Rachel, my darling, I would do anything if you would be my wife. I beg of you to covenant with me this very moment that you are in fact my wife, and this you will always be."

"Yes, my darling Akiva," she replied, the tears turned from sadness to overflowing joy. "Yes! Yes! Yes!"

And so it was that Akiva traveled to Yavne to make arrangements for his forthcoming extended period of study. So it was also that their private covenant of marriage was consummated without delay, and they cohabited as husband and wife to the extent that their difficult circumstances allowed.

At first, Kalba Savua was distraught over the impending loss of this his most extraordinary employee. However, it pleased him greatly to learn that this pagan was willing to go to great lengths to learn more about the one true God. Thus, in the end, he had no choice but to bless Akiva's decision.

Inevitably, some three months after their secret relationship had begun, and just a few days before Akiva's planned departure for Yavne, Rachel could no longer conceal her good news. "Akiva," she announced when they had come together for one of their frequent romantic rendezvous, "we can wait no longer to tell Abba that we are betrothed. We must hurry to get things settled here before you leave."

He sensed that there was something more by the tone of her voice and this sudden urgency. "Is there something else I should know?" he probed.

"Yes, my darling Akiva," she replied joyfully. "I am with child."

And so it was that the two of them stood before Kalba Savua that evening and confessed their situation, begging his understanding, indulgence, and support. Instead, in a fit of rage, he drove his daughter from his house and swore that he would never help her as long as Akiva remained her husband.

Akiva, with his young pregnant wife, therefore lived under the most impoverished and constrained circumstances. Indeed, so poverty-stricken did they become that Rachel had to sell her hair to enable her husband to pursue his studies.

Worse still, they had no choice but to live apart, she in a small hut in nearby Tiberias, where she begged for assistance from her girlhood friends with whom she remained close; all of this while Akiva struggled to survive under even worse conditions while he diligently pursued his studies.

According to the rabbinical literature and legend, Akiva and Rachel's self-imposed separation endured almost continuously for another twenty-four years, apparently interspersed by occasional conjugal visits that resulted in additional children, the number of which cannot now be accurately determined.

What is well documented, however, is that through all of his and Rachel's diligent sacrifices, Akiva not only grew to be considered as a great teacher at Yavne, but that he also emerged as their undisputed leader, a leader who has long since been acknowledged through all of the ensuing centuries as "the father of rabbinical Judaism."

Moreover, according to this same rabbinical literature, on the great day when Akiva returned to permanently reside with his wife and children after twenty-four years of only occasional visits, he did so as a famous scholar, escorted by twenty-four thousand disciples, who reverently followed their beloved master. When his poorly clad wife was about to embrace him, some of his students, not knowing who she was, sought to restrain her. But, Akiva exclaimed, "Let her alone; for what I am, and for what we are, to this noble woman the thanks are due."[2]

But there is even more to this happy ending. When Kalba Savua learned of Akiva's enormous success and the lofty position to which he had arisen, he at once canceled his vow against him and Rachel, immediately gave him half of his enormous wealth, and joyfully embraced them both as well as his several grandchildren.

Today, in death, once again, Akiva and Rachel remain apart, their tombs in Tiberias separated by a considerable distance. Even so, many thousands of Jewish pilgrims come each year to visit and revere them both, subscribing to them supernatural powers sufficient to answer the most difficult of petitions: "divine" healing, the conception of children, and all manner of other such needs requiring some higher plane of intervention.

Beyond this happy ending to his family's life story, Akiva, as the acknowledged "father" of rabbinical Judaism, left behind the theological and doctrinal foundation of what began as the religion of the Pharisees and today survives as the most orthodox and vital expression of traditional Judaism.

Perhaps the most enduring and distinctive among Akiva's many theological legacies is his remarkable and entirely unique system of biblical interpretation, the essence of which is that the rabbis were henceforth endowed with the authority to interpret the words of Scripture in such a way that Scripture was thus made to conform with the rabbinical interpretation or opinion.

In a way, Akiva's new hermeneutical system would seem to be a continuation of the fault Yeshua found with the Pharisees, as it is recorded in the Gospel according to Matthew: "These people draw near to Me with their mouth, and honor Me with their lips, but their heart is far from Me. And in vain they worship Me, teaching as doctrines the commandments of men" (Matt. 15:8–9).

The enormous impact of Akiva's hermeneutical system can be seen much later (circa 1168) as it was codified in the teachings of Maimonides, another notorious and highly esteemed rabbinical father. Maimonides' full Hebrew name was Moshe ben Maimon. To the Jewish world, he is known by the acronym of Rabbi Moshe ben Maimon, "Rambam."

Rambam was a Sephardic Jew, born in Spain shortly before the fanatical Muslim Almohades came to power there. To avoid persecution by the Muslims, who offered both Jews and Christians the choice of conversion to Islam or death, Rambam fled with his family, first to Morocco, later to Israel, then finally to Egypt.

One of Rambam's major contributions to Judaism and Jewish life in general was the Mishneh Torah, his meticulously detailed code of Jewish law that deals with virtually every aspect of day-to-day Jewish life. His intention was to compose a book that would guide Jews on how to behave in all situations just by reading the Torah and his code, without having to expend large amounts of time searching through the then already massive Talmud and other rabbinical commentary. Needless to say, this provocative rationale did not endear Maimonides to many traditional Jews, who feared that people would rely on his code and no longer study the Talmud, the other considerable commentaries, or, even worse, the Holy Scriptures of the Tenach. Even so, despite sometimes great opposition, the Mishneh Torah became a standard guide for Jewish living and practice.[3]

While the Mishneh Torah remains even today the very centerpiece of the "Oral Law" around which modern-day rabbinical Judaism virtually revolves, Rambam also formulated a credo of Judaism expressed in "Thirteen Articles of Faith" that continues to have, by far, a much greater impact upon all Jews in general and, in particular, upon some Orthodox-rooted Messianic believers; i.e., those Jews who have embraced Yeshua as Messiah.

Two of these Thirteen Articles of Faith formulated by Rambam upon which contemporary Judaism is so absolutely founded and inexorably entwined are the second and third of these articles:

2. The belief in God's absolute and unparalleled UNITY.

3. The belief in God's non-corporeality (inability to take on human form), nor that He will be affected by any physical occurrences, such as movement, or rest, or dwelling.

While Article Three was seemingly penned by Rambam to directly confront the core Christian doctrine of Yeshua's bodily incarnation, it is Article Two that has had and continues to have by far the greatest impact upon all of Judaism.

Moreover, I believe that with Rambam's seemingly innocuous paraphrase of the Sh'ma (Deut. 6:4), he personally became responsible for the huge, long-enduring, and perhaps irreconcilable theological gulf that exists today between rabbinical Judaism and Christianity regarding the nature and substance of the Godhead.

While both Judaism and Christianity worship Yahweh, the Lord God of Israel, the rabbinical understanding of the nature and character of the "absolute unity" of the Godhead is radically different from the Christian triune understanding.

It seems to me the central cause of the great and enduring rift between Judaism and Christianity, this seemingly insurmountable wall that stands between the Jewish people and their recognition of Yeshua as their Messiah, can be laid at Rambam's feet as a direct result of his paraphrase of the Sh'ma.

The words of the Sh'ma are: "Hear, O Israel: The LORD our God, the LORD is one!" (Deut. 6:4). The Holy Spirit's deliberate choice of the Hebrew word to designate the unity "one" here is *echad*. In this particular foundational verse, and in several other instances in the Torah, *echad* is used to describe a unity that specifically allows a plurality.

For example, in the following verse there are two single entities, the "evening" and the "morning," designated by a pluralized unity; first (*echad*), "God called the light Day, and the darkness He called Night. So the evening and the morning were the first day" (Gen. 1:5). Similarly, in this next example, there are two single entities, "man" and his "wife," designated by the pluralized unit, "one" (*echad*): "Therefore a man shall leave his father and mother and be joined to his wife, and they shall become one flesh" (Gen. 2:24). Finally, the most poignant example is found in the Sh'ma itself wherein the plural form used for "God" (*Elohim*) is described as a pluralized unity "one" (*echad*), which certainly makes a grammatical provision for three individual entities: Father, Son, and Holy Spirit.

> Hear, O Israel: The LORD our God, the LORD is one!
>
> —DEUTERONOMY 6:4

Article Two of Rambam's Thirteen Articles of Faith is a paraphrase of the Sh'ma:

> The belief in God's absolute and unparalleled UNITY.

Instead of using what should have seemed the obvious *echad*, Rambam chose instead the Hebrew word *yachid* in his Second Article of Faith.

Yachid appears only 12 times in the Tenach, while *echad* appears 464 times in the Torah alone, and in many other places elsewhere throughout the Tenach. *Yachid*'s meaning is "very self, only; solitary; lonely, unique, one."

It seems clear that Rambam chose *yachid* in this context to convey the idea of an absolute, indivisible unity. Moreover, I believe he did so quite deliberately for two reasons: first, to draw a line in the sand showing his agreement with the Pharisees' understanding of the indivisibility of the Godhead and, therefore, his disagreement with the Essene triune understanding, which was a legacy from their mainline ancient predecessors. Secondly, it would seem clear that Rambam chose to directly confront and discredit the then-flourishing Christian understanding of *echad* as it allows for a triune understanding of Yahweh (YHWH).

Finally, it would be a serious omission in this brief overview of the highlights of Rabbi Akiva's life not to include some mention of his almost single-handed instigation and leadership of the second Jewish revolt against Rome (132–135), the events leading up to this revolt, and the enduring fallout of this conflict upon the Jewish people.

Akiva began his studies at Yavne soon after the Sanhedrin leadership of that time adopted the nineteenth "blessing" to be recited three times each day in all synagogues beginning circa 90:

> For the renegades let there be no hope, and may the arrogant kingdom soon be rooted out in our days, and the Netzarim [Nazarenes] and the

> Minim [non-Jews] perish as in a moment and be blotted out from the book of life and with the righteous may they not be inscribed. Blessed are You, Lord, who humbles the arrogant.

This official venting of the emerging rabbinical sect's growing hostility upon those whom they called *minim* ("foreigners, sectarians, or apostates") was, for the most part, pointedly directed against Jews who had embraced Yeshua and in the process of doing so had, according to the Jewish law promulgated by the Pharisee-dominated Sanhedrin, forgone their Jewish ethnicity and heritage in the process.

It thus seems clear that Akiva held a strongly negative opinion of Yeshua and His followers from the outset, an opinion that under his hand later came to become strongly evident in the pages of the Mishna, which he became consumed in writing, and by other writings in the Talmudic commentary that followed what had become this central man-authored guide of rabbinical Judaism.

After the first "Great Jewish Revolt" against Rome failed in 70, the Roman authorities took measures to suppress the rebellious province by installing a senior official as governor and stationing an entire legion in Jerusalem under his command.

Things seemed to be taking a turn for the better in 130 when Emperor Hadrian visited the ruins of the city. At first he seemed sympathetic toward the Jews and promised to rebuild the city, but the Jews, who were greatly influenced by Akiva, felt betrayed when they learned that Hadrian planned to rebuild their holiest city as a Roman metropolis, with a new temple upon the ruins of the second temple that was to be dedicated to the pagan god Jupiter.

Hadrian then assigned a second legion to Judea to maintain order, and he began to reshape the city that was to be renamed as Aelia Capitolina. Moreover, Jewish unrest continued to be inflamed when Hadrian abolished circumcision (*brit milah*), which he held to be mutilation.

Because the Great Jewish Revolt had resulted in the destruction of Jerusalem, the Sanhedrin at Yavne provided spiritual guidance for the Jewish nation, both in Judea and throughout the Diaspora.

The Jewish leaders, with Akiva playing a key role, carefully planned the second revolt to avoid numerous mistakes that had plagued the first Great Jewish Revolt sixty years earlier. In 132, the second revolt, led by one Bar Kochba, quickly spread across the country, cutting off the Roman garrison in Jerusalem.

In 135, Akiva proclaimed Bar Kochba as the "King Messiah" and invited the Nazarenes to join the then-emerging rabbinical Jewish sect in this second armed revolt against Rome. When the Nazarenes declined to transfer their messianic allegiance from Yeshua to Bar Kochba, their persecution by other Jews began immediately and continued with a fury.

The Nazarenes, although greatly diminished in number and widely scattered throughout Israel and Syria (mostly restricted to remote mountain communities), lived on quite actively to the end of the fourth century, and then in a state of decline perhaps for another two centuries, but at least until the end of the fifth century when the "Church of the Circumcision" finally gave way entirely to the "Church of the Gentiles."[4]

Rambam, like Akiva and Rachel, is buried in an elaborate and ornate tomb, just a short distance from our home in Tiberias. Each day hundreds, sometimes even thousands, of Jewish pilgrims from elsewhere in Israel and from around the world come here to pray at the tomb of this long dead seer, seeking from him in the dust of his bones all manner of favor: believing that he has the power, even in death, to heal the sick, raise the dead, enable the conception of children—to perform the very same miracles subscribed in Scripture to Yeshua.

Chapter 6
Hannah's Story
Auschwitz–Birkenau Extermination Camp
(Poland: July 1943)

The four of them—Hans, Flora, Michael, and Hannah—huddled together in a corner of the crowded cattle car where they had managed to find a modicum of privacy during their now nearly ending four-day transport to the east.

Despite the stifling mid-summer's day heat and humidity, Hans visibly shivered as he pulled his dear ones together in a close circle where only they could hear what he had at last decided to share with them.

"I'm so very sorry for what I've done, my precious family. All of this is my fault, and my fault alone. If only I had listened to your father, Michael—"

"You are my other father!" Michael cut Hans off. "There is nothing to forgive; you did only what you thought was best for us, and none of us made a single protest! Hans, enough already!" he pleaded as he kissed his distraught father-in-law on the cheek in a vain attempt to bring him even a hint of relieving comfort and peace.

"Hans!" Michael continued sternly. "This is a time for planning, hope, and survival! It is not the time for self-recrimination!"

Hans now wept openly, unable to reply. He had now retreated for a moment to another world of his own making, mesmerized by the loud, clickety-clack of the train's cold steel wheels rhythmically, persistently making contact with the unyielding rails beneath—an onerous-sounding summons to oblivion. Such a summons was hideously magnified by the nearly overpowering din of human agony that spontaneously arose from their still-living fellow transportees who, like themselves, had somehow managed to survive these past horrific four days and nights. Only those dozen or so of the elderly, less strong, or less determined were now stacked like cord wood along the back side of the car where they had, at last, mercifully found their own eternal silence.

"Michael wisely speaks of survival," Hans finally spoke, forcing himself to once again embrace their terrible reality, groping for a glimmer of hope. "Each of us must struggle, yes relentlessly struggle, to survive as long as life remains!

"Flora and I have had a good life, filled with many happy memories," he continued, "but you, children, Michael and Hannah, you haven't even begun to live. Flora and I may survive, but you two must survive!

"Hear me well!" Hans continued, not waiting for a reply. "Before all of this began, before we left our beloved Bogenhausen, I opened two separate bank accounts in Switzerland—one at the Union Bank of Switzerland, the other at Credit Suisse. There are sufficient deposits in each of these accounts to see to all of our needs for many years into the future. Each of you, the four of us, are signatory for both of these accounts. To gain access to these funds, you need only to properly identify yourself. Of course, you must remember the account numbers."

"How are we to do that?" Flora protested. "How can we remember two many-digit account numbers when it is impossible for us to write them down without almost certain later detection? For that matter, Hans, how on earth are you able to remember them, if indeed you are able to do so?"

"It's really rather simple." Hans smiled at his own cleverness, for a moment breaking the deep pall that had come over him. "For the account at Union Bank, you only need to remember the name 'Hannah.' And for the account at Credit Suisse, the name 'Meyers.'

"Let me explain," he continued before any of them could interrupt. "Take each letter in the name 'Hannah' and assign to it its position in the alphabet, then add to this, the number four, representing the number of signatories on the account. Thus, 'H', the eighth letter in the alphabet, plus 4 equals 12. Then, 'a,' the first letter, plus 4 equals 5. Continue this process forward and the name Hannah translates to the account number 1251818512, and, in the same way, the name 'Meyers' translates to 1792992223."

"*Raus! Raus!*" [Out! Out!] The capos (Jewish collaborator who acted as a camp guard) shouted viciously as he grabbed Hans by one of his arms and pulled him abruptly from the now near empty cattle car onto the concrete ramp below.

Flora quickly jumped from the car onto the ramp, where she tearfully helped her grossly overweight husband to his feet.

Next came Michael, who was followed closely by Hannah, and the four of them took their places, two abreast in a line that was rapidly screamed into place by club-wielding capos supervised by a band of Nazi SS guards carrying machine guns.

The four of them, like the rest of their fellow new residents of this living hell, were terrified beyond the outer limit of human fear, their voices frozen in a universal eerie, horror-born silence. The putrid air they now breathed was thick with the deafening and confusing sound of screamed orders, barking dogs, and the stench of burning flesh and hair that spewed from the smokestacks of the camp's five crematoria.

Like unresisting lambs bound for slaughter, the line moved ever slowly forward as, from a nearby wooden platform, the camp orchestra played a hideously inappropriate yet somehow still beguiling Strauss waltz.

Hans was the first of the four to catch sight of the strikingly handsome SS officer who, in the midst of all this madness, agony, and death, seemed somehow out of place. His classically German face was set in a fixed, kindly smile; his uniform was impeccably tailored, cleaned, and pressed.

Now, as this sadistic madness unfolded before him, providing its own uniquely horrific visceral gratification, he cheerfully whistled along with the orchestra that had now shifted to its next selection, a vibrant Wagnerian overture.

To even the most assiduous observer, this recruiting-poster-perfect SS officer seemed almost completely detached from the totally appalling human tragedy that was being staged before him. Ironically, none but a few insiders knew it was he, and he alone, who was its sole author, producer, and director.

This was the murderous monster whom history would remember as the "Angel of Death." This was Doctor Josef Mengele, who now relished in the barbarous ecstasy of his favorite self-appointed camp activity.

In his right hand he held a military leather riding crop. As his mostly cowering, pathetic, newly arrived victims, whose only crime was to have been born a Jew, moved into a position directly before him, he pointed to them in turn, one by one for a fleeting moment in time that would forever determine their fate.

"*Links*" (left) or "*rechts*" (right), he pronounced his entirely arbitrary, sole judgment upon each of them, indicating which way they should turn.

While some of his victims most assuredly understood, many did not understand that this Angel of Death was selecting those who would immediately be sent to the gas chambers followed by cremation, and those whom he, by a momentary casual glance, deemed fit for slave labor, or worse still, candidates to participate in the hideously depraved so-called "medical experiments" of his own invention.

Those of the new arrivals who were sent to the left, usually less than one-third, were thus granted an indefinite continuation of life. However, the rest of them, those who were sent to the right, were thus condemned to immediate death without even a hint of mercy or due process.

For a fleeting moment in the vastness of time, the Angel of Death made eye contact with Hans. He smiled kindly, and like a snake about to strike at a helplessly cornered rodent, he pointed directly at this stereotypical, corpulent Jew with his riding crop, and gleefully pronounced, "*Rechts*!"

Then, a moment later, it was Flora's turn to capture Doctor Mengele's professional attention. He hesitated for a moment, more than usually required, apparently puzzled by the unseemly blonde, blue-eyed good looks of this middle-aged Jewish woman who stood before him. It was only for a moment, however. "*Rechts*!" he pronounced, touching the tip of his riding crop between her two prominent breasts.

Then it was Michael who became the momentary focus of Doctor Mengele's fateful life or death gaze. Here stood a young Jew who was every bit as handsome, masculine, and otherwise striking as his own Aryan judge. Unlike most who had preceded him in this hellish judgment, he stood tall, as if in a position of military attention as he stared back, defiantly and accusingly, into the Angel's own curiously exploring eyes. "*Links*!" Mengele pronounced, as he smiled with obvious satisfaction.

Finally it was Hannah who made her way into this unspeakable place of iniquitous judgment. Like Michael before her, she stood tall, thrusting her raised chin in the direction of her judge, an act that unintentionally gave emphasis to her full and perfectly formed body while her gorgeously featured, classic Jewish face remained expressionless, masking the raging turmoil that welled within her. The Angel of Death took far longer than his usual cursory glance to make his judgment as he explored every visible feature of this remarkably lovely young woman with his penetrating, evil eyes. "*Links*!" he pronounced as he smiled and unconsciously licked his lips.

Hannah sat totally naked on the crude, bare mattress of a steel-framed cot in the center of a small, private room on the second floor of block ten of the main camp. She was mesmerized, utterly shocked beyond tears as she stared unbelievingly at the burned, still bleeding pulp on her lower left arm. She began to shake, out of control, as she recalled her excruciating pain when two capos women had restrained her with all their strength as an SS guard heated a pen-like tool to red hot, dipped it in ink, and then burned into her flesh, dot by dot, her new tattooed identity: A-25232.

"There, there," a woman capos who had just entered the room comforted Hannah. "The pain will go away in a few days," she offered reassuringly. "Now we must do our very best to make you as beautiful and presentable as possible for Dr. Mengele. Never mind, my dear," she added her own evaluation. "You are already quite lovely, so my work will not be all that difficult.

"Please don't be afraid," the capos continued gently. "Dr. Mengele thoroughly examines and evaluates all of us whom he has selected. You have nothing to worry about, I can assure you. He seldom rejects any who have made it this far."

"What are we being selected for?" Hannah asked in a near whisper as she finally regained enough self-control to allow her to speak for the first time in more than an hour since she had entered the room.

"Continued life," the capos replied without emotion. "Come now, Hannah." She spoke her name for the first time as she pulled her to her feet. "You must do your best. We cannot keep Dr. Mengele waiting."

"It's OK!" Dr. Mengele assured Hannah comfortingly as, still entirely unclothed, she stood before him on an elevated platform while he, with mock professionalism, told her, now for the second time, to turn, slowly, completely around so that he might complete his initial examination. "I am now your doctor!" he continued. "I must decide if you are an appropriate candidate for my medical investigations. So, little one, please cooperate and help me."

With that, he rose from the chair where he had been sitting and took her hand. "Come, step down, and I will continue my examination."

Despite her emotional potpourri of sheer terror, shame, and embarrassment, some deep animal instinct arose from within her inner being demanding that she survive this terrible moment and what might lie beyond. Without any conscious thought, she smiled, feigning trust as he led her to the large marble-topped examination table that dominated the large room where he conducted his most unusual "medical" practice.

"Sit here," he pointed to the edge of the table. "I want to learn more about you before I proceed."

After Hannah had obediently taken her place, he began his bizarre inquiry. "Tell me, Hannah Ruth Meyers, are you married?"

"Yes," she replied simply, trying without success to mask her near overwhelming concern about Michael's fate and status.

"Is your husband here with you?" Mengele inquired.

"Yes," she replied, "he was with me when you, ah, pointed to me after we arrived."

"Oh, yes, I do remember him," Mengele announced. "He is very tall and very handsome, as I recall."

"Yes, he is," Hannah replied, now genuinely warming up enough to ask her own burning question. "Herr Doctor, may I ask how he is?" she ventured "And perhaps you may know something of my parents, Hans and Flora Meyers?"

"Oh yes," Mengele replied. "Oh yes, I do remember your mother. She is a rather striking woman for her age—you get your beauty from her, certainly not from your overstuffed father."

"Then you do know of them, Herr Doctor!" she replied with genuine encouragement.

"Of course I do," he smiled. "But never mind them for now. Let's get on with the business at hand. I need to gather much information for my medical database. "Tell me, Hannah, is your physical relationship with Michael satisfactory to you both?"

She struggled for a moment to frame an appropriate response and then replied simply but blushing, "Yes, Herr Doctor."

"Do you have any children?" he continued to probe.

"No, Herr Doctor," she replied, looking for a way to cut off this line of questioning. "We have only been married for a short time."

"For how long?" he continued, unwilling to let go.

"We were married at Westerbork, the day before we were transported here," she replied forthrightly.

"Very well, then, I will now complete my physical examination, and then we will be finished." He took a large pillow from a storage area near the table and placed it over a wooden block that served as the usual headrest. "Now, Hannah, please lie down and relax."

She complied, exposing herself to his probing explorations.

"*Mein Gott*!" he exclaimed with genuine surprise. "You're a virgin! You told me you were married."

Deeply embarrassed, Hannah haltingly explained. "Michael and I were married by a rabbi in the afternoon, and we were required by camp rules to sleep separately at night. Then we were transported the next morning."

While she struggled to explain what he had already surmised, Mengele took a long wooden swab from the nearby instrument stand and dipped its cotton tip into a bottle filled with innocuous-looking clear fluid. Then, in a well-practiced gesture, he thrust the now-soaked tip deep inside his unsuspecting victim, who was totally unaware that the caustic fluid he had applied would very soon burn closed the entrance to her fallopian tubes, making her permanently sterile.

Mengele's breath now quickened as his terrible intentions began to become apparent. "Would you like to see your Michael again, my dear?" he asked arrogantly, conveying to Hannah that he and he alone held this possibility in his own hands. "And your parents?"

"Of course I want to see them, Herr Doctor!" she exclaimed, grasping at his unseemly suggestion—even so, thrilled by the newfound hope that was only now registering in the depths of her conscious mind as something achievable that could be produced by this suddenly bigger-than-life man who menacingly hovered over her.

"Then, my dear," he commanded lustfully as he leered at the totally vulnerable lovely innocence he held under his monstrous control, "first I shall complete the duty of your absent Jewish husband!"

"No!" she screamed in pointless protest, as she felt the sharp physical pain of his intimate presence and then lost consciousness.

When he was finished, Mengele slapped her sharply on both cheeks, returning her to the full awareness of the terrible thing that had happened. She began to weep, sobbing deeply and out of control. "There, there, my dear," Mengele comforted. "A promise made is a debt unpaid. Now you shall see your Michael and your parents. Come with me, come!" he commanded as he pulled her to her feet and led her toward a large iron-barred window facing the main compound.

She stood by his side, trembling. Even now she foolishly hoped in the horror of her own despair that some miracle was about to be revealed in return for the unspeakable forced payment she had already made in fulfillment of the devilish contract proposed by this supposed man of medicine.

"Look, over there," he pointed between the iron bars toward the two tall smoke stacks that towered side by side over the camp crematorium. "Do you see the building with the smoke stacks?" he asked. "Do you see the smoke?"

"Yes," she replied in a scarcely audible, horrified whisper.

"Then look very carefully, Hannah," he laughed loudly—gleefully. "Michael and your parents, they are all right there—there in the smoke!"

Dr. Josef Mengele delighted in the absolute, unchallengeable, visceral power he wielded over the members of his impressive professional medical staff. He particularly relished standing before them, the martinet that he was, each Monday morning at his weekly staff meetings. It was then that these seven "men of medicine," who were at once his military subordinates and professional colleagues, assembled to hear his current maniacal pronouncements and to report on the status of their own various individual medical experiments.

On this particular Monday morning, as was his custom, he turned first to Professor Dr. Karl Clauberg, who was acknowledged by all present to be Mengele's favorite. "So, Karl," he began, "what do you have to share with us this morning?"

"Good morning, Herr Doctor Mengele, gentlemen," he began with expected formality and deference. "I can now report with confidence that the unique method of mass sterilization I have developed is now completely perfected. Furthermore, I am ready to assure you, as well as our highest authorities, that one experienced physician, with an appropriately equipped office and the aid of ten auxiliary personnel, will be able to carry out in the course of a single day the sterilization of hundreds, or even as many as one thousand, women."

"Remarkable, Karl! Remarkable!" Mengele heaped praises upon his favorite colleague as he began to loudly clap his hands together, thus evoking an immediate standing ovation from the entire staff.

"You are far too modest, Karl," Mengele continued after quiet had once again been restored. "Just yesterday I applied your technique to a particularly attractive specimen who, remarkably, came to us as a virgin. "She wasn't even aware of your simple procedure that I was able to apply, entirely without assistance, during a routine examination. She has already been assigned to the SS officers' brothel, where you can be sure she will be of great service to our well-deserving comrades in arms."

Again, the staff stood in yet another round of spontaneous applause.

When quiet had been restored, Mengele next turned to Dr. Horst Schumann. "Horst," he began sympathetically, "you have a hard act to follow after what we have just heard from Karl, but I trust you will be able to rise to the occasion."

"Of course, Herr Doctor!" Dr. Schumann, a specialist in male sterilization, replied confidently. "As you all know, I have long opposed radiation, in all of its various applications, as neither an effective nor reliable method of mass male sterilization. The fact is, none of our extensive radiation research has produced an approach that did not also carry with it permanent collateral damage that invariably rendered its recipients incapacitated, often by serious physical limitations. "Such limitations," he continued professorially, "clearly defeat the central purpose of our program by variously limiting the amount of post-procedure hard labor these Jews are able to perform.

"If I may, Herr Doctor Mengele, I would now like to demonstrate for you my findings that surgical castration, if properly performed, is by far the better technique. Using the technique I have perfected, the entire procedure can be accomplished in less than seven minutes and carries with it no collateral damage. Furthermore, men so sterilized can return to work within twenty-four hours and continue at hard labor without further reference to our own medical contribution to their effectiveness."

"It seems to me," Mengele interjected skeptically, "that only seven minutes to achieve such a remarkable result may be a bit of an exaggeration. Perhaps fifteen minutes or even thirty is more realistic and as such hardly conducive to anything like the goal of at least several hundred per day per surgical team."

"I anticipated your skepticism, Herr Doctor Mengele," Dr. Schumann replied, "and therefore, with your permission, sir, I would like to present a demonstration right here and now of the surgical castration technique I have perfected. I propose to perform this procedure with complete success on two of our candidates and to do so in a total of twelve minutes or less."

"By all means," Mengele responded, both very pleased and impressed. "You may proceed."

"Gentlemen," Schumann beckoned his fascinated colleagues, "if you will kindly gather around the examination table in the back of the room, we will proceed."

As Mengele and the rest of his staff complied by taking their places, Schumann clapped his hands to signal a capo who waited just inside the entrance door.

Within moments, two young men were led into the room. The first was a muscular gypsy who sweated profusely like a cornered animal.

The second was Michael Silberman.

When the promised dual task had been accomplished in slightly less than ten minutes, the resounding applause Dr. Horst Schumann's work provoked was both spontaneous and, in the eyes of those who stood cheering, abundantly well deserved.

October 1944–January 1945

Hannah and two other uniformed female capos stood close by Dr. Josef Mengele as he examined one of two twelve-year-old twin girls who were cramped together in the bottom deck of a triple-tiered wooden bunk in Lager B. This was the place he had reserved for more than one hundred sets of twin girls who were the subjects of his own intensive medical experiments.

"There is no point in even examining the other," he lamented, as if speaking to himself. "Since this one will live only another week or so, there is no need for us to sustain the other. Syringe!" he commanded as he reached his hand behind him.

It was October 1944, and Hannah, who after the past sixteen months of other daytime capos duties had recently graduated into this totally unsolicited and dreaded position as Mengele's "special technician assistant," understood well as she removed one of several syringes, already filled with 15 milliliters of phenol from his black leather medical bag, and handed it to him.

"There, there, little one," the Angel of Death offered in mock comfort as he plunged the needle directly into the struggling child's heart and released its lethal contents.

His victim's physical resistance began to cease almost immediately as her executioner watched her final moments with scientific interest until he had verified that her heart had stopped beating. "Time?" he demanded.

"Fifteen seconds, Herr Doctor," Hannah, who had been closely monitoring a stopwatch, replied.

"Excellent!" Mengele exclaimed with satisfaction. "Syringe!" he again commanded as he now turned his attention to the other healthy surviving twin.

Hannah was deep in soul-wrenching, near hysterical self-contemplation as she mindlessly tidied up Mengele's private laboratory late that same afternoon. As a matter of her own emotional and physical survival, she seldom allowed herself the luxury of even considering, much less acknowledging the horrific, total degradation her life had become in the service of her "benefactor" who held her tenuous continued existence subject to any passing whim that could pronounce her immediate extinction.

Even now, as she fought to suppress the chilling reality of her ongoing service in the SS officers' bordello, she marveled at her well-learned ability to weep silently while smiling outwardly, to shout her outrage, heard only in the depths of her own soul, while speaking fetchingly to the next in the seemingly unending line of those who waited to further use and abuse her terribly worn, totally defiled body.

Even so, once again she inwardly screamed her silent pledge to the memory of those whom she still most loved, those who, to her knowledge, had long ago vanished forever in the unceasing sick, yellow-gray smoke of the camp's crematoria. "I will do whatever is within my power to survive. This was my promise to you, my beloved Michael, and to you, my precious parents!"

"Good afternoon, Hannah!" Mengele, who had entered the laboratory unnoticed, snapped her back from her tortured recollections to the terrible reality of the moment. "We've had a very busy day!"

"Yes, Herr Doctor," she replied obligingly through her instantaneously reestablished albeit fragile mask.

"You have fared very well, Hannah," he continued in a very rare moment of congeniality. "In fact, you are still just as lovely as the day we first met."

He took the immediate red flushing of her face to be a blush of modesty rather than the outward sign of the inward outrage that was its true genesis. "You seem to be thriving upon your evening activities."

Her flush of outrage deepened as she struggled to suppress the indescribable horror of what amounted to her gang rape by five to seven SS officers during her two-hour shift in their private bordello, an unspeakable, total defilement she had been forced to endure for six evenings of every week for the past sixteen months. "Yes, Herr Doctor," she repeated, even managing what she hoped would be a convincing modest smile.

Then, in an unprecedented moment that caught her entirely off guard, her tormentor, this murderer of all whom she held dear, spoke to her as if he were a suitor.

"Hannah," he confessed, "I have grown quite fond of you. That's why I have seen to it that you were properly fed and made as comfortable as possible—that is why, when this war is finally over, you will have survived. You will owe your life to me, Hannah!"

"Of course I do, Herr Doctor," she replied with just a hint of feigned warmth. "How can I possibly thank you enough?"

Even he could see through the veil of her insincerity. He raised his right arm and slapped her full across the face, knocking her to the floor. "You already have thanked me enough!" he shouted as he turned and made his way toward the door.

"You'd better hurry! You'll need to fix your face before you begin your evening's work!" he added, trying to cover this momentary lapse from his vicious and complete control over this dreadful sub-human Jewess, who despite himself and his inspired racial insights and understandings had somehow managed to touch him deeply.

A very pregnant, dingy-white, short haired stray cat finished the last of her fortuitously pilfered late afternoon meal of assorted meat scraps gleaned from the large uncovered garbage cans behind the SS officers' dining hall. She breathed deeply of the effluvium-filled air emanating from the rotting refuse of her immediate surroundings, made even viler by the pervasive, inescapable, stench of burning human flesh.

She looked left, then right, instinctively awaiting the moment that would afford her safe escape before she lunged across the two hundred meters to the secret place behind the camp's gas chamber where she had made her nest, deep among the discarded, now empty, metal Zyklon B canisters that had collected there in a huge heap nearby the place where they had been wantonly and murderously expended.

Now, safely removed from any immediate danger, she succumbed to reality; her time had come. Slowly, methodically, the already protesting and struggling new life came forth from her swollen womb as she, in turn, frantically licked clean each of her newborn kittens, forcing them to take in their first samplings of the putrid air of their horrific surroundings, thus, at least for a time, assuring them of the blessed gift of life.

When at last she was finished, she slept as the little ones struggled with one another for their turn to suckle nourishment and succor from her now fully flowing udder.

January 27, 1945

Hannah shivered as she pulled herself from the warmth and comfort of her bed in her small now unheated room near the laboratory. Would this be the long expected day of her release from this hellhole, she wondered as she hurriedly dressed and went to the single barred window of her room.

Her heart quickened as she noted once again that the smokestacks of the crematoria no longer spewed forth their terrible yellow-gray smoke—the winter sky was once again a perfectly clear, lovely blue.

The roaring sounds of nearby artillery fire underscored her growing feeling of elation as she hurried from her room and into the laboratory from which Dr. Josef Mengele had suddenly disappeared more than two weeks earlier without a word to anyone.

Just yesterday, she noted, there had been several other capos and a single SS guard watching over this very large block, and this morning, even they were gone.

She hurried from the building and joyfully noted that there were no SS in sight, yet even so, those prisoners who had miraculously managed to survive to this point remained, still huddled in their respective places.

Then she saw the first of the Russian Army vanguard making its way across the camp in her direction, and she rushed to greet them. She was filled with a weird admixture of conflicting emotions: an overwhelming sadness from all that she had lost; a deep, all-consuming guilt because of the unspeakable things she had consciously done to survive; and a nearly unbearable, soul-wrenching hatred for her fellow Germans, those who had brought all of this upon her, simply because she was a Jew.[1]

Hannah frantically looked for familiar faces among the relatively small number of her fellow-surviving former inmates who were well enough to gather for what to them was the incredible gift of a full and nourishing breakfast in what had only recently been the SS officers' dining hall.

"Could it all have been a terrible lie, a cruel mistake? Could it be? Could it be?" she screamed inwardly in her desperate hope for a miracle. But no, she understood, there would be no miracle. The stark reality and pain of this unbearable truth overwhelmed her as her momentary inward vain hope gave way to yet another flood of outward tears. They were gone, all of them gone forever. Nowhere among this small contingent of relatively viable survivors were the faces of any of those whom she had so dearly loved.

It was as if Mengele, the Angel of Death, had thrown a switch and she had suddenly become the subject of yet another one of his horrendous experiments. The pain and terror of even the worst of the former atrocities he and others had visited upon her had given way to new chamber of horrors. Alone. Hannah suddenly realized that she was utterly alone in a world with which she was no longer even vaguely familiar.

It was then, in this moment of her greatest despair, that she felt his hand as he reached out from another dimension to touch her shoulder. At first she did not recognize his voice. "Hannah? Hannah Silberman?"

She turned and focused intently on the gaunt, severely worn, heavily bearded face. "Rabbi Cohen—Yakov Cohen!" she exclaimed in the sheer delight in the wonderful recognition of a familiar face in what until this moment of relief had been her own private chamber of human emptiness.

After they had exchanged their joyful greetings, Yakov, fearing the near certainty of what would be her response, dutifully inquired, "What of your beloved Michael? Your dear parents?"

When she had confirmed his worst fears, they comforted one another with the solace of their mutual tears.

Chapter 7
Hear O Israel
The First Holy Crusade
(Claremont, France: November 27, 1095)

SINCE 325, THE time of Constantine, Christians from all over the world have gone on pilgrimages to Jerusalem and other sacred sites in the Holy Land. Even though Muslims had ruled Jerusalem since 638, Christians were still allowed to visit the city. By the eleventh century, however, the situation had changed. The Seljuk Turks had taken over control of the Holy Land, and all future religious pilgrimages were forthwith disallowed.

The entire church of that day was incensed at what these Turks had done, and their collective anger coalesced in a famous speech delivered by Pope Urban II to a large assemblage in Claremont, France:

> The noble race of Franks must come to the aid of their fellow Christians in the East. The infidel Turks are advancing into the heart of Eastern Christendom; Christians are being oppressed and attacked; churches and holy places are being defiled. Jerusalem is groaning under the Saracen yoke. The Holy Sepulcher is in Moslem hands and has been turned into a mosque. Pilgrims are harassed and even prevented from access to the Holy Land.
>
> The West must march to the defense of the East. All should go, rich and poor alike. The Franks must stop their internal wars and squabbles. Let them go instead against the infidel and fight a righteous war.
>
> God himself will lead them, for they will be doing His work. There will be absolution and remission of sins for all who die in the service of Christ. Here they are poor and miserable sinners; there they will be rich and happy. Let none hesitate; they must march next summer. God wills it![1]

"*Deus vult!*" (God wills it) became the battle cry of the Crusader.

Pope Urban II had called the Christians to join him in a Holy War to reclaim the Holy Land as an act of Christianity, but there were many activities that took place that were anything but "Christian." The Crusaders had originally been charged with helping the churches in the East, but now their purpose was to reclaim the Holy Land, especially Jerusalem, from the Muslims. Pope Urban II stayed in France until September 1096 in hopes of providing leadership for the participants of the First Crusade. Urban had originally hoped the crusading army would be composed of mostly knights and other warriors, but his speech had already begun to spread throughout the west, and many people of different social classes started joining the crusading army. Thus, presumably, Pope Urban II lost control, which led to the slaughter of Jews along the convoluted journey that ultimately took them to Jerusalem. It seems that the rallying cry had changed from driving the offending Turks from Jerusalem to a fanatical orgy whose objective was to slaughter Jews wherever they could be found as "revenge" for their alleged murder of Jesus Christ.

By January 1096, the crusaders began attacking Jewish communities outside of the Land of Israel, slaughtering those who refused baptism. In Germany, Jewish communities along the Rhine—Speyer, Worms, and Mainz—were virtually "cleansed" of all Jews. Of those many thousands of Jews forced to choose either baptism or death, most elected to die as martyrs.

The Crusaders reached the Land of Israel in the spring of 1099 and headed toward Jerusalem. When they reached Jaffa and Ramle, they found them empty as the entire populations had fled in terror. On June 7, they arrived at a mountain overlooking Jerusalem, where they prayed and prepared for the upcoming siege of the holy city.

At noon on July 15, with the sound of trumpets and shouts of encouragement, the Crusaders forced their way into Jerusalem from the north, entering the city's Jewish Quarter. As they streamed into the city, its panic-stricken defenders and residents fled through the narrow streets. A massacre of the city's residents ensued. Tens of thousands of Muslims and Jews were slaughtered. Many of Jerusalem's Jews were burnt alive as they were forced into their synagogues, which were then set aflame. Others desperately attempted to hide but were hunted down and slaughtered. The few who survived were sold into slavery.[2]

Chapter 8
Messianic Synagogue *Beth Emeth Jerusalem* (Shabbat, January 15, 1099)

Benjamin Ben Haim extended his arms drawing Vered, his beloved wife, and their two young sons, Matthew and Mark, close to him in a comforting embrace as he struggled to suppress his already great and growing concern for his precious family's well-being—even safety.

"Dear ones," he spoke, trying to sound reassuring, "We must remember that these Crusaders who have come into our city to liberate it from the Turks are also followers of Yeshua. We, like them, are 'born again' by the shed blood of our Lord, so we have nothing to fear from them. In fact," he continued more confidently, "Rabbi Steven has encouraged us all to gather together in our synagogue so that we will be on hand to welcome these dear brothers as a congregation of like-minded believers and invite them to join us in a time of thanksgiving and praise."

"Abba," Matthew, their eldest, sounding older than his twelve years, questioned, "How is it that we have heard these brothers are killing Jews wherever they go? Aren't we also Jews?"

"Of course we are Jews, my son," Benjamin replied. "But we are also members of one of the only two Yeshua-believing congregations in Jerusalem." He paused for a moment, trying to reassure himself before he continued. "Rabbi Steven tells us these Crusaders who call themselves Christians are standing with us in our ever-continuing struggle with the Pharisees who have now taken over almost all existing Jewish religious expression. Even now, their rabbis are working very hard to have us renounce Yeshua and accept their way of thinking."

"Come," Vered interjected, her voice reflecting her still shaky confidence. "We'd better hurry to be with the congregation; we'll be safe there. Who can say when these visitors will arrive in our part of the city?"

Rabbi Steven had just finished the introductory liturgy preceding the Lord's Supper when there was a great commotion just beyond the large wooden door of their sanctuary. Before he could collect himself to continue, the door was thrust open in a loud crash. Several knights of the Crusade in full armor burst into the room with swords drawn.

Godfrey of Bouillon, his armor spattered with blood, cried out in English, a language no one in the congregation except their rabbi only vaguely understood. "Jews! Jews! Filthy Christ-killing Jews!" he screamed.

"Yes, we are Jews, born again in Yeshua!" Rabbi Steven screamed back in Aramaic, a language unknown to Godfrey or any of the other knights. Seeing their lack of communication, Rabbi Steven held up the filled chalice and the loaf of bread, shouting as he did, "Yeshua! Yeshua! Yeshua!"

Without any further communication, the knights withdrew from the sanctuary, slamming the door behind them.

For a moment, Rabbi Steven and his congregation breathed a sigh of relief, but only for a moment. The loud pounding of spikes sealing the door showed him he'd best hurry with his last official clergical responsibility. Hurriedly, he held up the chalice and the loaf, blessing them and calling for the elders, Benjamin being one of them, to come forward and serve the congregation who waited in their seats.

The first sign of smoke began to leak into the room just as the last of them had been served.

"This is my body which is given for you," Rabbi Steven chanted as flames now began to lick at the door from the inside and move toward the walls of the sanctuary.

"Ema! I'm afraid!" Mark, just turned eight, cried out as he stood by his mother's side.

"Be at peace, my dear son," Vered replied lovingly through her tears as she placed a tiny piece of the Communion bread she had saved for him into his mouth. "Take, eat, this your first and your last Communion, for today we will all meet our Lord Yeshua in heaven."

Following their long day of carnage, the knights of the Crusades changed their blood-stained clothes and went to pray at their holy places, where they offered prayers of thanksgiving. Over the following days, the Crusaders sacked the city, plundering its wealth. Each marauder claimed the house he entered, as well as its possessions.[1]

Chapter 9
Hannah's Story
Munich and Freising, Germany
(April 1945)

Hannah, deeply overcome by her abject sorrow, noticed nothing of this glorious Bavarian spring morning as she, utterly alone, laboriously made her way on foot from the empty, burned-out shell where the Silbermans' once stately mansion had stood, to nearby Maria Theresia Strasse 27, the beloved, equally magnificent villa where she had been born and lived out the naivety and innocence of her first eighteen years.

She had just beheld all that remained of the glorious place of Michael's birth and youth—like Michael, whose ashes she painfully accepted she had seen rising anonymously upward into a grotesquely gray, yellow-tinted sky—turned into the nothingness of ashes and rubble by a single, gone-astray Royal Air Force incendiary bomb whose intended target had been elsewhere in central Munich.

As she approached her own home of remembered happiness, she bravely forced herself to look up from her fixed, intently sullen downward gaze, emotionally bracing herself for yet again another tragedy in the seemingly never-ending collection of tragedies that had filled her life since she had been forced to leave this place of her now long-lost youthful happiness and innocence.

For a fleeting moment she had the flicker of returning joy as she saw from a distance that the Meyers' residence still stood, like those immediately around it, apparently untouched by the relentless bombings that had flattened all of central Munich beyond recognition. Then, as she quickened her step and drew closer, she began to notice that her formerly magnificent home and those around it, indeed, all of what remained of once posh Bogenhausen, had been taken over by literally hordes of displaced Russian Jews.

Because of the providence of geographic distance, many of these much more fortunate Eastern European children of Abraham had managed to escape the ravages of the Final Solution and had instead found their way to Bogenhausen and other formerly exclusive German Jewish neighborhoods that had, for a time during the war, been occupied by members of the Nazi elite who were now dead or in hiding.

Hannah soon saw to her dismay that Maria Theresia Strasse 27 did not escape this uniquely Russian Jewish squatter occupation. Even worse, now standing immediately in front of the mansion, she saw that it had been transformed into a place of black-market enterprise. Several American soldiers, she noticed, each bearing multiple cartons of their various brand cigarettes, one of the universal currencies of postwar Europe, waited in line at the front door for their turn to barter for the treasures waiting within. An antique grandfather clock could be purchased for two cartons of Camels; a beautifully framed Bavarian landscape by a well-known artist could be "stolen" for even less.

Hannah wept silently, even when she thought no tears remained, as she saw laundry hanging to dry from almost every window, clothing obviously needed by the seeming hoard of universally filthy, disheveled children who played roughly among the ruins of the once immaculately appointed and maintained grounds.

As she took all of this in, she had a strong desire to leave this place, now and forever. However, she felt compelled to do one final thing before making her retreat.

Much to her surprise and delight, she managed to make her way, unnoticed, into the backyard and to the gazebo that still stood, apparently untouched, at its center. How bittersweet it was for her to sit in the swing where she and her beloved Michael had so often shared their dreams of what was to have been their lifelong future together. Even now, as she once again sat among the sweet scented lilacs, in the seeming, near palpable reality of her memory, she could almost feel the touch of his hand, the taste of his lips, and the depth of their precious, uncorrupted love.

Hannah had a special love for Freising, a medieval, charmingly Bavarian city a short distance north of Munich. Freising was just large enough and far enough away to have escaped the indignity of being labeled a "bedroom community," yet near enough to have carried with it much of the traditional

German heart and spirit that still somehow characterized the now war-ravaged metropolis.

When Hannah had fled from the postwar shattered ruins of Bogenhausen, the utopian sanctuary of her innocent youth, she instinctively turned to Freising, where she sought and found physical and emotional refuge in a small modestly furnished flat in the center of the city. It was here where she chose to dwell, a recluse among unknown neighbors whom she deliberately avoided.

Certainly she was not in any state of mind to have friendly contact on any level with those fellow Germans around her who were most certainly not Jewish, so deep was her emotional destruction at this point that even the slightest hint of forgiveness of those whom she held in common as the perpetrators of her inhuman suffering was beyond her capability, much less desire.

But there was more to her self-imposed isolation than simply her now soul-deep mistrust, even hatred for all non-Jewish Germans. She did not care to be called upon to explain the older man with whom she had chosen to share her apartment and, in an entirely platonic relationship, her very life.

Hannah and Rabbi Yakov Cohen had bonded together on the morning they were released from the immediate terror of Auschwitz. The two of them stood alone, in the world of their understanding, entirely stripped of family and friends. For Hannah, Yakov almost immediately became a growing substitute for the father she had lost in the gray smoke of the crematorium. For Yakov, who now appeared much older than his fifty-seven years, Hannah had become a twenty-five-old daughter who was desperately in need of restoration at every level: physical, emotional, and to his thinking, most of all, spiritual.

Thanks to the fruit of her biological father's rare wisdom in the form of a huge stash of diamonds secure in a Swiss bank safe deposit box, money had not been and never would be an issue. While she could have lived in absolute extravagance at every material level of her existence, she chose instead the anonymity of a lower middle-class city dweller who spent most of her waking hours with Yakov in her simple, sparsely furnished flat, struggling to ward off the terror of her horrific memories, all the while dreading the night when her torturous nightmares afforded her no such escape.

Yakov, for his part, strived to understand then meet her every need. He saw to the maintenance of the apartment, did most of the cleaning and shopping, and, dearest to his heart, read to her from the Torah and Talmud and even counseled her when, on rare occasions, she was willing to listen.

Freising, Germany (June 1967)

Shabbat, the holy Jewish Sabbath, had become Hannah's only respite from her otherwise nearly total isolated existence. From the very beginning of her now twenty-three-year residence in Freising, she had continued to reenact a long-held family practice established by her father when, almost without exception, late each Saturday morning he had transported his adoring and appreciative family to Freising's famous Weihenstephan, the oldest brewery in the world where the best of Bavarian beers had been continuously created since 1040.

Now, on this lovely June morning, as was her custom of these many years, she sat alone at the very table in the enormous, yet still quaint beer garden where she, now forty-seven, and her dear ones had so often joyfully sat together.

Almost mystically, it was here that Hannah found her weekly needed respite from tending to the needs of Yakov, now seventy-eight, and the still painfully lingering horrors of the past as she ever so slowly sipped from her second masse (one liter glass mug) of the amber-colored brew while she took occasional small bites of *obatzer*, a delicious house blend of cheese, onion, and paprika spread generously on heavy dark bread.

It was here that she had already spent most of this particular Shabbat rest basking in happy, even sometimes joyful, memories, somehow resurrected from the sea of those blatantly tragic and terrifying recollections that continued unrelentingly to dominate her very soul.

Even so, as she smiled inwardly at the fleeting memories of long past lovely moments, she knew within the far reaches of her understanding that something deeply compelling and important was missing from her empty and horrendously scarred life.

She knew that this terrible aching void was the absence of God, a God, who despite Yakov's frequent efforts to reveal Him, remained painfully unknown to her. Certainly, even during her most demeaning times at Auschwitz, she had sought solace in this comforting entity, this Creator of the universe who somehow had always remained nearby but just beyond her own clear understanding and personal grasp. Even so, she had never given up her quest for such divine solace as the longing within her became increasingly more demanding, almost unbearable.

While she had, from time to time, attended synagogue with her mother, those occasions for her had had no meaning beyond their mostly traditional, secular implications. Neither had any of Yakov's deeply sincere testimonial outreach found any root in her being.

Now, in the remaining ashes of her war-torn Germany, virtually nothing Jewish remained, and even if it had, she seriously doubted that the secular Judaism of her youth could possibly afford her any release from the torment that had overtaken and still controlled every aspect of her existence.

It was thus, out of sheer desperation, that she, unbeknown to Yakov, and however tentatively, had superficially explored the refuge purportedly offered by the Roman Catholic Church. The ancient twin-spired cathedral known as the Dom Kirche was only a short walk from her flat, and she had made many desperately seeking visits to this supposedly holy place that had begun as a Benedictine monastery in A.D. 738.

Day by day, hour by hour, over a period of several months, she had sought the joyful relationship with the God that she had seen so radiantly shine forth from the Holy Spirit–filled faces of Theo and Gerta de Goede, the precious Christian martyrs who had selflessly laid down their lives for her and her family.

So deep was her longing that she undertook six weeks of formal pre-baptismal discipleship under the loving care of Father Friedrich Folz, a parish priest. However, at the end of this, despite her deep longing and constant seeking, she had found nothing of any lasting value, absolutely nothing except perhaps even more longing and with it growing despair among the grotesquely ornate statues and cold marble, heavily frescoed walls as she sat alone on hard oak pews praying, seeking, and in the end weeping until there were no more tears.

Hannah was well read and had a good academic understanding that there was yet another Christian option open for her exploration. However, she couldn't yet bear to even begin its investigation.

How could she explore, much less embrace, the religion of those regular army officers whom she was forced to service along with their SS colleagues in their upscale Auschwitz bordello, those whose silver belt buckles shined forth from the uniform trousers she neatly hung up prior to each of their lustful assaults upon her, boldly emblazed with the raised words "*Gott Mit Uns*."

This God whom the Nazis claimed was with them, Hannah reasoned, was the very same God who was worshiped and adored by Martin Luther, the Great Reformer whose virulent anti-Semitism was the wellspring of Adolf Hitler's personal theology as well as the *modus vivendi* of his Final Solution.

Hannah was so engrossed with her own gnawing, inward despair that she had, up to now, only barely noticed the obviously American couple in their thirties seated at an adjacent table. She had not seen them as they approached, and she was startled by their sudden intrusion.

"Pardon me, madam," the man began warmly. "Do you speak English?"

"Yes, I do," Hannah replied, trying to hide her own extreme discomfort with the beginnings of a long-practiced forced smile.

"My name is Frank Featherstone," he continued, "and this is my wife, Martha. I'm the Protestant chaplain assigned to the American Air Force Radar Squadron at Vimy Kaserne. Please forgive us if we are intruding, but we noticed that you seem very upset, and we wondered if there might be some way we could help." Now, as she sat alone in the Weihenstephan beer garden, she once again became inwardly and outwardly tormented over the sheer magnitude of her horrific loss: her beloved Michael, her treasured parents, her lifelong protected honor—all gone in the name of Jesus Christ as He was presented to the world by this Martin Luther, a universally adored patriarch of the non-Catholic Church that he founded. If this was the God who was with them, how could she, or any Jew, tolerate His existence, much less seek His face?

Hannah sat alone in the otherwise empty back pew of the Vimy Kaserne Chapel. She marveled at how immediately drawn she had been to Frank and Martha Featherstone, whom she had met just the afternoon before.

She had badly needed someone to talk with, and when they had been very willing to listen, it had given her much comfort to pour out the torture of her aching heart to them in a long, intimate meeting, capped by their invitation that had brought her to this place.

Hannah was especially happy to accept their invitation when Frank had told her that the guest speaker for this service was, like herself, a Jew. Thus she now listened attentively as Frank introduced this speaker, her fellow Jew.

"It is my great pleasure to introduce Chaplain Captain Andrew Scott Sterling to you this morning," Chaplain Captain Frank Featherstone warmly intoned as he invited Drew to deliver the message at the eleven o'clock Sunday service.

"Chaplain Sterling and his lovely wife, Carla," Frank continued, "come to us from the chapel family at McChord Air Force Base, Washington. They are both our close personal friends, and he is my greatly admired colleague. Chaplain Sterling has already distinguished himself as a rising star in the chaplaincy, and if I were a betting man, I would wager that he will one day be the chief of Air Force chaplains. Chaplain Sterling," he concluded, "won't you come now and bless us."

Even before he began to speak, Drew made eye contact with the strikingly attractive, middle-aged woman who sat on the aisle in the back pew. To Drew, their unspoken exchange was at once electric and mystifying. This momentary connection was so compelling that he found himself struggling to collect himself sufficiently to begin.

"Thanks so very much, Chaplain Featherstone," Drew began with genuine warmth, under the anointing of his profound calling. "Carla and I are so pleased to be with you all, here in this lovely chapel. This may be our first visit to West Germany, but I can assure you it won't be our last if we have anything to say about it—which, of course, we won't!"

The congregation laughed in response, already caught up in this man of God's innate ability to attract the riveted attention of a congregation, like iron filings drawn to a magnet. "In any event," he continued, "you can be sure that Freising will become our first official choice for an accompanied overseas assignment, just as soon as we get back to McChord and are able to update our 'Dream Sheet.'

"Of course," he joshed, "just in case you haven't noticed, we do have a war going on in Southeast Asia, so I would imagine I'll be getting a little side trip to where the fighting is before Carla and I are blessed with an assignment to Europe."

While the Air Force has already given me many blessings," Drew continued, "the greatest of these indeed is my darling wife, Carla, a former Air Force nurse who captured my heart seven years ago during a TDY to Eglin. Stand up, darling, and show these dear ones I am not one to exaggerate."

Carla, blushing at the unexpected words of her husband, stood briefly and waved modestly to the congregation, who responded with applause as she sat down again next to Martha Featherstone in the front pew.

While he had no idea why, Drew suddenly had a clear understanding in his spirit that his next words, and those of his message to follow, would be directed to the mind and heart of the very attentive, obviously sorrowful woman with whom he had earlier made eye contact and who now, trying to be inconspicuous, remained huddled and very much alone in the back pew.

"Chaplain and Mrs. Featherstone, brothers and sisters," Drew continued, "even though more than twenty years have passed since the end of the terrible Holocaust that nearly consumed this land, there are still physical signs of the mass destruction that came with it evident all around us. Even in this very building where we now meet, there are scars from bullet holes on its outside walls marking a battle that was fought here, where blood was shed and hearts were broken.

"Yes, there are physical scars from this hate-initiated tragedy of war everywhere around us. But, worse still, even after twenty years, there are spiritual scars still lingering in the souls of many of those dear ones who somehow managed to survive, those who even now are still struggling to put their lives back in order but, try as they might, find themselves unable to do so. These spiritual scars I speak of are nothing like the physical scars that remain on the face of this building; these may eventually be repaired, or for that matter simply ignored with little or no consequence.

"However," Drew continued with deep feeling, "the not so visible spiritual scars on the souls and spirits of some of those who have survived have a much deeper and more lasting significance. These are the scars that must be healed if those who have been so deeply afflicted are to find peace and meaning for the rest of their time upon this earth.

"We read our Lord's words in the Gospel according to Mark: 'And whenever you stand praying, if you have anything against anyone, forgive him, that your Father in heaven may also forgive you your trespasses. But if you do not forgive, neither will your Father in heaven forgive your trespasses.'

"Paul tells us in his letter to the Romans: 'Beloved, do not avenge yourselves, but rather give place to wrath; for it is written, "Vengeance is Mine, I will repay," says the Lord. Therefore, if your enemy is hungry, feed him; if he is thirsty, give him a drink; for in so doing you will heap coals of fire on his head. Do not be overcome by evil, but overcome evil with good.'

"My brothers and sisters," Drew continued, "I want to share some thoughts with you this morning about the one true road to eternal life—some considerations that go a bit beyond the simple, wonderful understanding that Jesus Christ, Yeshua, is the one and only way to salvation—the great mystery that He came down from heaven to dwell among us, that He came to teach the wondrous things as they were given to Him by His Father, and then, like a lamb led to slaughter, He went to His cross where He willingly shed His precious blood so that we all might have eternal life in Him."

Drew paused for a moment before he continued, looking out over the large congregation and knowing with pastoral certainty that he had captured their rapt attention.

"Certainly," he continued, "the Scriptures teach us that our individual salvation is made possible by the shed blood of our heavenly Lamb. But they teach us much more as well on this eternally important matter of our salvation.

"From the Scriptures we learn that we cannot be saved until we are first drawn by the Father. The prophet Jeremiah speaks of this truth in his divine revelation: 'The LORD has appeared of old to me, saying: "Yes, I have loved you with an everlasting love; therefore with lovingkindness I have drawn you."'

"The apostle John teaches us: 'There is no fear in love; but perfect love casts out fear, because fear involves torment. But he who fears has not been made perfect in love. We love Him because He first loved us.' And so, dear ones, we learn from the Scriptures that our salvation depends first upon God's initiative, not upon our own.

"Brothers and sisters," Drew asked rhetorically, "whom did He choose? Whom did He first love? Whom did He first draw? Whom did He first save?

"Let me tell you clearly," he continued out of his own strong conviction. "Yeshua came to save us all, Jew and Gentile alike. But He came first to the Jews. By the end of the first century there were literally hundreds of thousands—some scholars say even up to one million Jews—who were praising and worshiping Yeshua in the Holy Land that is now the modern State of Israel. Sadly, however, today, there may be as few as twenty thousand such Jewish believers in the entire world.

"You may reasonably ask: Why are there so pathetically few Jewish believers in Yeshua in the world today? I believe there are several reasons. And it is one of these that I want to discuss with you today. The title of my message this morning is Forgiveness: the Key to the Door of Salvation.

"I'm certain that some of you are questioning what I have already shared. Some are surely wondering, 'Who is this wandering Jew from back home who has skipped over the obvious, fundamental truth we all learned in Sunday school, the universally understood teaching as Paul shared it with the Ephesians: 'For by grace you have been saved through faith, and that not of yourselves; it is the gift of God, not of works, lest anyone should boast.'

"Let me assure you, these words of Paul concerning our salvation ring just as true today as they did even before they passed from the apostle's lips to feed a hungry, waiting world. We who were first loved and chosen by God are drawn to Him so that we might be saved—that's what grace is all about! But there's more to salvation than just this!" Drew continued. "Paul was talking about God's side of the salvation contract. There's another side to the wonderful gift of salvation and eternal life. Indeed, there is another requirement not mentioned here by Paul that is entirely our own—personal responsibility.

"This is the way Yahweh, the Lord God of Israel, goes about His eternal business. The Torah, the first five books of the Old Testament, is filled with numerous examples of this sort of contractual relationship between Yahweh and His people.

"He rescued Noah and his family from the great flood, but Noah, as part of his side of the covenant, was forbidden from eating meat while its life blood was still in it.

"He gave the land of Canaan to Abraham and his descendants as an everlasting inheritance, but in exchange He required of them that their sons be circumcised on the eighth day.

"He led the Jewish people out of captivity in Egypt, but in turn He demanded their obedience.

"Dear ones, the eternal life in Yeshua that comes to us hand in hand with our salvation in Him is a great gift we are freely given because He first loved us, then drew us, and then through His grace enabled us to have the faith we needed to believe what He had said and what He had promised was indeed God's truth. This is His side of the bargain, but let me tell you, as believers, our relationship with Him also depends very much upon each of us personally.

"Yeshua Himself taught us clearly, 'If you have anything against anyone, forgive him, that your Father in heaven may also forgive you your trespasses. But if you do not forgive, neither will your Father in heaven forgive your trespasses.'

"Moreover, He taught us how to pray, saying, 'Forgive us our trespasses as we forgive those who trespass against us.'

"So, here we can clearly see it is necessary for us to be proactive in this process of living our lives in and for Yeshua. Even after He has chosen us, even after He has given us the faith through His grace to believe, even then we must continue to forgive anything and everything we may have against others.

"I can almost hear many of you thinking," Drew continued with conviction, "'Hmm, forgiving all others really isn't too onerous a burden when one considers the greatness of walking with our Lord.'

"Let me tell you," he now spoke with passion. "There are some 3.5 billion people in the world today, and I would venture to guess that at any given moment most every one of them, including each of us gathered here this morning, has a very real need to forgive someone for some real or imagined offense we believe they have committed against us. Certainly some of these offenses are very serious matters, but taken as a whole, most are minor day-to-day offenses like unkind words spoken in a family argument, parking your car in an unauthorized space, and so forth.

"However, I ask each one of you to carefully consider this: In 1939 there were some 17 million Jews in the world. Only six years later, in 1945, at the end of the war, there were only some 11 million. Today, twenty years after the end of the terrible war, there are still fewer than 12 million Jews. Together these amazing surviving chosen of God make up less than one-thousandth of the entire world's population.

"It is an easy matter to calculate that some 6 million Jews were murdered at the hands of the Nazis during the Holocaust, known as Hitler's Final Solution. Stated differently," Drew involuntarily raised his voice in a pained emphasis born in the depths of his soul, "more than 35 percent of the world's Jews were wiped from the face of the world by the very hand of Satan himself who undeniably used Germany and the German people as his personal instruments of destruction.

"To get a better idea of the sheer horror of what we're talking about here, please consider what would have been the outcome if by some unspeakable, yet equally murderous mechanism 35 percent of the 3.5 billion Gentiles in the world today were to meet with a similar fate. Yes, when you look at the Holocaust in this light, you must consider that we are suddenly talking about well over one billion people, people just like each of you and just like the vast majority of the rest of the non-Jewish people in the world. More than one billion people, more than three times the entire population of the United States, or more than the entire population of China, or more than the entire population of Western Europe. Can anyone even begin to imagine the extent of the world's rightful outrage if any of these horrific scenarios were to become a reality?

"'Unthinkable!' some of you are thinking. 'Something like this could never happen!' Dear ones, I am certain that many of the six million Jews who were slaughtered would also have viewed the terrible possibility that became a horrific reality in the same way: 'Unthinkable!'

"Now, I ask you, please put yourself in the shoes of a Jew, a Jew who somehow by the grace of God managed to survive this almost indescribable outrage against himself, his family, and his people. What would you tell some well-intended Christian who shared the gospel with you, a gospel that promises salvation with one little attached caveat—'Come and walk with Jesus, my Jewish brother and sister. Repent, rejoice, but first you must forgive!'

"Is it any wonder there are so relatively few born-again Jews in the world today? Is it any wonder that evangelistic outreach to my people, the Jews, is a very difficult undertaking? I challenge each one of you who thinks of himself as a called evangelist: Go out and share the gospel and its promise of eternal life with an unsaved Holocaust survivor. Show him or her that the way to salvation is through Jesus Christ. Show this unsaved Jew that he must eventually forgive the likes of Adolf Hitler, Heinrich Himmler, Josef Mengele, and the rest of their murdering cronies; then see just how great or how small is the harvest from your well-intentioned outreach.

"Impossible, some of you might say.

"It certainly wasn't impossible for Joseph, who forgave his brothers who had sold him into captivity.

"It wasn't impossible for Stephen, whose dying words were a whispered prayer begging our heavenly Father to forgive those who had stoned him.

"Nor was it impossible for our Lord Yeshua, who, while suffering so terribly upon His cross, at the end of His unspeakable torment cried out, 'Father, forgive them for they know not what they do.' Earlier He had said, 'But I say to you, love your enemies, bless those who curse you, do good to those who hate you, and pray for those who spitefully use you and persecute you, that you may be sons of your Father in heaven; for He makes His sun rise on the evil and on the good, and sends rain on the just and on the unjust.'

"Brothers and sisters," Drew continued, "there is a true story of a Holocaust survivor who had witnessed the Nazis brutally and hatefully murder his wife and three young children by shooting each of them in the back of their heads execution style. Later, this deeply shattered man who had lost everyone in his life that he treasured cried out, 'Now there is nothing left for me to do but to love them all—those who planned and then implemented the annihilation of the Jews; the SS officer who, on a passing whim, personally ordered the execution of my wife and my children, those whom I most loved, and the guards who gleefully carried out these orders before my very eyes. Yes, I can only love and forgive them—because I have seen what hate can do.'

"In conclusion," Drew returned to the title of his message, "there is a locked door through which each of us must pass in order to reach the glorious salvation in Yeshua, who waits for us just on the other side.

"Dear ones, this is my message to you today: the key to this door is forgiveness. If there is someone in your life whom you have not yet forgiven, now, right now, as you sit here in this chapel, now is the time to forgive! As hard as it may be, now is the time to genuinely forgive any person or persons who have committed any wrong, great or small, against you. Now is the time to forgive so that you also can be forgiven. Let us pray."

After the service, Drew and Carla stood together at the exit with Frank and Martha Featherstone greeting the parishioners as they left the chapel. Suddenly, there she was, the woman with whom Drew had earlier established a mystifying, strangely enthralling and focused contact.

"Good morning, Chaplain Sterling," she greeted Drew warmly, yet somehow hesitantly, in perfect accent-free English as she took his proffered hand. "I'm Hannah Silberman. This is my first time to attend a service here in your chapel."

"Are you and your husband newly assigned to Freising?" he asked, genuinely interested in learning more about this person.

"Oh no!" she replied defensively. "I'm a widow. I'm German; I live here in the city."

"Your English is remarkably good," Drew complimented. "Have you spent some time in the United States?"

"Oh no!" Hannah replied. "I attended a fine private school in Munich before the war. I learned your language there.

"Chaplain Sterling," she continued earnestly, "I don't know why I am telling you this, but I want you to know—I am a Jew, and try as I might I have been unable to forgive the terrible things I experienced during the war."

"Excuse me, Drew," Carla interrupted, "but I would like to introduce you to Colonel Howard, the base commander, and to Mrs. Howard."

"Excuse me for a moment," Drew quietly pleaded to Hannah, as he turned to the unavoidable matter of protocol at hand.

Only moments later when the ill-timed formalities were finished, he turned to resume his engaging conversation with this dear woman, who seemed so terribly in need.

To his great disappointment, she was no longer there.

Hannah was filled with deep foreboding as she approached her apartment late that evening. She assigned this emotion to her guilt that she would be late in preparing and serving Yakov's evening meal. She unlocked the door and called out to him in her usual warm, greeting, "Shalom, Yakov!"

There was no response, so she called out again, assuming that he had fallen into a deep sleep while studying the Talmud, which was his every late afternoon and evening practice. "Yakov! Hello! It's time for you to get ready for supper."

In the next moments, however, she realized that they would not be sharing another meal together. The beloved old man was beyond any earthly awakening as he sat, Talmud clutched in his hands, having passed beyond this earthly realm.

CHAPTER 10
HEAR O ISRAEL
GOLDA MEIR AND THE LAW OF RETURN
(JERUSALEM: 1969–1970)

SINCE ITS FOUNDING in May 1948, the modus operandi of the government of the State of Israel has been to place the champions of the political Left in opposition to those of the political Right. Additionally, "centrist" parties have surfaced from time to time that have offered a seeming compromise between the two polar positions and agendas. In theory, when the opposing parties have made their case to the voting public, it is this collective constituency of voters who determine through their ballots which of the opposing points of view—right, left, or center—will guide the state until the next election.

The seeming simplicity of this system, however, immediately breaks down given that the number of votes won by any given political party, expressed as "mandates" or seats in Israel's governing body, the Knesset, must equal a majority of at least sixty of its one hundred twenty seats.

It takes sixty-one votes in Knesset to get a government approved and seated. Since no one party alone in the eighteen Knessets formed since 1948 has ever gotten all of the sixty-one required mandates by itself, the successive leading political parties have needed to look to the various minority parties in order to build a coalition of two or, more often, several parties. This necessity to form such successive political coalitions has led, historically, to often unstable and compromised governments. In return for joining and then remaining in such a coalition, the smaller parties are rewarded in part with some, often key, ministerial positions, their (to use the Western expression) "pork" written into the budget, and plum Knesset committee chairmanships. More importantly in the context of our present discussion, their own sometimes-extremist minority political agendas are, by means of "payment," turned into law.

Such was the situation when Golda Meir succeeded Levi Eshkol, who died in office in February 1969.

Golda Meir, the fourth prime minister of Israel, was an unabashed "secular humanist." When asked if she believed in God, she replied, "I believe in the Jewish people, and the Jewish people believe in God."[1]

This remarkable woman was one of twenty-four signatories (two of them women) of the Israeli Declaration of Establishment on May 14, 1948. She later recalled, "After I signed, I cried. When I studied American history as a schoolgirl and I read about those who signed their Declaration of Independence, I couldn't imagine these were real people doing something real. And there I was sitting down and signing a declaration of establishment."

Golda Meir, known, not always affectionately, as the "Iron Lady" of Israeli politics, served in a number of important government positions; most notably she was Foreign Minister from 1956 until 1966 when she retired from government service.

After Levi Eshkol died in office in February 1969, the surviving leaders of his left-wing government decided that the Iron Lady stood the best chance to become his enduring successor, so they persuaded her to come out of retirement and appointed her to that office.

Later, the newly appointed prime minister's far-left "Alignment" party prevailed in the October 1969 elections, and she took the reins of the existing broad-based coalition that was the legacy from her predecessor.

A key player in the government the Iron Lady thus inherited was Haim-Moshe Shapira, an Orthodox Jewish rabbi who had long served in the successive governments of Israel since he, like his new boss, had been fellow signatories of the Declaration of Establishment.

An obviously shrewd and deeply religious politician, Shapira had already, since 1959, served ten years as Minister of Internal Affairs (today's Ministry of the Interior). In this capacity, he and his ministry had absolute control over who would and who would not become citizens of Israel, as they chose to interpret the Law of Return (Law of Return 5710-1950, July 5, 1950).

Thus it seems reasonable to conclude that very soon after the new secular humanist prime minister took office, her deeply religious Minister of Internal Affairs likely seized upon the opportunity to leverage his own religious agenda against the prime minister's corresponding need to shore up the governing coalition she had inherited.

Shapira's motivation to bring a change to the Law of Return came as a result of two famous cases in the early 1960s. The first was *Roffeisen v. The Minister of Interior*, where a Jew who had become a Catholic monk wanted to immigrate under the Law of Return but was denied. The Supreme Court of Israel determined that a Jew who changed his religion is not entitled to immigrate under the Law of Return and determined that it is not possible to be ethnically Jewish and part of a different religion at the same time. The second case was *Binymin Shalit v. the Minister of Interior.* Here a non-religious Jewish father requested to register his child who was born to a non-Jewish mother, as a Jew by race with no religious affiliation. The court accepted Binyamin Shalit's petition and determined that Binyamin Shalit's child would be registered as a Jew. Also, it ruled that the Interior Ministry must accept a person's personal declaration regarding his religious affiliation if such a declaration was given in good faith. As a result of these cases, an amendment was made to the Law of Return. This amendment defined a Jew as a person born of a Jewish mother and who is not a part of a different religion. Subsequently, an additional amendment granted the right of return to family members of Jews. However, this right was limited to relatives who did not willfully change their religion.

The resulting legislation, Law of Return (Amendment No. 2), 5730-1970, finalized by the Knesset on March 10, 1970, brought both good and bad news for Jews who sought to become citizens of Israel.

The good news was that any Jew with as little Jewish ethnic heritage as one grandparent on either side of their family could become, at the very least, a "permanent resident" (if this person was a fourth-generation Jew) or more often a full-fledged citizen (if this person was a second- or third-generation Jew).

The bad news was that any Jew, irrespective of ethnicity, who had "changed his religion" was no longer considered to be a Jew and therefore was not entitled to enjoy the benefits of the Law of Return. He could only obtain residency status by means of the Law of Entry into Israel and the Law of Citizenship, in the same manner as any other "alien." This provision had an immediate devastating impact that is still in force on the Aliyah ambitions of those Jews who had embraced Yeshua as Messiah. While there is no way to accurately assess how many otherwise qualified born-again Jews have been denied citizenship based entirely upon their religious beliefs, to my own personal knowledge, I can attest to many who have endured this persecution and would presume that, over the forty years since this provision became law, many hundreds, perhaps thousands of Jews have been turned away from taking up their biblical inheritance of the Land of Israel.

During these forty years since it was enacted, the true intent of this provision has become abundantly clear. Ironically, in 1970 the "Messianic Jewish" movement was just beginning to take root in the United States, evidently not quietly enough to escape notice by Minister Shapira of Israel, who apparently immediately sought to interdict its eventual transference to Israel. In support of this contention, please consider the following:

Thousands of orthodox Jews, worldwide, have embraced and are still awaiting the imminent return of the false messiah, Menachem Mendel Schneerson, who died in June 1994. Many already have made Aliyah to Israel, and, presumably, the rest would be welcomed with no opposition based upon their out-of-the-mainstream messianic beliefs.

While, presumably, even thousands of Jews have been denied citizenship exclusively because they have been deemed to have "changed their religion," many other thousands who are professed atheists may have been granted citizenship with no regard to their complete denial of the Lord God of Israel, who is embraced by those born-again Jews who have been sent packing.

Halikah (Jewish religious law) unequivocally establishes that there is absolutely no way that a Jew (including converts to Judaism) can voluntarily give up his or her Jewishness or by any other means cease to be a Jew. The principal of "Once a Jew, always a Jew" is clearly etched in the heart of legal Jewish ordinances.

The founding fathers of the State of Israel wrote in their "Declaration of Establishment" that the new State "will be faithful to the principles of the Charter of the United Nations." As I mentioned earlier, the United Nations' Universal Declaration of Human Rights states: "Everyone has the right to freedom of thought, conscience and religion; this right includes freedom to change his religion or belief, and freedom, either alone or in community with others and in public or private, to manifest his religion or belief in teaching, practice, worship and observance."

From the perspective of the many born-again Jews who have been denied Israeli citizenship based upon their religious beliefs alone, it is not difficult to propose that this Second Amendment to the Israeli Law of Return is in reality a modern-day continuation and restatement of the anti-Yeshua teachings and practices formulated by Rabbi Akiva and first promulgated by the latter-day Pharisees of Yavne and those who were to follow.

CHAPTER 11
HANNAH'S STORY
TIBERIAS
(NOVEMBER 2008)

DREW FELT A surge of his deep, abiding love for Carla, his wife of now almost thirty-nine years, as he stood in front of a Jacuzzi outlet in the naturally heated water of Tiberias' hot springs. He watched her on the other side of the wonderfully therapeutic outdoor pool as she diligently forced herself to complete the rigorous daily regimen of water exercises prescribed by her orthopedic surgeon to speed her recovery from a recent hip replacement.

"Dear Lord," he closed his eyes as he prayed from the depths of his soul, "how I love this life's partner You have given me, and how I thank You for bringing us back to the Land of my inheritance where we have served you together for these nearly twenty-nine years. I thank You for birthing Kehilat Emet [the Congregation of Truth] and for calling me to lead this new gathering of believers here in Tiberias. I thank You for the Jewish and Gentile believers You have already called forth to worship You together in this new, growing body. O Lord, I ask that You would continue to bless us, protect us from all opposition, and grow our numbers according to Your will. Once again, dear Lord," he continued, "I commit myself and all the remaining days of my already long life to Your service and pray that You will use me in any way You please according to Your will and for Your glory. In the precious name of Yeshua I ask You for these blessings that I might in turn be a blessing to others. Amen."

As he opened his eyes, Drew looked to the place where Carla had been exercising before he began to pray. She was no longer there, and in her place there was a still strikingly attractive, white-haired pensioner. She was staring at him intently with her somehow inexplicably familiar dark brown eyes. She seemed to be very alone and pensive, qualities that were emphasized by her stooped, introspective body language and the very plain, black, long-sleeved shirt she wore over a very conservative olive drab bathing suit.

While both of them struggled to do so, neither could immediately recall the specific origin of their far-distant memory of the other, but it was Drew, after several moments of unspoken curious non-recognition, who moved toward her and inquired simply, "Excuse me, but I have the strangest feeling that we have met some time in the past. My name is Andrew Sterling."

"Ahh!" she replied with sudden recognition. "You are Chaplain Sterling! I am Hannah Silberman. You may not remember me, but we met briefly in Freising, Germany, where you were speaking many years ago."

"Indeed! I remember you well," Drew replied as Carla made her way to join them. "It is so good to see you again, Hannah. This is my wife, Carla."

"Oh, yes, Carla," Hannah replied as the two women instinctively hugged one another. "You are just as lovely now as you were then," she offered sincerely.

Later that same evening, after Carla had served them an impromptu but delightful supper, the three of them shared a long time of warm fellowship in the Sterling's lovely penthouse apartment overlooking the Sea of Galilee. It took Drew quite some time to get to the point where he felt comfortable resuming his conversation with Hannah that had been interrupted many years earlier.

Up to now Hannah had revealed only that she had lost her entire family during the war and that after the war she had lived in Freising as the caretaker of an aging rabbi, a fellow survivor of Auschwitz, until his death. Then, she had gone on to share, out of sheer loneliness and growing despair, she had made Aliyah (immigrated) to Israel where she hoped she would be able to finally find herself and begin a new life.

At first she had lived alone in Jerusalem for several months and then moved to Tel Aviv where she had lived for many years as a self-imposed recluse until just a month ago.

Then, she had continued, since she had still been very lonely and unable to escape the almost constant torture of her horrific memories in Tel Aviv, where she had made only a few very superficial friends, she had decided to investigate the possibility of moving to Tiberias in the hope of becoming more at peace with the past and more intimately integrated into new and hopefully more inviting surroundings.

"Hannah," Drew ventured cautiously, "if I may be so bold as to take up our conversation where we left it back in Freising, as I remember, you reacted quite negatively to my message on forgiveness, and I had hoped to ask you why before we were interrupted. Perhaps Carla and I could help in some way if we better understood why you have been carrying such a burden all these years."

Hannah paused for only a moment, then, resolutely rose from where she had been sitting and stood between the two of them, who remained seated. "I have never shown anyone this before," Hannah replied tearfully, as she rolled up the left sleeve of her loose fitting blouse.

Drew and Carla were deeply shocked as they beheld a clearly visible dark blue tattoo "A-25232" indelibly etched on Hannah's lower left arm.

"Do you know what this is?" she asked, unable to conceal the depth of her bitterness and long suffering.

The two of them wept as Drew replied softly, "Yes, Hannah, we know."

For the next hour, with almost no interruption, Hannah poured out the details of her tragic story, even the most intimate detail of the horrors she had never before shared with anyone. The three of them knew with certainty that this was Hannah's greatly needed catharsis of long-suppressed pain, the outpouring of which started as a trickle but quickly became a mighty, unrestrained torrent.

When she spoke of her treatment at the hands of Josef Mengele and the other horrors of her life at Auschwitz, she sobbed unabashedly as Carla held her close, offering what loving comfort she was able to provide.

Finally, when this outpouring from the depths of her soul was finished, Hannah further confessed. "Chaplain Sterling, I want you to know that your message that Sunday morning in Freising touched me very deeply. For all of my long life I have never really known God.

"My dear parents," she continued, "may they rest in peace, went through the motions of practicing their Judaism, but their expression had nothing of the heart. It was," she struggled to find the right words, "it was a traditional, socially obligatory, really meaningless series of religious things we did as a family. It never really meant anything to me.

"God knows," she continued, "I needed Him desperately, especially during and then after the war, but after the Final Solution, there was nothing Jewish left in Munich or in Freising. I had no place to turn where I could search for anything meaningful and real in the Judaism into which I had been born.

"Then," she continued her sad confession, "out of my great despondency I looked for God in the Roman Catholic Church. But all I could find there were man-made idols, trappings of paganism, and the same kind of meaningless religious superficiality I had already endured in Judaism. I could find nothing of the Lord God of Israel in the church, nothing of the comfort, nothing of the love I had been so desperately and earnestly seeking.

"After several months of this unproductive search," she continued to pour out her story, "when I had reached the very depths of my longing, I met Chaplain and Mrs. Featherstone. I now know that it must have been God who led me to them, and then to their chapel where I was obviously supernaturally called to hear your message on forgiveness. Yes, I had no doubt that it was the God whom I had been seeking who spoke to me through your words.

"Drew, Carla," Hannah used their first names with trusting tenderness, "you must forgive me, but I tried, I honestly tried to forgive Mengele, those who used me and abused me like I was some sort of an animal, and all the rest; those who murdered my dear parents and my beloved Michael, but I just couldn't. I tried to forgive them that very day, right there as I sat there in the pew. I prayed for the ability to do so, but when I tried, the very words froze in my mouth.

"Then, when we started to speak at the end of the service but were interrupted, I took the path of least resistance. I ran away, back to my apartment in the city, but I didn't stay there long; only for a few more miserably lonely, empty months without this God whom I still sought, but by then I was convinced I would never come to know.

"Then, when it seemed I had no other alternative, I decided to make Aliyah with the hope, even the expectation, that I might be able to find this elusive God among other Jews who presumably already knew Him—among my people, here in the Land where I knew all Jews have been called to return.

"At first I looked for Him in Jerusalem, but all I could find there were even more religious Jews who seemed to be going through their own unique and apparently endless rabbinical, orthodox ritual. I could find no comfort there among them, nor could I find any one of them who had any apparent concern or even the slightest interest in me.

"And so, after a few months of again coming up spiritually empty-handed, I rented a nice apartment on the beach in Tel Aviv. At least the ocean is pleasant there, and the restaurants and cultural things are enjoyable."

"Hannah, have you found God?" Drew interrupted.

"No—at least not up until today," she replied forthrightly. "But," she continued, "I have never felt closer to Him than I do at this moment. I know that my meeting you and Carla again, here in Israel, after all of these many years—I know this was no coincidence. I had never been to Tiberias before today, but I somehow knew that I was to come here, to this spa."

"Don't be surprised by this," Carla commented. "This is the way our God manages to accomplish His will. He frequently makes these divine appointments, but it is up to us to keep them."

"I'm so very, very happy I listened to Him today," she replied, for the first time joyfully.

"And so are we!" Drew answered in the same happy, newborn spirit, like the glorious light of the sun rising beautifully after the bleak darkness and terror of a long storm-filled night. "Perhaps you can spend a couple of days with us until you return to Tel Aviv. There are many more things we need to share."

"There is absolutely nothing that keeps me in Tel Aviv," she replied. "If you would be kind enough to point me in the right direction, I would like to spend the next day or so looking for an apartment here in this lovely city. For the first time in many years it seems to me that at last I have come home."

Chapter 12
Hannah's Story
Tiberias
(May 2009)

Drew and Carla were savoring their second cup of morning coffee together as they looked over their adopted city, the Sea of Galilee, and the Golan Heights beyond from the awesome vantage point of their penthouse apartment balcony. Drew looked at his watch and announced, a bit hesitantly, not wanting to give up the joy of this morning ritual they were sharing, "Well, it's about that time. Hannah will be here in a few minutes."

"You can count on it," Carla replied, instantly lifting his somewhat faltering spirits with her contagious bright smile that so clearly illuminated the Holy Spirit who dwelled within her. "Honestly, the dear woman is absolutely amazing. Even after all she has been through in her life, no one would ever guess she was in her eighties; she looks and acts as if she were so very much younger. Isn't it wonderful how she is never a minute late for any of these Wednesday morning meetings? She's so hungry, so deeply seeking."

"I wish I could find a way to get beyond the teaching of her Rabbi Yakov," he replied with just a hint revealing his continuing frustration. "He packed her head so full of his Talmudic understandings, it may still be a long battle before we can find a way for her to see beyond them."

"Of course we will," Carla comforted. "Don't forget that everything happens in His time, not ours. If you are looking for an opinion, I think your approach of showing her the three parts of the Godhead entirely as they are revealed in the pages of the Tenach is brilliant—just trust the Lord; it will eventually work. The question is really just a matter of God's timing."

"As usual, Carla you are right," he agreed, his momentary tension lifted. "I'm going to stick to this approach until the shades are finally lifted from her precious Jewish eyes."

When the three of them had taken their usual seats at the Sterlings' large wooden dining room table facing the now closed glass panel sliding doors leading to the balcony and the awesome view beyond, Drew began their morning session with the Lord's Prayer. He then closed with a plea that the Lord might this very morning show this dear sister the wonderful truth in what they had been sharing from the Tenach all of these now many months.

"Hannah," he began, "you have been such a wonderful, seeking listener all of these many months. We have carefully reviewed the entire Bible together, both the Old and the New Testaments. I would imagine that you could write a credible thesis on Yeshua, the Messiah, as He was prophesied in the former and fulfilled in the latter." He stopped abruptly when he noticed the tears beginning to flow from her lovely brown eyes. "What's wrong, Hannah?" he asked with deep concern.

"You are so right, Drew," she confessed in an emotional outburst revealing her very deep frustration.

"I found Yeshua in the very first verse of the Torah: 'In the beginning Elohim.' Then He cried out to me again and again a bit later in this same beginning book: 'Let Us make him in Our image.' How could it have been any clearer? Right here we have the Lord God of Israel revealing to us that He manifests Himself in multiple ways!"

She continued without pause as Drew and Carla listened attentively. "I do understand, Drew, just the way you pointed out; Rambam distorted the Sh'ma: 'Hear O Israel the Lord is one' when he changed the original biblical Hebrew *echad*, meaning a plural unity, like a man and woman will become *echad*/one flesh, and made it instead *yachid*, meaning an indivisible unity. It is so obvious to me that he did the same sort of thing with his second article of faith, where he declared that God could not take on flesh. Surely he wrote these things to directly discredit Yeshua and those who would follow Him!

"You've taught me well, Drew—you and Carla. You have shown me Yeshua in the pages of the Tenach. While there is no mention of His name, I have seen Him there in exquisite, unmistakable detail as if this were His biography. The prophet Daniel beheld 'one like the Son of Man coming with the clouds of heaven' to take up His dominion and glory and an everlasting kingdom where 'all peoples, nations, and languages would serve Him.'

"Dear ones," she continued through her tears, "I have so many of these wonderful words etched on my soul. These are the words I whisper each night before I sleep, and when I wake up in the morning, I find them still on my lips:

> Go and tell My servant David, "Thus says the Lord... And it shall be, when your days are fulfilled, when you must go to be with your fathers, that I will set up your seed after you, who will be of your sons; and I will establish his kingdom. He shall build Me a house, and I will establish his throne forever. I will be his Father, and he shall be My son; and I will not take My mercy away from him, as I took it from him who was before you. And I will establish him in My house and in My kingdom forever; and his throne shall be established forever."
>
> —1 Chronicles 17:4, 11–14

> Who has believed our report? And to whom has the arm of the Lord been revealed? For He shall grow up before Him as a tender plant, and as a root out of dry ground. He has no form or comeliness; and when we see Him, there is no beauty that we should desire Him. He is despised and rejected by men, a Man of sorrows and acquainted with grief. And we hid, as it were, our faces from Him; He was despised, and we did not esteem Him. Surely He has borne our griefs and carried our sorrows; yet we esteemed Him stricken, smitten by God, and afflicted. But He was wounded for our transgressions, He was bruised for our iniquities; the chastisement for our peace was upon Him, and by His stripes we are healed. All we like sheep have gone astray; we have turned, every one, to his own way; and the Lord has laid on Him the iniquity of us all. He was oppressed and He was afflicted, yet He opened not His mouth; He was led as a lamb to the slaughter, and as a sheep before its shearers is silent, so He opened not His mouth. He was taken from prison and from judgment, and who will declare His generation? For He was cut off from the land of the living; for the transgressions of My people He was stricken. And they made His grave with the wicked—but with the rich at His death, because He had done no violence, nor was any deceit in His mouth.
>
> Yet it pleased the Lord to bruise Him; He has put Him to grief. When You make His soul an offering for sin, He shall see His seed, He shall prolong His days, and the pleasure of the Lord shall prosper in His hand. He shall see the labor of His soul, and be satisfied. By His knowledge My righteous Servant shall justify many, for He shall bear their iniquities. Therefore I will divide Him a portion with the great, and He shall divide the spoil with the strong, because He poured out

> His soul unto death, and He was numbered with the transgressors, and He bore the sin of many, and made intercession for the transgressors.
>
> —Isaiah 53:1–12

"I could go on and on, my dearest Drew and Carla," she continued unabated. "I have seen the Father, and the Son, and yes, I've seen the Holy Spirit. And I've seen all three of them in the same place at the same time at the moment of Yeshua's baptism."

> When all the people were baptized, it came to pass that Yeshua also was baptized; and while He prayed, the heaven was opened. And the Holy Spirit descended in bodily form like a dove upon Him, and a voice came from heaven which said, "You are My beloved Son; in You I am well pleased."
>
> —Luke 3:21–22

With that, she bowed her head and began to sob uncontrollably. Carla went to her, embraced her, and stroked her thick snow-white hair comfortingly. She continued for a time until Hannah regained her composure and lifted her head. It was only then that Carla spoke.

"My dear Hannah, you have learned so much. Your mind is like a sponge, like that of a young girl. Surely through all of this you have come to know Him."

With that, Carla had deliberately opened a long-sealed door through which Hannah leaped. "God help me!" she almost screamed. "I know of Him! I know of Him in my mind, but I do not know Him in my heart!"

"You will know Him in your heart, Hannah." It was now Drew who responded. "Yeshua told us to knock, and the door would be opened. Yeshua is God, and God does not lie. Your salvation is only a matter of His timing, so let's join hands, all three of us, and bow before Him in prayer as we have done at the close of each of our times together."

The three of them were now on their knees, Hannah between the two she now intently loved, those who had discipled her. They faced the morning sun, still streaming through the closed glass doors leading to the balcony. Their heads were bowed and their eyes were closed as Drew began to pray:

"Abba, we rejoice at what you have brought forth in our sister, Hannah, this precious woman who has lost everything dear to her in her life and who now so reverently and earnestly seeks a heart knowledge of You. We do ask in the name of Your Son, Yeshua, that You would have mercy upon her, that You would take the scales from her precious Jewish eyes, eyes that have seen indescribable horrors. Abba, we beseech You to open these eyes so that she might finally see the blessed face of Yeshua and know Him in her heart for who He is. Abba, we beseech You in the name of Yeshua to touch her as you did the apostle Sha'ul in the house of Ananias, to remove the scales from her eyes and soften her heart that she might come to know You and be baptized. Blessed be your holy Name. Amen."

As they opened their eyes, the three of them at once saw the magnificent large dove perched on the wrought iron railing that surrounded the balcony. It was silhouetted against the azure blue morning sky, and the sun highlighted its dark gray and white feathers, making them seem as if this beautiful creature had been outlined in pure gold.

Wordlessly and in awe the three of them remained on their knees as the heavenly visitor jumped down from its perch onto the tiled floor of the balcony and slowly proceeded toward them, where they waited just on the other side of the closed sliding glass doors. Closer and closer it came until, if the door had been open, they could have reached out and touched it.

Now, in fulfillment of what the three of them took to be its holy mission, the dove raised its head and cooed loudly enough to be clearly heard on the other side. This done, it stepped back enough to give it space to raise its wings, and in a sudden burst of motion, it flew away toward the Sea of Galilee.

"I have seen His face!" Hannah cried out joyfully from the depths of her soul. "Praise God! At last—at long last I have come to know Him in my heart!"

Tiberias (May 2009)

Rabbi Mordecai Ben Shlomi cherished his appointed position as the leader of the Tiberias branch of Shomrei Israel (Guardians of Israel). Like many ultra-Orthodox Jews, he vigorously opposed and greatly feared all Christians, as well as everything associated with these *minim* (apostates).

For Mordecai, this characteristically militant anti-Christian bias had a much deeper and more personal dimension that had drawn him to join and wholeheartedly devote his life's work to the activities of this nationwide "anti-missionary" organization. Mordecai had done so with passionate dedication born out of sheer anger and frustration when his lovely Sarah, the one who had been chosen by their two respective families to be his wife, instead, in violation of everything he held most dear, had allowed her very soul to be stolen by a particularly persistent Christian missionary. Then, adding an equally grave insult to the terrible injury she had already caused, Sarah had changed her religion and joined a flourishing, so-called "Messianic Jewish" congregation in Jerusalem.

In keeping with the ultra-Orthodox Jewish traditions of such arranged marriages, Mordecai hadn't, in any more than a very superficial way, gotten to know Sarah before she had fled from him on what was supposed to have been their wedding day.

It therefore wasn't that he, in a manner of speaking, loved Sarah in any romantic sense. After all, she was only eighteen, and he was already nearing forty.

The truth was, Sarah was gorgeous, a stereotypical, Israeli Jewish beauty, who, even behind the concealment of her very conservative Orthodox dress and whatever other genuine efforts her mother had used to try to veil the reality, was an exquisitely full-figured, classically beautiful, virginal young woman. She had become the object of Mordecai's long suppressed sensuous nature and, by the nearness of their promised union, had become increasingly the focus of his own self-admitted, nearly all-consuming preoccupation.

There was nothing especially distinctive about Mordecai's appearance that would cause him to stand out in a crowd of his ultra-Orthodox peers. He was simply average looking in the sense that his average height, average build, nondescript facial features, near total baldness, and thick horn-rimmed glasses, among his other indistinctive features and characteristics, simply did not add up to the lifelong mate to whom a genuine beauty like Sarah would be drawn.

In the end, however, it wasn't the physical attractiveness or unattractiveness of the man to whom she was betrothed that snatched her from beneath the chuppah under which she was to become his wife. Rather, it was a genuine drawing to her Lord Yeshua that turned her away from the arranged marital alternative that had been promised by her family.

It was thus that Mordecai, on the very day that was to have been his wedding to the now-forever lost Sarah, motivated by a soul-deep longing for vengeance, joined the local chapter of Shomrei Israel and vowed to give its anti-Christian mission his fully committed attention.

Mordecai was a native of Tiberias, the last of five sons of a typically large ultra-Orthodox brood of fourteen. Mordecai's father, Shlomi Ben David, like Mordecai and his four brothers, was himself an Orthodox rabbi.

The old man was seriously shrunken and stooped from his more than ninety years of fastidious bobbing to and fro while offering perfunctory, ritualistic whispered readings from the pages of his badly worn and yellowed *Siddur* (Jewish Prayer Book).

It was deeply sad for the old man, and the many who loved him, that Rabbi Shlomi's thus precariously contorted posture forced him to stare fixedly at the floor beneath him rather than to feast his eyes upon the horizontal view that took in the faces of those he most loved and the awesome beauty of the Land of his inheritance.

Even so, despite the physical encumbrances life had thus thrust upon him, Rabbi Shlomi nevertheless took enormous pride and found great comfort in the fact that his own generation, like every preceding generation of his venerable family back to the time of Rabbi Akiva (A.D. 50–135), had been headed by, like himself, a staunchly Pharisaic-rooted Orthodox rabbi.

Now, as Rabbi Shlomi's many years were drawing to their inevitable end, the large, prospering Tiberias congregation he had long led was quietly preparing for the ascension of Rabbi Avraham Ben Shlomi, who, from the moment of his birth as the first son, had been ordained to one day take the place of his father.

Rabbi Mordecai, as the last of the old man's four sons, had never for a moment questioned the validity or inevitability of this deeply embedded cultural tradition. Sadly, given the relatively vast number of such sons, like himself, who had "worked" their way from *Gan* (kindergarten) through the several layers of the independent, yet government-funded Yeshiva educational system until their ordination, there were far more fully qualified Orthodox and ultra-Orthodox rabbis than there were congregations for them to lead.

Never mind. For Mordecai and the many other Yeshiva-trained but uncalled potential congregational leaders, there was a genuinely appealing alternative that offered them a different fulfillment and meaning for their lives.

Since they were exempt from compulsory military service, and only rarely were inclined to seek gainful employment in the mostly secular, materialistic world around them, they most often opted for a very appealing modus vivendi. After all, hadn't their God commanded them to "multiply and fill the earth"? Most assuredly, theirs was a calling to procreate, to raise their large families with freely offered government financial assistance, and if they were to so choose, to simply live out their often long years in relatively strife-free comfort.

Of course, life for Mordecai Ben Shlomi and his kind was not at all that simple and undemanding. Along with being outstanding reproducers of their own kind, they were, each of them, highly educated, ordained, very special "holy" men of God's own choosing. They were modern-day sages dressed in starched white shirts worn under conservatively cut uniform black suits, topped off with very large broad-brimmed black hats.

These were rabbis, highly oriented and focused along strict sectarian lines, scholars steeped in their knowledge of an ever-changing "Oral Torah of Moses" as they were taught to believe it and that had been recorded and periodically redacted in the multi-volume commentary upon the Mishna treatise known as the Talmud.

From the moment of their circumcision on the eighth day of their lives, the pattern had long been established. Never mind, they were to spend their youth and early manhood in deep and focused sectarian study. Never mind that the bill for all of this would be footed by the rest of Israeli society, mostly comprised of immigrants who, if they managed to survive two years of compulsory military service, worked long, hard hours in return for marginally adequate, heavily tax-burdened wages.

Indeed, as modern-day sages without another calling Mordecai Ben Shlomi and his kind could remain at home, procreating and assisting their genuinely overburdened wives care for their growing broods. Then, in whatever time might be left over from such domestic duties, they were free to continue their study and meditation upon the Talmud, the commentaries upon the Talmud known as the *Gemara*, and other related rabbinical writings that made up their extensive portfolios derived from the commandments of men.

If the truth were known, Mordecai had spent all of his nearly forty years pursuing this singular vocation of government-financed study. While he lived alone under very comfortable conditions, all the while vainly hoping for yet another opportunity to marry, he was bored—even profoundly so. It is for this reason that he so excitedly seized upon the opportunity to become a "soldier" in the army of the "Guardians" and, after doing so, excelled at his new vocation.

Even now, as he was about to address the Tiberias branch of the "Guardians," whom he had called to gather at his father's synagogue late Friday evening after the last of the services, he felt a deep surge of empowered righteousness at the "operation" he would set into motion the next afternoon. Like a centurion about to lead his legion into battle, he began to speak with an obvious bitterness born of sought vengeance that colored his carefully chosen words.

"My brothers," he began, struggling to make his normally high-pitched voice somehow sound more commanding. "Tiberias has long been of little concern to our national organization, that is, until recently. For the past several years we have only had to contend with three such 'Christian missionary' congregations, each of them relatively innocuous and posing no significant threat to the precious Jewish souls who we are sworn to protect from spiritual pollution.

"The largest of these three, Congregation Bethel, has maintained its membership of nearly three hundred for several years. To their credit, they have never made any concerted, congregational effort to evangelize here in our city. This is likely so since they have obviously paid attention to the time we stoned their meeting place during one of their early gatherings. Most of this particular group of minim are Gentiles, and most of these are transient volunteers from the United States.

"Moreover, most of them live together in a closed residential community away from the heart of our city. Then there is the second so-called 'Messianic Jewish' group who call themselves 'Bet Yeshua.' Their leader, although he was born a Jew, takes virtually no notice of Jewish traditions to the extent that he includes nothing of our sacred feasts in his almost entirely Brit Hadisha [New Testament] teachings.

"There are just over fifty regular attendees at this group's weekly Shabbat service, and the vast majority of these are new immigrants from the former Soviet Union who were spiritually polluted before they ever came to Israel.

"Then," Mordecai continued, "there is the third congregation that is hardly worth mentioning in this context. Saint Agnes Church is a small local branch of the Church of England that provides spiritual services for local transient Christians and a handful of expatriates who live here in Tiberias. They have never been and are not now a threat, in that they clearly avoid any evangelistic activities among our people.

"Thus, my brothers," Mordecai's voice began to rise again with growing emotion, "all would be well here in our city if it were not for yet a fourth group of *minim* that has only recently arisen like a den of vipers in our midst. Ironically, they call themselves 'Kehilat Emet' [Congregation of Truth] when they teach nothing but lies, such as fabrications that Yeshua is the Messiah, and worse still, that He is God Himself come in the flesh and all manner of other 'Christian' rubbish.

"Their leader, Andrew Sterling, was born a Jew but then later changed his religion to Christianity. Worse still, he then devoted much of his life to his new false religion as a chaplain in the United States Air Force, where he rose to high rank and prominence. He and his wife, Carla, managed to make Aliyah, and they have lived here in Tiberias ever since.

"Up to now, this so-called Rabbi Drew and his followers have pretty much stayed to themselves, and while they have many other *minim* in their circle of friends, they have posed no significant threat to our people. While Rabbi Drew has written several books relating to his understanding that Christianity arose from Judaism and is not a separate religion, but rather a fulfillment of Judaism, his audience has been mostly the Christian church in North America. None of his writings have been translated into Hebrew, and none of them are offered for sale to the general Israeli public.

"Therefore, up to very recently, we have not seen this Rabbi Drew or his followers as a significant missionary threat to our precious, vulnerable people—that is, until he took it into his head to found this so-called Kehilat Emet.

"Satan himself must be in this work!" Mordecai screamed in almost uncontrolled rage. "After only two months there are over sixty, most of them dear, precious Jews who have blindly converted to this despicable *minim* religion! It seems that each day more and more of our innocent, vulnerable, dear Jewish brothers and sisters are flocking to this Rabbi Drew, only to be duped by his false teachings and blindly follow this vicious enemy of his own people!"

Mordecai stopped for a moment for effect before he came to his next dramatic pronouncement. "This Rabbi Drew—the Reverend Andrew Scott Sterling—must be stopped!" He shouted hatefully. "And Kehilat Emet must be disbanded and silenced forever. My brothers of Shomrei Israel, it has fallen upon us to accomplish this great work for HaShem.[1] He has placed us here in this holy city, and He now calls us to this sacred purpose.

"I have learned," he continued with resolve, "from one of our own who has been attending their meetings that tomorrow afternoon Kehilat Emet will be conducting a so-called 'baptism' ceremony at an out-of-the-way site on the Jordan River. My brothers, this will be both a perfect place and a perfect opportunity for us to take a stand, to commence our open verbal and even physical opposition to this band of *minim* and their missionary leader. Come now, my brothers; we have much planning to accomplish before we soon confront the enemy on the banks of the Jordan."

Chapter 13
Hear O Israel
A Compendium of Sorrows

The Law of Return (1950) in its original form allowed any Jew in the world to immigrate to Israel and become a citizen. The central question begged by this legislation that is still being debated is, "Who is a Jew?" The historically unanswerable question seems to be: Is Jewish identity a matter of ethnicity, nationality, religion, or some combination of these determinants? In 1958, Israel Bar-Yehuda, then Minister of the Interior and a member of the Labor Zionist Party, decreed, "Any person declaring in good faith that he is a Jew, shall be registered as a Jew and no additional proof shall be required."

Later, in January 1960, with respect to the determination of "Jewishness," it was decided, at the discretion of the Ministry of the Interior (only as an internal directive, not as a law) that religion and nationality were the same. To be a Jew, it was then determined, one must declare in good faith that he is a Jew and is not a member of a different religion. However, two years later this simple directive was hotly challenged before the Supreme Court in the landmark case of *Brother Daniel in Rufeisen v. The Interior Ministry.*

Brother Daniel was born Oswald Rufeisen, a 100 percent ethnic Polish Jew. After he had heroically helped to save many fellow Jews from the Nazis, he disguised himself as a nun and lived among them successfully, thus avoiding capture by the Germans through the remaining years of the war.

Perhaps because of his great exposure to Christianity during these several years, he proclaimed himself to be a Christian and changed his name to "Brother Daniel." Even so, the new convert continued to have strong Zionist identification and loyalty. Hence he hurried to Israel in 1948 to fight for the new state's independence alongside those he felt were his fellow Jews.

Afterward Brother Daniel sought to be entered in the Population Registry as a Christian with Jewish nationality and thus receive automatic citizenship under the Law of Return. However, the Minister of the Interior at the time denied him this, according to discretionary authority, since he was in fact religiously a Christian. Brother Daniel, who did not accept this decision lightly, petitioned the Supreme Court in 1962.

A long and passionate debate ensued, wherein Brother Daniel argued that he identified himself as a Jew and fought for Israel; thus his nationality, despite his religion, was most certainly Jewish. He declared, "My religion is Catholic but my ethnic origin is and always will be Jewish. I have no other nationality. If I am not a Jew, what am I? I did not accept Christianity to leave my people. It added to my Judaism. I feel as a Jew."

In the end, the result was a 2-1 decision against Brother Daniel on the basis that he had refused Jewish nationality by converting to Christianity. He had thus "severed" himself from his "historic past."

However, even though Brother Daniel had been denied Israeli citizenship, out of compassion for his earlier heroic rescuing of Jews during the war, he was granted the lesser status of "permanent residency" and thus was able to live out the rest of his years in the Land of his inheritance.[1]

Since *Rufeisen*, there have been other cases denying Aliyah rights based on a person's belief in Yeshua as Messiah. *Hatshins v. the Minister of Interior* deals with a Christian family who decided to convert to Judaism in order to immigrate to Israel under the Law of Return. They intended to establish a congregation that taught Jews it is possible to believe in Yeshua and still remain Jewish. Once the Ministry of the Interior discovered their plan, it immediately annulled their conversions, along with their right to immigrate to Israel. In his decision, Justice Berenson wrote words that have echoed in the decisions of similar cases. "Concerning Yeshuim who are considered and recognized as Jews, we have never yet heard of. This is absolutely unacceptable…ask any Jew on the street if this phenomena is probable and their definite answer will be: 'no.'"[2]

Two years after this, *Dorflinger v. The Minister of Interior* came before the court and was decided. This case involved a Jewess, Esther Dorflinger. Her request for Israeli citizenship as a Jew was rejected because the Ministry of the Interior decided she was part of a different religion. Ms. Dorflinger fervently insisted that there was no contradiction between her Jewishness and her belief that Yeshua is the Messiah. However, to the regret of the members of the Messianic Jewish community, she did not succeed in convincing the judges. In the words of Justice Victon, "She has raised many extended and tortuous claims as to the possible link of a Jew believing in Yeshu as the Messiah, as if we are living today at the beginning of the first century, and as if since then nothing has transpired as it relates to different religious structures that have been established and that have disconnected themselves from Judaism, and from all those who choose to join those different paths."[3]

After this very solid and broad precedent was established regarding Jews who believe in Yeshua, *Beresford v. the Minister of Interior* further cemented the issue. Here a Messianic Jewish family attempted to immigrate to Israel under the Law of Return but was denied. In spite of the fact that this issue had already been settled, as dictated by very negative precedent, this family decided to appeal to the Israeli Supreme Court of Justice. In a court decision by Justice Elon (an obvious religious judge), which is spread over dozens of pages, it was determined that any Jew who believes in Yeshua in any shape or form or any Messianic Jew is part of a different religion and has decided to willfully change his own religion.

Shortly following the Beresford decision, the next case to be decided was *Kendel v. The Minister of Interior.* The Kendel family claimed that they were no longer active in Messianic Jewish activity and that a separation needed to be made between their inner beliefs and their external activities. Justice Netanyahu rejected the Kendel family's claims.[4]

The most recent court decision addressing this issue followed in 1995 with *David Yochanan v. the Minister of Interior.* In a very short decision (approximately a paragraph) written by Justice Aharon Barak, David Yochanan was denied citizenship. While David Yochanan claimed to be a Messianic Jew, he did not provide any documentation proving he was Jewish.

In summary, all court petitions for Israeli citizenship submitted by Jews who have embraced Yeshua as their Messiah have been denied. Sadder still is the reality that some incalculably large number of such Messianic Jews have been found out at one stage or another of the immigration process and have been abruptly turned away from taking up their biblical inheritance in the Land.

Although Israel is presumably a democratic nation, groups that refer to themselves as "anti-missionaries" are freely allowed to advance an agenda of religious ethnic cleansing in the Jewish homeland. Propelled by a so-called religious duty, these radical groups function like a secret police unit, overstepping legal boundaries and impeding individual rights. Their goal? To stalk, harass, and persecute any group perceived to be a threat to their worldview. On their list of targets are not only Messianic Jews but also Reform Jews, Conservative Jews, and Kabbalists.[5]

Israeli citizenship is a great and wonderful blessing. However, for many of those believing Jews who have managed to attain it, there have been associated trials and tribulations making their lives in the Land something less utopian than they might have envisioned at the outset of their quests.

There is a well-documented and deeply saddening reality that oftentimes the radical Orthodox Haredi (7 percent) minority discriminates against non-Jews, or those whom they do not consider to be Jewish. By the grace of God, the Jerusalem Institute of Justice (JIJ) and other dedicated advocates in the Land have often provided pro-bono and/or highly subsidized litigation and consultation services and spearheaded other projects to stand at the forefront of the ongoing and often intense battle for religious freedom and religious tolerance in Israel.

Dear reader, please recall from our earlier discussion how the Israeli coalition form of government has often led to greatly out-of-proportion influence demanded by the religious parties as their price for joining the majority party in order to form a majority government. Particularly germane is the example when Golda Meir, a secular humanist (atheist), gave way to the demands of the religious Left and in 1970 allowed the Law of Return to be amended to the great detriment of the tiny minority of Israeli Messianic Jews and those like-minded believers who would, during the ensuing years, seek to make Aliyah.

History does indeed have a way of repeating itself. Following our elections in March 2009, Benjamin Netanyahu (right-wing Likud party) was asked by President Shimon Peres to form a coalition government, a mission that proved to be more difficult than expected. At the end of lengthy negotiations Netanyahu was forced to include Shas, (the current-day Haredi, ultra-Orthodox religious party representing 7 percent of the population) in the coalition, the result of which was to once again create a narrow right-wing/religious minority–dominated government. What does this mean in plain English? The militantly anti-Messianic, ultra-religious are very much, once again, back in the seat of power in Israel.

Following is a direct quote from the coalition agreement between the Likud and Shas parties, under a section titled "Religion and State":

> The government will look into the claims regarding the expansion of the scope of illegal missionary activity in Israel and the steps required to deal with it, to the extent necessary.

According to the JIJ, you can be sure that the ultra-Orthodox Shas party did not have a narrow legal definition of "missionary" in mind when this seemingly carte blanche coalition agreement was signed. Every Messianic Jew in Israel, for instance, is profiled by Shas' rabbis as "an illegal missionary," regardless of their actual vocation or behavior.[6]

To my knowledge, the impact of this coalition agreement was both immediate and profound. Many within the leadership of the tiny Messianic minority have received repeated letters from the Ministry of the Interior demanding that they appear before them with their Israeli identity cards and passports in hand. Reportedly, some of those who have complied and did so without legal representation trustingly turned over these crucial documents to ministry clerks who sought to "examine" them. They were not returned. In other cases involving those who have sought legal representation, the Ministry of the Interior has simply refused to renew their passports on the alleged ground that these documents are a privilege and not a right.

In one recent development, the ministerial and administrative leaders of one of the largest Messianic congregations in the Land have been threatened en masse with the revocation of their citizenship in part because of their alleged "missionary activities," but mainly because of the claim that they immigrated into Israel based on falsified information.

Certainly, this potentially devastating discrimination against the Messianic minority has been and remains cause for great concern. Even so, however, the problem goes much deeper than its administrative implications when time and time again it has deteriorated into outright Jew against Jew violence. What follows is by no means all-inclusive but rather a brief compendium intended to illustrate the much greater profusion of such instances that have occurred within Israel during recent years.

The Messianic Congregation in Arad

Since its founding in the late 1990s this mixed Jewish and Gentile congregation in the Northern Negev has been the target of almost perpetual harassment and physical attack by Shomrei Israel and other local ultra-Orthodox groups. Even before they were able to acquire a communal meeting place and met in homes instead, every morning, as a matter of course, as many as fifty black garbed ultra-Orthodox extremists assembled outside the pastor's home, where they taunted, screamed anti-Yeshua commentary, and threatened violence upon anyone who dared to enter or leave this residence.

Simultaneously, another such group carried on a parallel daily harassment over a period of years against a young widow and her three children who attended a local Messianic congregation and who lived in a small house elsewhere in the city.

These events led to the Supreme Court of Israel's decision in *Amutat BeZedek v. The General Police Commander and Others.* This case involved the gathering of up to 700 members of a fundamental religious group for the purpose of demonstrating outside the private homes of members of the Messianic community in Arad. The police refused to approve of the demonstration in the proposed setting. It would only grant approval on the conditions that it would be limited in time, limited in the number of participants (up to two hundred, including ushers), and without the use of loudspeakers or vulgar and provocative speech.

When this issue was raised before the High Court of Justice, two apparently opposing values were considered: the right to privacy, property, and the freedom of religion of the Messianic community, challenged by freedom of speech and demonstration of the fundamental religious group.

In its decision, the court indicated that "according to some opinions, a collective and degrading speech aimed at a minority group has the ability to imbed the existing hierarchy in the society and to strengthen it, and as a result cause damage to the value of equality. According to this opinion, the Messianic community should be looked upon with preference, improving their social legitimacy and to limit all the more the freedom of speech which had been aimed against them for their elimination." These claims have been staple positions of courts around the world in defense of minority groups that are entitled to receive legitimacy within a society. Even though the court ruled in favor of the Messianic community, by enforcing the police requirements, it could only accept or reject the petition of the religious group. However, the fact that religious Jews are even able to demonstrate outside the private home of Messianic believers is already a disturbing occurrence, which should be prevented in a healthy democratic society that values the rights of minority groups.

I have just received an e-mail from this "young widow," who I will call "P.S." This message has already been widely distributed within the Messianic community and beyond. I immediately spoke with her by phone and received her enthusiastic permission to include her message, dated 13 February 2011, in this present context, an excerpt of which follows:

> Hello to those who might be concerned:
>
> March is the anniversary time of the year for the ultra orthodox to have their BIG demonstration [three hundred, four hundred, seven hundred people] to protest the existence of Messianic Jews here in Arad. This has become an annual event and as usual it will take place in front of my house.
>
> Throughout the year there are numerous smaller demonstrations in front of all the homes of the believers of Arad. For the Orthodox Jews of Israel this annual event has become a platform for them to voice their disagreement, even hatred, of Messianic Jews. Of course it saddens us to see and hear our Jewish brothers outside our homes screaming curses against us and our families, trying to entice our neighbors to join their efforts to make our lives so miserable that we would choose to just pack everything and flee our birthright country, Israel. This has been going on for seven years now.
>
> "What do we do about it?" you ask? We have tried many things over the years, but mostly we pray. We pray for protection over our families and property.
>
> But mostly we pray for THEM. We pray that God would have mercy on them and would reveal to them the TRUE identity of their own Messiah whom they so desperately wait for. We pray that the scales would fall from their eyes, that their ears would be cleared so that they can HEAR the WORD of the heavenly Father. We pray that their necks be massaged and their hearts be softened so that they can receive HIS message. We pray for them to find the Pearl of great price so that they will receive their rightful inheritance! We pray for their SALVATION!

In another display of violence in June 2005, a different Messianic ministry acquired a small building, formerly used as a chess club, to use as a social gathering place. After two attempts, the ultra-Orthodox extremists, using Molotov cocktails, managed to burn the facility to the ground. It was regarded by many as a miracle that those inside at the time managed to escape without harm.

As earlier noted, the believers in Arad are both Jewish and Gentile. One of the couples, the Beckfords, are racially mixed. The Jerusalem Post reported a confrontation between this couple and the ultra-Orthodox, an excerpt of which follows:

> He (Beckford) has taken a lot in Arad. "They slashed six tires on our car and van. They scratched the car; they wrote [epithets] all over it.... I went to the police over and over again, and they'd tell me to wait here, sit

> over there, go to some other office. I'd be there for four hours, six hours, and nothing ever got done."....A Jewish shopkeeper in the market says: "Everything that happened to him...are a result of the provocations by the haredim....They'd come by the dozens every week...there'd be hundreds of them, blowing a shofar. They called him and his wife terrible names...him 'nigger'...her 'whore.'....Eddie's a good man, peaceful; he has his own ideology, but he doesn't bother anybody."[7]

Beckford was indeed pushed beyond the limit during one such especially vitriolic attack by these intruders wherein they threatened violence upon his wife and child. He, a former US Marine, rushed into the crowd and physically "decked" the one who had voiced this ugly threat. As a result, Beckford was arrested, tried, convicted of assault, and sentenced to an extended period of house arrest.

The Israel-born leader of one of the Arad congregations, Yoyakim Figueras, reportedly makes every effort to avoid direct confrontation with his ultra-Orthodox neighbors. Accordingly, when two young women, just over the legal age of eighteen, recently came to the Lord in his congregation and sought baptism, in order to avoid further inflaming those who so strongly opposed him and his group, he thought it best to administer this sacrament in what is a sort of sister congregation in nearby Beersheva (about twenty miles to the west).

Congregation Yeshua's Inheritance (Beersheva)

As it turned out, transferring the celebration of baptism from Arad to Beersheva was anything but a solution to the out-of-control anti-messianic hatred that now pervaded both communities.

Even before the two young women who were to be baptized arrived at the Beersheva congregation's meeting place, as many as six hundred black-suited ultra-Orthodox protesters and other law breakers had surrounded and then begun to violently crash their way into the small facility.

The congregation had planned a picnic following the baptisms, which of course was canceled. Eventually the two young women were baptized elsewhere.

Howard Bass, the local pastor, at first did his best to welcome the intruders and invited them to be seated. Their response was to throw several objects into the baptismal and then to physically shove him into this sacred place as well. In the process, his multi-focal glasses were destroyed.

The now out-of-control attackers sang and danced as they physically assaulted many members of the congregation, all the while breaking or damaging equipment and shattering glass.

Three policemen finally arrived and, realizing the large scope of the confrontation, immediately called for reinforcements. All the while, the chief orthodox rabbi of Beersheva and leaders of the local unit of Shomrei Israel conferred just outside the building.

After more than three hours that it took for the police to finally dispel the last of the intruders, three of the ultra-Orthodox protestors were arrested and then released with no charges brought against them.

Pastor Howard Bass reportedly decided he had finally had enough of this outrage, and later, after consultation with other Israeli Messianic leaders and legal counsel, he filed suit against both the chief rabbi of Beersheva and the local unit of Shomrei Israel for damages and for their involvement in instigating the three hours of mayhem.[8]

Unfortunately, the verdict that was given by Justice Iddo Ruzin was not in favor of Pastor Howard Bass's claims, who posted on his congregation's website:

> A verdict has been handed down by Judge Iddo Ruzin.... The judge did exactly what we have been praying and hoping... that he would *not* do! Judge Ruzin has determined that the two defendants are innocent of any wrong-doing concerning the events before, during, and after 24 Dec 2005, and that we did not produce sufficient evidence to prove any personal liability on their part in our civil suit against them. Judge Ruzin has ordered that we pay 1000 ILS to each of the defendants, graded percentages of our claims against them for violations of Israeli law, attorneys' wages for their clients' defense, and the five appearances in court for the trial, for a total of approximately 155,000 ILS ($40,200 or GBP 27,800). This miscarriage of justice is a sad commentary on the state of affairs, and should be seen, too, as a wake-up call to all who care for truth and righteousness.[9]

In an e-mail sent to me, dated January 5, 2011, Pastor Bass emphasized, "Again, the judge's verdict did not accurately or fairly represent the facts of the testimonies of either side." See Pastor Bass's endorsement of this current writing on page ii.

Bible Burning in Or Yehuda

Or Yehuda, a town of about twenty-eight thousand located near Tel Aviv, was the scene of a massive burning of hundreds of New Testaments collected from the local residents in June 2008.

According to the deputy mayor of Or Yehuda, "The missionaries passed out a kit, which included the New Testament and two additional booklets, in a new, well-to-do neighborhood in Or Yehuda. The whole essence of these pamphlets was incitement against the Jews."

Reportedly the deputy mayor drove through the streets, asking residents over a loudspeaker to turn over New Testaments in their possession to yeshiva students who would be collecting them. When hundreds of these New Testaments had thus been collected, they were thrown into a huge pile next to a neighborhood synagogue and set on fire.

The deputy mayor, who was caught on camera at the scene of the fire, reportedly told the media that he had come there to stop the students after he saw what they were doing.[10]

The Horrendous Crippling of Ami Ortiz: Ariel, March 2008[11]

Purim may be a religious holiday, a time when the entire Book of Esther is read by most Israeli families, but for many Israelis, Purim is perhaps more of a holiday of good will, a time focused upon the children when families and friends exchange holiday baskets filled with candies, baked goods, and other such treats.

Even so, Messianic Pastor David Ortiz, highly respected and loved by his large congregation in Ariel, a thriving Jewish city behind the so-called "Green Line," found it necessary to go to extreme lengths to protect his wife, Leah, and their six children from the never-ceasing threat of terrorist attack from their Arab neighbors. Even more, as incomprehensible as it may seem, he also found it necessary to protect his family from the very real and growing threats of physical violence from their fellow (ultra-Orthodox) Jews.

And so it was that Pastor Ortiz installed a state-of-the-art, expensive, and highly efficient series of security cameras that would accurately record any penetration of the area surrounding their home. He felt certain that the cameras that were clearly visible to any potential intruder would in themselves deter any overt attack. Sadly, he was wrong in this assessment, nearly dead wrong.

Ami Ortiz, at fifteen, was the youngest of the Ortiz children. He was widely known and admired for his great prowess and skill as a basketball player. He had a dream that was shared by his coach and many of his teammates that one day he would become a professional player. Not only did Ami have the clearly demonstrated talent that would seem to guarantee his achieving this lofty goal, but he also had the enormous drive and winning spirit that was a rare gift in one so young. So it seemed Ami had a bright and promising future when, on March 20, 2008, he decided to stay home from school because it was Purim, a Jewish festival he greatly adored.

A number of holiday baskets were delivered to the Ortiz home that morning. One, an attractively wrapped large package, was left on the front doorstep, where it was picked up by the family cleaning lady and brought into the house.

A short time later Ami's life and future were tragically transformed when he excitedly picked up the package and opened it. In a blinding and deafening flash, the package exploded in a huge blast that shook the house and threw Ami onto the floor, where he was bathed in his own blood gushing out of him from over one hundred pieces of shrapnel that had torn at his young body. Pieces of metal, safety pins, screws, and other such objects penetrated deeply within him, blasting away some of his toes and for a time causing him to completely lose both his sight and hearing. Moreover, both of his hands were severely wounded, seeming to shatter Ami's dream of playing professional basketball. But at that moment his very survival was a far more urgent concern.

Heroically, the cleaning lady pinched off an artery that was gushing blood, most likely saving the young life that she held in her hands, until the ambulance arrived and its highly skilled paramedics could take over.

Israeli medicine is rightfully reputed to be among the very best in the world, and Ami's amazing professional team of caregivers underscored this sterling reputation. Ami survived under their care after, at first, clinging perilously to his life. Amazingly, after literally dozens of surgeries and almost continuous severe pain that he still endures more than a year and a half after the incident, Ami's condition continues to improve.

Many attribute Ami's amazing and continuing recovery as a direct answer to the prayers of unknown thousands of Christians around the world who have been faithfully interceding on his behalf. Add to this worldwide outreach the skills and dedication of his medical caregivers, then further season them both with Ami's undaunted spirit, and behold—Ami is back on the court, once again tentatively playing his beloved basketball.

Most likely Ami will never be able to achieve his goal as a professional player. He is not able to grasp the ball adequately, nor is he able to see or hear sufficiently. Moreover, his missing toes have greatly hampered his once deft footwork. But that is the way things are now. There are many more planned surgeries, the prayers on his behalf will continue, and Ami's amazing spirit remains strong and unbowed.

A police investigation was opened after the bombing. However, from the outset the Ortiz family has believed that the Israeli police have been extremely indifferent and apparently negligent in conducting their inquiry. The surveillance cameras that had been installed by the Ortiz family actually filmed the person who delivered the package. They handed this recording over to the authorities, but to their dismay, no arrests were immediately made, and the police refused to return the tape to the Ortiz family. Finally, a year after the tape was confiscated by the police and after repeated refusals by the police to release their property, the family brought the matter to court. With Ami and his parents present, the judge ruled to return the tape to the Ortiz family.

In an interview on Israeli television in May 2008, Ami's mother, Leah Ortiz, made it clear that the family believed that the perpetrators of this incident were ultra-Orthodox, radical Jews. Along with the security camera evidence, the family has revealed that they were warned repeatedly and threatened prior to the incident by these radical Jewish groups who were strongly opposed to their so called "missionary" activities. Moreover, pictures of Ortiz family members had appeared throughout the Ariel area on posters placed there by members of these same radical groups, warning all Jews to beware of this family.

As I am writing this account, it has been a year and a half since the unthinkable—the attempted murder of an innocent fifteen-year-old Messianic Jewish boy in Ariel, Israel. After a year and a half of excruciating rehabilitation, twelve operations with at least four more required, Ami and his family have received another miracle. A suspect was finally arrested in early November 2009, presumably a year and a half after he was clearly photographed by the Ortiz security system while perpetrating the attack. The suspect, Yakov "Jack" Teitel of Shvut Rachel in the Shomron, a region in the "occupied territories," is charged with the attempted murder of the

Ortiz family. Teitel is also suspected of being involved in a string of other murders and bombings that have occurred over the last twelve years.

In reacting to the arrest, Prime Minister Benjamin Netanyahu said in a statement that Israel must fight a "marginal minority" of extreme nationalists threatening Israel's democracy.[12]

It is heart-breaking for me to report what appears to be the final outcome of this case. It seems that the suspected Jewish terrorist, Yaakov Teitel, has been deemed unfit to stand trial for his alleged attack against Ami Ortiz, other such attacks, and two suspected murders, as reported in *Haaretz*, May 4, 2010.

> Suspected Jewish terrorist Yaakov (Jack) Teitel, who was arrested late last year on the suspicion that he was responsible for the murder of two Palestinians, is unfit to stand trial, Jerusalem's district psychiatrist said in an evaluation submitted Tuesday.
>
> Teitel, a resident of the settlement Shvut Rachel, was charged last November with murdering two Palestinians and attempting to murder three people, including Hebrew University Professor Zeev Sternhell and Ariel teenager Ami Ortiz. Ortiz, a member of a family of Messianic Jews, was gravely wounded by a bomb packaged inside a Purim gift in March 2008.[13]

Car Torching in Beit She'an, December 3, 2009

In a recently reported incident in nearby Beit She'an in the Jordan Valley, two Haredi men have been arrested as suspects in the torching of the family car belonging to the Eliav Levine family, Messianic Jews who made Aliyah from Russia eighteen months ago.

Last April, unknown assailants tried to torch another automobile belonging to the Levine family when it was parked outside their house. The fire, ignited outside the bedroom of their children, aged three and five, was extinguished, but it caused thousands of shekels in damage.

According to attorney Calev Myers, chief counsel of the Jerusalem Institute of Justice, the family subsequently moved, but the harassment continued, with unknown people spreading rumors about the family to their neighbors. The harassment included an incident around a month ago, when Haredi men drove around the Levine family's neighborhood in a car with speakers on top, announcing that the neighborhood must expel "the Christian missionaries who are paying neighborhood children money in order to baptize them as Christians."

The Levines have flatly denied all such accusations. "We are not missionaries; we are Jews who believe in Yeshua and pray with other Jews from Russia who also believe in Yeshua," Eliav Levine said.

Levine said the family drives to Nazareth Illit on Shabbat, where they attend prayer services in the home of other Messianic Jews. Levine said that in spite of the harassment, the family has no intention of leaving Beit She'an.

"We want to stay here. We don't see any reason for us to leave," Levine said.

Levine said the family has installed a security camera outside their home, partly because they feel that police have not done enough to stop the harassment.

Levine recalled several incidents of harassment, including a landlord who demanded they leave their apartment only two months into a one-year lease after he found out they were Messianic Jews.

He also said one of his children reported being taken out of class at school and questioned by Beit She'an religious authorities about the family's religious beliefs, without her parents being notified.

Myers said in the wake of the arson that "the apparent indifference exhibited by the police toward extremist Haredi activists leaves innocent citizens exposed to grave danger, simply because of their religious affiliation."

In a press release, Myers, who provides legal representation for Messianic Jews in Israel, said that "Haredi extremists" had turned the life of the Levine family "into a living hell just because of their religious beliefs," adding that the family "lives in fear for their lives."[14]

Chapter 14
Hannah's Story
On the Jordan River
(Shabbat, May 9, 2009)

"How are you going to deal with this, Drew?" Carla spoke softly for only his ears as she, along with the rest of their group of nearly eighty, noted with growing trepidation the crowd of more than one hundred black-suited ultra-Orthodox, the local chapter of the Shomrei Israel and some of their supporters, who had come to challenge their very presence and purpose. These uninvited intruders had quietly positioned themselves in a circle that extended on both sides of the river, surrounding Drew and his entire group who were now assembled on the east bank.

"I'm going to do nothing for the moment," Drew replied. "Nothing but follow the leading of the Holy Spirit, who has been rescuing our people from this sort of opposition since the very first of us gathered on Mount Zion."

"Welcome to you all!" Drew shouted his greeting to both the invited and potentially hostile uninvited guests. He then turned toward Hannah who, dressed in a white robe, stood by his side. "Don't be frightened by these misled people, my dear sister," he comforted. "In their ignorance, they can do us no lasting harm."

"Remember me, rabbi?" Hannah made light of the situation unfolding before them. "I'm the one who went through much harder times than this. Nothing or no one is going to take away the great joy of this wonderful moment in my life."

"Praise God!" Drew replied warmly as he led her into the water and they moved together, arm in arm, toward the other shore until they had reached the depth where the water flowed just above Hannah's waist.

"Stop this insanity!" Rabbi Mordecai screamed, setting off a rancorous chorus of inharmonious, virulent verbal abuse from the well-rehearsed black-suited band that had come to interrupt, even prevent, Hannah's sacred moment.

"Let us curse these slandering believers in Yeshua![1]" Mordecai screamed to his now incensed band of followers as he then began to intone the Birkat HaMinim, "Blessing" of the Amidah, a vitriolic curse against all Messianic believers that was instituted in the early first century and, ever since, has been included in the daily ritualistic prayers uttered in a somewhat less severe version in many Orthodox synagogues throughout the world.

> Let there be no hope for these sectarians (Messianic Jews)! May all their evil be destroyed in an instant! O Lord our God, may all of Your enemies be swiftly cut down! May these evil ones soon be uprooted, broken, destroyed, and utterly humbled. Blessed are You, O Lord our God, who breaks down Your enemies and humbles sinners!

"Cursed be the Messianic Jews! Cursed be the Messianic Jews! Cursed be the Messianic Jews!" Mordecai and his band of brothers shouted again and again.

Carla, led by the Holy Spirit, quickly picking up the moment, unhesitatingly entered the water and began to make her way toward her two dear ones, who were already in the river. Instinctively, the entire congregation, along with their guests, followed, and when they reached Drew and Hannah, they formed a tight protective circle around them.

"My dear sister Hannah, precious brothers and sisters of Kehilat Emet," Drew spoke in a loud voice so all of them could hear, even above the din of the shouting objectors. "Let us together renounce our sinful ways." They all now repeated Drew's words as he paused between each phrase:

> With all of my heart—with all of my soul—with all of my spirit—I totally and completely renounce Satan and his legion of demons and all the evil works of their creation.

When this was finished, Drew continued, "And now, Hannah, I will anoint you with oil," which he accomplished by pouring olive oil over her head from a small flask he had carried with him.

When Hannah had been thus anointed, Drew continued, "Hannah, and any of you others who would like to join her, I now ask you to repeat, after me, your confession of faith." Again, pausing between phrases, Drew led them:

> Heavenly Father, I confess with my mouth and believe with all of my heart that Yeshua is the promised Messiah, Your Son. I believe that He reigns with You and the Holy Spirit as the Holy God of Israel. I believe that He came into the world to dwell among us as God incarnate—to

> forgive our sins and to show us the way to our salvation and eternal life in the kingdom of Heaven. I believe that He willingly went to His cross and suffered death, shedding His precious blood there, as a perfect blood sacrifice for us all. I believe that He died as a man, was buried, and that He arose from the dead on the third day. I believe that He ascended into heaven, and I believe that He will return at the end of days to take up His throne on Mount Zion where He will reign in glory. I repent of my sins and will worship You all the days of my life because Your word is truth. I confess with my mouth that I am born again and cleansed by the blood of Yeshua. In Yeshua's name, amen.

When this was finished, Drew continued, "May God richly bless you, my sister Hannah, and may He also richly bless each of you, who are my sisters and brothers in Him. Hear now the words that were recorded in the sacred scrolls at Qumran many years before Yeshua came and walked among us." Drew recited:

> And he will atone for all the children of his generation, and he will be sent to all the children of his people. His word is like the word of the heavens, and his teaching according to the will of God. His eternal sun will shine and his fire will burn in all the ends of the earth; above the darkness his sun will shine. Then, darkness will vanish from the earth, and gloom from the globe. They will utter many words against him, and utter every kind of disparagement against him.[2]

"And now, my brothers," Drew continued, "hear the words that Yeshua spoke to each of us in every generation: 'I am the light of the world. He who follows Me shall not walk in darkness, but have the light of life.'[3]

"Now, let us once again complete the ancient purification rite of our people," Drew continued as he moved to a position directly in front of Hannah, the two of them effectively shielded by the several layers deep, protective circle formed by the congregation.

Drew now made the sign of the Taw (an equilateral cross) on Hannah's forehead with a bit of olive oil. He then placed his hands on her head and applied just a hint of pressure, proclaiming, "I baptize you, Hannah Ruth, in the name of the Father." As he spoke, Hannah squatted down in place until she was totally immersed, a condition ensured by the water that for a moment covered Drew's hands that remained in their place on top of her head.

At the very moment Hannah had become totally immersed, Mordecai in his absolute frustration and anger, now out of control, threw the first medium-size stone toward the assembled group in the water. He quickly reached for another as the first fell several feet short of its mark.

Following the example of their leader, many of the other black-suited opposition who had by now grown hoarse from their incessant, repetitiously shouted cursing, also began to search for and hurl stones toward those in the river, who were all now leaning forward, covering their heads with their hands for a semblance of protection.

Even so, despite their dedicated efforts, stones of throwing size were hard to find in the dense vegetative covering along both banks of the river, and even when these potentially dangerous missiles were found, then hatefully hurled, not a single one of them reached its intended target. Most fell a few feet short; a few others fell to just one side or the other of the assembled congregation.

Now, as Hannah once again stood in front of Drew, after he had again used a bit of oil to make the sign of the Taw on her forehead, he repeated his supervision of her immersion in the same manner, this time proclaiming, "I baptize you, Hannah Ruth, in the name of the Son." Then, when this was concluded, a third anointing and immersion followed with Drew proclaiming, "I baptize you, Hannah Ruth, in the name of the Holy Spirit."

When this was finished, Drew began to lead them out of the water. As he did so, all of them spontaneously began to shout out joyful praises to God for the wonder of His salvation and great goodness He had bestowed upon them.

As Drew and the rest neared the riverbank, the black-suited intruders who had just moments before been shouting curses and hurling stones suddenly fell silent and backed away a considerable distance, making way for the congregation to gather on the shore.

When all who had followed Drew had come up out of the water, they again began to form a protective circle around Drew and Hannah. When this was finished, Drew once again poured anointing oil over Hannah's head and lifted his voice toward heaven. "Hannah Ruth," he spoke with faith-filled confidence, "be baptized in the Holy Spirit."

Immediately, Hannah cried out in a previously unknown to her Middle Eastern–sounding language with a profound depth of joy, the likes of which she had never before experienced or even imagined.

Spontaneously, the congregation and a few of their invited guests joined in their own praises to God in previously unknown to them foreign tongues. So loud and gloriously compelling was the combined divinely orchestrated harmonious outpouring that it sounded to those who heard it like the sound of rushing water being offered up by a chorus of angels.

When they were finally able to recover from the utter shock of what they had just witnessed, the black-suited Shomrei Israel and those ultra-orthodox friends who had come to support them sheepishly retreated toward the city.

But this was not to be the end of the Shomrei Israel's hateful opposition to Drew and his rapidly expanding Congregation of Truth. It was only the beginning of what was to become a long and ferocious battle.

The next morning, after an early breakfast, Drew and Carla left their apartment building to shop for produce in the public market in the center of the city.

"Oh, Drew!" Carla exclaimed as she was the first to see the very large poster picturing her husband and her attached to a lamppost directly in front of them. It was emblazoned with the words in very large bold print: "BEWARE OF THESE MISSIONARIES WHO HAVE COME TO STEAL YOUR CHILDREN AND CURSE US ALL WITH THEIR FALSE MESSIAH YESHUA."

As they made their way toward the market, they could see that Mordecai and his people had done their work well. There were dozens of these posters scattered throughout the city. And as they walked into the market, it was obvious that this utterly false and vitriolic warning against them had not gone unnoticed.

This hateful poster distribution had already had an impact, as was evident from the several onlookers who recognized them from their widely displayed images and were now pointing toward them and speaking of them to others with apparent disdain.

"Drew, darling, what are we to do?" Carla asked as she struggled to put down her growing dread.

"For starters, I would suggest that we pray; beyond that, the strawberries look wonderful. Let's buy a few kilos and make some jam."

"Drew!" she objected. "How can you be so nonchalant about all of this? Don't you realize that most likely every Orthodox Jew in this city has come against us? These are people of God, Drew. They may not know Yeshua yet, but they are His chosen people! They aren't wrong, Drew; they are just ignorant and incomplete!" she nearly screamed in her growing frustration.

"How can you simply just blow off all of this opposition?"

Drew paused for a few moments before he replied thoughtfully. "Yes, these are Jews—each of them chosen by God. Those who have come against us are following the Torah, the first five of the sixty-six books of the Bible, the same Bible that we love and adore. How sad it is that they virtually ignore the remainder of the Tenach (Old Testament) and, of course, have never even considered the Brit Hadeshah (New Testament).

"But much worse, they have relegated their precious Torah, the very Word of God, to an inferior position of authority beneath their Mishna and Talmud that make up the very heart of the Oral Law. These are the commandments of men, created and written down by their Pharisaic Orthodox rabbis.

"Carla," he continued emphatically, "we have nothing to fear from these followers of the commandments of men, these sadly misguided lost souls who have often chosen to give second place to the commandments of God. It is not for us to fear them. We are called to reach out to them in love, to show them that God's Word, all of it, is the truth, to teach them about the pathway to their eternal salvation through the shed blood of Yeshua."

He paused for a few moments before he continued soberly. "Sweetheart, you've got to look at this situation from their perspective as well. Christians to them are all who believe in Yeshua, Jesus Christ: Catholics, Jehovah's Witnesses, Mormons, all manner of Protestants, and of course their fellow Jews, the handful of us who are their would-be loving neighbors. Worse still, these fellow Jews who hate us so deeply blame all of us collectively for the wrongdoings that have been wrought against our people starting way back at the Council of Nicea. We are collectively held at fault for the legions of their and our forebears who have been slaughtered over the centuries, all the rivers of Jewish blood wantonly spilled in the name of Jesus. When they look at us who would now dare to dwell in their midst, those who would dare to call themselves Jews while embracing who they can now only see as the Christian Messiah, is it any wonder that they view us with such disdain? Carla," he tenderly held her close, "we must reach out to them in love and understanding while offering them peace in exchange for their hatred, lest we forget the words of the Master who told us to turn our other cheek."

With that, standing there arm in arm, in the midst of a curious and mostly unfriendly crowd of onlookers who now surrounded them, they purchased three kilos of strawberries, then bowed their heads and began to pray.

Chapter 15
Hannah's Story
Tiberias
(Motze Shabbat, May 16, 2009)

DREW WAS GENUINELY amazed as he looked out over his congregation, still gathering for this, their first meeting at a new location, the large auditorium of Kibbutz Galilee Alpha, just two kilometers beyond the city limit to the south. As he quickly estimated the number of attendees, many of them there for the first time and unknown to him, he found himself both greatly pleased at the sudden, almost explosive growth of the congregation, yet at the same time he was just a bit concerned that this success would surely bring with it even more intense opposition from Shomrei Israel, who had been ratcheting up their campaign against them since their direct confrontation at Hannah's baptism.

By now, he reflected, it would be hard to find any one small street section in the entire city where Carla's and his face were not displayed along with inflaming words on huge posters warning all who read them that these "Missionaries from Satan" had come to steal their souls and the souls of their children. He had shared with Carla just this morning, "Thanks be to God that our three girls and their families are going about their own lives in their own sheltered worlds totally oblivious to the increasing outright confrontation the two of us are enduring on the other side of the world."

Later, after their time of worship and congregational prayer, Drew found himself strongly led to turn over the morning message to the leading of the Holy Spirit and had the wonderful experience of knowing that the words he had just begun to speak in English, translated simultaneously into Hebrew and Russian, then delivered through headsets, were flowing from the heart of the Lord to his gathered flock who waited hungrily and attentively to be fed.

"We have a saying in America," he quipped. "'Advertising pays!' It would seem there is much truth in this as it applies to us even here in Tiberias. So let us all give thanks to those who so strongly oppose us and the gospel of

Yeshua. They have done well to more than double the size of this congregation in such a short time. Obviously," he continued after the congregation had responded with a resounding guffaw, "this was by no means their intention in plastering our pictures up all over the city, and just as obviously, it seems to me that many of you who are here for the first time have come out of curiosity regarding just who we are and specifically what we have to share that would so greatly incite so many of our Orthodox brothers and sisters. Thus, especially for you first timers I want to speak this evening about why we followers of Yeshua have been so strongly opposed from the beginning and how all of this relates to our situation today here in the modern State of Israel, the Land of our biblical inheritance, an inheritance we share with all other Jews, whatever they may believe or not believe or wherever in the world they may find themselves.

"First of all," he began to introduce the central points of his message, "Yeshua did not come to start a new religion called 'Christianity.' He told us quite clearly in His Sermon on the Mount that He had come to fulfill the Torah, not to replace it. Quite emphatically He told us that His appearance and ministry had not even slightly changed the substance or the meaning of a single word of Scripture.

"Let me make it abundantly clear," Drew continued. "No one, neither Jew nor Gentile, however sincerely or passionately they may seek salvation through the shed blood of Yeshua, will be thus saved, 'born again,' until they have first have been given to Yeshua by His Father. The very first Jewish believers on Mount Zion passionately believed that the Father, according to His own will, chose who, specifically, were to be given to His Son and who were not, and that this election was made before the beginning of time and that it is inalterable. A large portion of the church of today continues to embrace this doctrine known as predestination, an understanding that is deeply rooted in ancient Judaism.

"My point here is simply this: If you are hearing these wonderful truths about Yeshua for the first time this evening, and if you, by His grace, are among those who have been given to Him by the Father, no earthly power—the prime minister, the Minister of Interior, Shomrei Israel—absolutely no one except you, yourself, can cancel out, by your own outright rejection, this pearl of great price, the wonderful, eternal destiny God has ordained for you, eternal life, freely given in Him.

"Are you beginning to get my drift?" Drew continued. "Yes, there is a slight catch to this incredible destiny that may await you, a destiny that can be yours beginning even this evening. You see, a gift given must also be a gift received for its wonderful promise to be fulfilled. Of what benefit is a beautifully wrapped gift if it remains unopened by its intended recipient, and then once opened, it is not joyfully received?

"Thomas Gray, an American poet, shared with us:

> "'Full many a gem of purest ray serene
> The dark unfathom'd caves of ocean bear:
> Full many a flower is born to blush unseen,
> And waste its sweetness on the desert air.'"[1]

Led by the Spirit, Drew spoke on for nearly another hour with words that had many of his congregation enthralled. In the end, with the clear leading of the Holy Spirit, he extended an invitation to those who had been drawn by the Father to come forward. There was an immediate and wonderful response. When those who came to the front of the sanctuary were later counted, there were more than thirty new believers who would enter into a time of personal structured discipling to properly prepare them for their baptism. All but a few of them were first-time attendees of the congregation. All of them were Jews, mostly young adults.

Drew and Carla stood together greeting those who had been with them on this exciting evening as they left the auditorium to go their separate ways. Drew recognized one of the last two who were about to leave, an attractive young woman who had been among those who came forward in response to the invitation and who had been later briefly counseled by long-standing members who would continue to disciple them over the coming weeks.

"Greetings in the name of Yeshua, ladies," Drew extended his hand in their direction, which they warmly received, introducing themselves in turn: "I'm Segal Cohen," offered the most vivacious of the two. "I'm Anna Feinberg," offered the other. "It is so good to meet you," Drew addressed them. "I am so thrilled for you, Segal, for the decision you made this morning to give your life to Messiah Yeshua." Turning to Carla, he continued, "These two are much younger than our own girls but certainly just as lovely; don't they remind you of them?"

"Oh yes!" Carla replied, noting that the two of them were typically beautiful young Israeli women, and thus, not surprisingly a bit immodestly dressed for the occasion. Being a bit more discerning than her too often over exuberant husband, Carla took this opportunity to ask matter-of-factly: "Our three girls are probably old enough to be your mothers—just how old are you two anyway?"

"You don't look anywhere near old enough to be our grandparents," Segal, who seemed to be their self-appointed spokesperson, offered quite sincerely. "The fact is, we served in the army together and have been out for nearly a year—so that makes us both pushing twenty-one."

"Then let me return the compliment," Drew responded. "You both look young for your age as well. We will certainly look forward to getting to know you and hopefully your families as well."

Chapter 16
Hannah's Story
Tiberias
(Wednesday, May 20, 2009)

It took less than a week before Carla's almost invariably accurate discernment proved frighteningly true concerning the nature and calling of the two young women who had "come to the Lord" on Shabbat.

As was their long-treasured practice and the high point of each day, the two of them had just concluded their morning time together with the Lord.

"What's for breakfast?" Drew inquired, as he had done at this point each morning since Carla had prepared their first morning meal together so many years before.

Before she could reply, however, there was a loud repeated banging at the door of their apartment, a clenched fist demanding an immediate and urgent response.

"Probably just the Orthodox collecting money again," Drew spoke comfortingly, trying to mask his own rising disquiet. "Have you got any change, dear?"

With that, he opened the thick security door that protected them from the constant threat of violence and immediately saw that a donation was not the object of this loud intrusion. Those who stood before him were not the expected black-suited ultra-Orthodox but rather two expressionless uniformed police officers.

"Are you Andrew Scott Sterling?" the officer nearest to Drew snapped.

"Yes, I am he," Drew replied, smiling, doing his best to be friendly.

However, his attempt at civility fell on deaf ears as the tone of this agent of the government who stood menacingly before him now ratcheted up a notch as he snapped. "Is Carla McKenzie Sterling at home?"

"Yes, I'm Carla Sterling," Carla, who had moved to her husband's side at the open door, replied as calmly as she was able, trying to match her husband's attempted warmth. "What can we do for you?"

"Mr. and Mrs. Sterling," the officer introduced himself and his partner officiously. "I am State Police Captain Isaac Katz. This," he continued, pointing to his partner, "is Police Lieutenant Benjamin Rothberg. We represent the Criminal Investigation Unit of the Afula Office of the State Police. You are directed to accompany us to our office for questioning regarding your alleged violation of Criminal Code Sections 174(a) & (b) and section 368 of Penal Law 5737-1977."

"Pardon my ignorance," Drew tried but failed to keep his voice from trembling. "But just what is Criminal Code Sections 174(a) & (b) and section 368 of Penal Law 5737-1977?"

"It is the anti-missionary law!" Police Captain Isaac Katz replied accusingly. "You both are under investigation for having violated this statute. Now please come along with us," he insisted.

"May I call my attorney?" Drew inquired. "We have no intention of responding to your questions without his presence."

"Suit yourself!" Katz replied. "You can attempt to reach him on our way to Afula."

"Thank God you came!" Hannah nearly screamed as she rushed into Carla's arms after the iron-barred door of Afula's Police Station holding cell had slammed shut behind them.

"What are you doing here?" Drew asked his frantic congregant incredulously.

"They came to my apartment and arrested me! They wouldn't tell me anything—just that I was accused of violating some law. I didn't understand what they were talking about, so I told them to please call you. I'm so glad they did!"

As grim as the moment seemed, Drew somehow found a humorous vein in their unseemly situation and began to laugh, slowly at first and then almost uncontrollably. Within moments, Carla and Hannah had joined in, and it took them quite some time to regain their self-control.

"They never called us, Hannah," Drew exclaimed. "They bagged the two of us as well. Here we all are, mighty warriors in the army of Yeshua locked up in an Israeli pokey!" With that, he began to laugh out loud again, but this time the others did not join in, as they simultaneously realized that their earlier seeming hilarity was a self-generated defense mechanism offered up from their inner beings to mask their deep inner terror.

"The Lord is my shepherd—" Drew began to pray, joined almost immediately by his two cell mates.

They were still praying when Pat Riordan, the Sterlings' family attorney, arrived about three hours later and was allowed to join the three of them.

Patrick Riordan, a late middle-age Irishman who had fallen in love with and married a local Israeli beauty during a tour to the Land many years prior, had been admitted to the Israeli Bar after four years of intense Israeli law and Hebrew language training. Following this, he had built a thriving family law practice in Tiberias, where he had long represented the Sterlings and many other primary-English-speaking residents of the city and the Lower Galilee.

"Thank God you're here!" Drew exclaimed as he vigorously shook Pat's hand in greeting and relief.

"Have they questioned you about any of this yet?" Pat immediately inquired. "Or have you made any kind of a written statement?"

"Nothing like that," Drew replied. "We've been left here by ourselves since we arrived several hours ago. I guess they took me seriously when I told them we would not answer any of their questions without the presence of our attorney."

"Excellent!" Pat replied. "Just a few guidelines before they begin. Don't answer any question, no matter how trivial it may seem, until I give you a clear nod of my head one way or the other that you should or should not respond. And, keep your replies brief and precisely on point; a simple yes or no when possible. The main thing is, volunteer absolutely nothing! Is this all clear to the three of you?"

"Yes," they replied together as they each nodded affirmatively.

They didn't have long to wait for their grueling interrogation to begin. A few moments later two uniformed officers, who were to be their initial interrogators, opened the holding cell and escorted the four of them to a nearby small and intimidatingly appointed room designated for that purpose.

When the preliminary introductions and formalities were completed, the lead interrogator, who introduced himself as Police Lieutenant Colonel Haim Bezalel, got down to the core business at hand. He took an 8 x 10 photograph from his briefcase and set it before the three who were under suspicion. "Do any of you recognize these young women?" he asked accusingly.

Drew was the first to respond. "Yes," he replied forthrightly. "The two of them attended our congregational meeting last Motze Shabbat."

"Mrs. Sterling," he asked in the same accusing voice, "do you recognize them as well?"

"Yes." She replied simply.

"What about you, Hannah Silberman, do you recognize them as well?"

Hannah visibly trembled as this interrogation brought back the terrible memory of earlier similar interviews she had endured at the hands of those she knew to be her life-threatening enemies.

"Yes!" she replied defensively. "I gave them cookies and punch after the meeting. Is there anything wrong with that?"

Police Lieutenant Colonel Haim Bezalel loved to interrogate Christians. They were naïve to the point that when asked questions, they told the simple truth, so unlike the usual band of local thugs he was often required to confront.

"And what did you 'feed' them, 'Rabbi' Sterling?" he raised his voice accusingly.

"Don't respond to that, Drew!" Pat intervened. "Colonel Bezalel," he answered for his client, who had briefed him in detail about the incident during their initial telephone conversation. "Andrew Sterling has never represented himself to be a 'rabbi,' and on the day in question, he had nothing to do with serving snacks to those attendees who desired to partake of them after the meeting."

"Thank you, counselor," Bezalel replied, not missing a beat. "I will rephrase my question: Andrew Sterling, just what specifically was your function at the meeting in question?"

"I planned and conducted it," he responded unhesitatingly.

"Was part of your function at this meeting to invite those in attendance to come forward and change their religion by embracing Jesus Christ as their messiah?"

Patrick Riordan again intervened. "Andrew Sterling, as a matter of regular practice, gave a general invitation to anyone among the hundreds of attendees who voluntarily, of their own free will, were at this meeting, to come forward if they were persuaded to do so. He did not extend this general invitation to any specific person or persons."

Bezalel once more picked up the photograph from the table, this time pointing to the more attractive of the two young women. "Do you recognize this person as one of those who came forward that day?" he asked Drew as he went for the kill he had so carefully planned and implemented.

"I do." Drew responded, as he inwardly found himself silently questioning the wisdom of what he genuinely understood to be the truly unchallengeable biblical promise that "the truth shall make you free."

"Did you speak to her that day after she came forward?" Bezalel probed.

"Only as a member of the fairly large group of which she was a part."

"What did you say to them as a group?"

"I simply welcomed them and told them that they would now enter into a time of learning."

"Learning that would lead to what?" Bezalel honed in.

"Baptism and full membership in our group."

"Mrs. Sterling," Bezalel suddenly switched his focus, "did you speak with this young woman after the service?"

"I did."

"What was the substance of the message you conveyed to her?"

"I congratulated her for making her life-changing decision and invited her to attend her first discipleship meeting on Thursday evening."

"I just fed her cookies and punch," Hannah, to Pat's dismay, voluntarily interjected.

"I believe that this about wraps it up for today," Bezalel responded, ignoring Hannah. "But before we go our separate ways, let me more properly introduce you to these two," he offered as he once again picked up the picture.

"The girl on the left is Anna Feinberg, and the one on the right is Segal Cohen; she is the dear one whom you convinced to give her life to your Yeshua and then fed cookies and punch. Both of them are seventeen years and a few months old. By Israeli law they are not young women at all. They are children."

"Segal made a point of telling me she was twenty!" Carla exclaimed incredulously.

"Kids all over the world lie about their age!" Bezalel replied, savoring what he had accomplished.

"Pat, what's your take on what just happened?" Drew pleaded, as he struggled to suppress the waves of near panic that unrelentingly sought to overwhelm him after the four of them had gathered around the Sterling's car in the Afula Police Station parking lot.

"It's really hard for me to say, Drew," Pat responded contemplatively. "I suppose it would depend upon which agency or agencies are driving this thing and where, if anyplace, they want take it from here. This may be just another ratcheting up of the harassment of you believers that has been going on with ever-increasing intensity over the past several months, or it may be that they are looking for some basis for an indictment. For now, my counsel is that we see what happens next."

Carla could not contain herself. "Are you saying that they might actually bring criminal charges against us?"

"What I'm saying," Pat replied somberly, "is that they may or may not be headed in that direction. Again, we will just have to wait and see."

CHAPTER 17
HANNAH'S STORY
TIBERIAS
(WEDNESDAY, JUNE 10, 2009)

THE THREE OF them—Drew, Carla, and Hannah—didn't have long to wait until the next move against them by the government of Israel unfolded in the form of a summons and a soul-shaking letter.

The State Attorney's Office didn't send them letters of indictment for violating Criminal Code Sections 174 (a) & (b) and section 368 of Penal Law 5737-1977, missionary laws. Instead, only two weeks following their interrogation by the Afula police, Drew, Carla, and Hannah now held in their hands a summons to appear before the Nazareth District Court, as well as a letter from the State Attorney's Office. The State Attorney's Office's letter was a request to the District Court to revoke their citizenship. The Nazareth District Court had thus, in response, summoned them for a preliminary hearing regarding this onerous State Attorney's Office request. The three of them, now officially the "respondents," were required to submit their responses at least seven days before the hearing, which was set for ten o'clock Wednesday morning, September 9, three months from the written notice.

"There is no need for us to panic about this thing!" Drew declared, trying to reassure himself as much as Carla, who was deeply shaken by the reality of this yet another summons. "We need to get together with Pat as soon as possible and try to get some better understanding about what this is all about and how we are to deal with it."

To Drew's relief, he was able to contact Pat by phone without delay, and without further discussion he shared with him the contents of the short summons, identical in content and separately addressed to the three of them.

"What do you make of this, Pat?" Drew pleaded.

"First of all," Pat replied, "I'm utterly amazed at the timing of this whole thing. Actions involving multiple agencies can take several months before they reach this level. It seems to me that this summons is the next step of a very well thought-out plan whose end has not yet been revealed by its instigators."

"Are you saying that this is likely not just another increased level of harassment?" Drew pleaded, looking for comfort.

Pat, clearly puzzled by this recent development, replied thoughtfully. "Given that the State Attorney's Office has already taken this matter to the District Court level, it is clear that they are trying to establish a precedent on this issue."

"What are we to do?" Drew, struggling to maintain his self-control, demanded.

"They really haven't given us any other choice," Pat replied as gently as he was able. "I will prepare an appropriate initial response to the State Attorney's Office. Then, I will accompany the three of you who will appear, as directed, for what apparently will be a merged hearing. We'll just have to see what unfolds there and then do our best to respond appropriately."

Chapter 18
Hannah's Story
Nazareth Illit
(Nazareth District Court: Wednesday, September 9, 2009)

Drew navigated the ancient Sterling family Toyota up the twisty road that wound its way from the densely populated, sprawling city of Nazareth, to Nazareth Illit, a much smaller, almost entirely Jewish suburb of the entirely Arab-populated city below.

"What a striking contrast," Drew observed as much of the modern-day architecture of the upper city skyline came into view when he rounded the last curve.

"It looks like an entirely different community in an entirely different world," Pat Riordan, who sat beside Drew, replied. "Nazareth is entirely Israeli Arab, huge and still growing. That's why the government established Nazareth Illit in the late 1950s—in order to better preserve the Jewish character of the Galilee."

"This is all very interesting," Hannah, who had remained mostly silent alongside Carla in the backseat during the half-hour drive from Tiberias, nervously interjected, "but I'm really much more concerned about what the judge may decide in this preliminary hearing."

"So am I!" Pat responded, since he had personally prepared the response to the request to revoke his clients' citizenships. "If it's any comfort, we won't have much longer before we find out. We're almost there.

"Drew," he continued, pointing to the imposing twelve-story, postmodern Jerusalem stone-faced high-rise just off to their left, "That's the court house, just ahead."

After going through standard security checks, except for Pat, who presented his license and was allowed a VIP entrance into the court building, they took the elevator to the second floor and entered a semi-circular "dock" that faced the judge's seat at the front of the large, imposing room. They had arrived about fifteen minutes early, and there was another hearing of some sort that appeared to be winding to a conclusion while they waited for their turn before the bar.

"Your case will be next," Pat explained to them, as he pointed to chairs where he preferred they sit, several feet to the rear of where the current respondent, or perhaps it was an attorney, was now shouting at the judge in Arabic, who apparently had just rendered what was an unappreciated verdict.

"Will there be an English translation?" Hannah whispered. "My Hebrew is woefully inadequate to understand all of this legal bantering."

"I don't think so," Pat replied, as the respondents to the just-concluded proceedings sullenly retreated and cleared the area. "I have no idea what this case was all about, but I know enough Arabic to understand that these folks just got hit with a huge fine."

"It looks like we have drawn Judge Salim Habash," Pat continued. "He's a well-known Israeli Arab with a good reputation."

"Doesn't it seem a bit bizarre that three Israeli Jews are being judged by an Israeli Arab in a proceeding that has to do with their citizenship?" Drew commented nervously.

"This could work in our favor," Pat replied. "We could just have easily drawn one of the Orthodox Jewish judges, and that would surely have been worse."

They didn't have long to wait as Judge Habash and the prosecuting attorney and his party, who had taken a short break between proceedings, returned to the bench area promptly at ten o'clock as all present in the courtroom rose out of traditional respect as the judge once more took his seat.

Judge Habash: All may be seated. I call case numbers: 7964/09 and 7975/09, *The State of Israel v. Andrew Scott and Carla Sterling* and *The State of Israel v. Hannah Silberman*. Are the respondents present in the Court?

RIORDAN: Yes, Your Honor, they are present and represented by their counsel, myself, Patrick Riordan.

JUDGE HABASH: Very well, Mr. Riordan. Who will represent the State Attorney in this matter?

HILDEBRAND: I, Howard Hildebrand will so serve, Your Honor.

The contrast between the advocates on opposite sides of this proceeding was as remarkable as it was striking. Howard Hildebrand was the only offspring of two German Gentile converts to Orthodox Judaism who prided themselves in their long and ethnically pure Prussian heritage. It seems that Christian and Margit, Howard's parents, were among those Germans who, in the early 1930s, had long been attracted to the teachings of Judaism as it stood in its simplicity against what to them was the uninspired state-administered Lutheran Church of their upbringing. Perhaps even more important was their clear prophetic wisdom that enabled them to foresee the unspeakable horrors that would soon overtake the Land of their birth. Thus, as unseemly as it may have appeared, even to them, they immigrated to Israel and almost immediately entered into their lengthy Orthodox conversion process. By the time Christian Hildebrand was ready to conceive Howard, his son, he did so as a newly circumcised member of the covenant.

HILDEBRAND: Your Honor, the Minister of Interior has requested that the State Attorney petition the District Court to revoke the citizenship of the respondents Andrew Sterling, Carla Sterling, and Hannah Silberman and that they be permanently deported from the State of Israel. Said action is requested by the Minister of Interior on the basis that the respondents, individually and collectively, violated the Nationality Law and the Law of Return by obtaining their Israeli citizenship according to false information they provided to agents of the ministry. They stated that they were Jewish when they were in fact Christians. Furthermore, their only intention for cheating the system was in order to obtain Israeli citizenship and break Israeli missionary laws. Moreover, Your Honor, the State Attorney has thoroughly reviewed the preponderance of administrative evidence upon which the Ministry of the Interior initiated these requests and has found revocation of citizenship and permanent deportation of the three respondents entirely appropriate and in keeping with Israeli law.

Riordan *(jumping to his feet and protesting in a loud voice)*: Your Honor, there is no credible evidence that the respondents have ever presented false information to anyone. Furthermore, my clients are loyal citizens of the State of Israel. The only time my clients were ever in opposition with any government was when Ms. Hannah Silberman was persecuted for being Jewish in Nazi Germany. A little over a month ago, the state police investigated alleged suspicions against my clients' religious worldview. However, the police decided not to pursue these suspicions, as the State Attorney's office never submitted a letter of indictment against my clients. In fact, my clients were certainly never pronounced guilty in a court of law for any of these frivolous allegations. They may have violated minor traffic laws, but no sound-minded or reasonable person would classify that as criminal, which is also irrelevant to these proceedings, as this is an administrative hearing and not a criminal hearing. Furthermore, may I remind this honorable court that even Igal Amir, the assassin of our late Prime Minister Itzhak Rabin, was declared a citizen by the Supreme Court of Justice. His citizenship was recognized, even after the State Attorney's offices attempted to revoke it for treason and disloyalty to the State of Israel. This attempt to revoke Igal Amir's citizenship took place before clear definitions for treason, as a basis to revoke a person's citizenship, were given in the Law of Citizenship. My clients' minor traffic violations do not rise close to the level of Amir's disgraceful actions. Further, they do not meet the definitions of treason and disloyalty according to the Law of Citizenship. Therefore, the central issue of this case is whether the respondents falsified information during immigration, not treason or disloyalty.

Judge Habash: Mr. Riordan and Mr. Hildebrand, after I have read both the request of the state, the responses of the three respondents, and in light of the extraordinary questions that were raised in the request, I would like to recommend that I implement my authority according to section 28 of the Administrative Court Regulations–2,000, and transfer this hearing to the Supreme Court. However, I will hear both of your opinions on this matter before proceeding.

RIORDAN: I do not have any objection to Your Honor's recommendation, but I do have two requests: that my clients may be granted permission to submit a longer and more thorough response to the claims raised against them and that they may be permitted to acquire new counsel, as I am the Sterlings' family attorney and would rather see to it that my clients are represented by an attorney whose expertise is in Supreme Court cases.

JUDGE Habash: Granted.

HILDEBRAND: I have no objections, Your Honor.

JUDGE HABASH: Thank you very much, gentlemen. I will transfer these hearings to the Supreme Court, and you will receive notification at the address indicated on the court proceedings.

The three of them and their attorney were too stunned to speak as they exited the court building and proceeded across the sprawling parking lot. Pat Riordan was especially dismayed that the State Attorney's office would invest so much time and resources in an attempt to revoke his three clients' citizenships. To his thinking they were loyal and totally dedicated citizens of the Land who individually and collectively should be its treasured assets and not the targets of its concerted rejection.

He finally spoke when they reached Drew's car. "The good news is that Israeli attorney Jeremiah Levine and his several associates in the Israel Society for Religious Freedom in Jerusalem have provided pro bono and/or highly subsidized litigation and consultation services and spearheaded other projects to stand at the forefront of what is the apparent battle for religious freedom and religious tolerance in which you three have become embroiled. I know Jerry personally and hold him in the highest personal and professional regard. I feel certain he will undertake your case before the Supreme Court. I will call him as soon as we get back to my office and ask that he see the three of you as soon as he can work you into his busy schedule."

Chapter 19
Hannah's Story
Jerusalem
(Office of the Israel Society for Religious Freedom: Tuesday, September 15, 2009)

Jeremiah Levine had a great gift of visible concern for his clients, along with a natural air of confidence that was both compelling and contagious, qualities that had carried him far in the practice of Israeli law. He most often prevailed but never failed to win the respect and even love of those he represented and always the great admiration of those whom he opposed.

"It was so good of you to see the three of us on such short notice, Jerry." Drew immediately warmed to this deeply committed brother as they grasped hands in the tastefully appointed reception area of the Israel Society for Religious Freedom located a short distance from the Old City in Jerusalem.

From his physical appearance Jerry could easily be lost in a crowd of typical Israeli men. There was nothing about him that was visually distinctive or especially attractive. His large round face was crowned with a thick crop of unruly jet black hair just beginning to show first hints of gray, while his thick, horn-rimmed glasses rested perpetually downward on his large Semitic nose. Even so, there was something about this five foot six, somewhat overweight, potbellied man who was just now approaching fifty that seemed to subliminally cry out to those who sought his representation: "Yes, I will be your advocate because I deeply care!"

"Shalom, Carla," Jerry greeted, extending his hand, which she ignored and instead instinctively hugged this man whom she had just now met. "I can see why your husband has kept you under wraps," he teased. "And I'm told you two have three gorgeous daughters to match." Not waiting for a response, he quickly continued.

"And, of course, you are Hannah," he greeted the white-haired self-appointed ex-officio matriarch of the Sterling family with particular warmth and familiarity, who in turn, like Carla before her, responded with a 'I feel like I've known you all my life' hug.

"Well, let's move to my office," Jerry exclaimed when Hannah had released him, "and take a look at what my favorite ministry and our dear black-suited brethren are up to this time."

It took Jerry nearly two hours to meticulously examine even the seemingly irrelevant aspects of his three new clients' religious backgrounds, Aliyah, and current ministry, all of which they freely shared as he skillfully probed and drew the information he sought from them, taking several pages of notes as they spoke.

When he was finished, Jerry, who was seated across from the three of them in a simple office chair that matched their own, put down his pen, took off his glasses, and thoughtfully put his hands behind his head as he leaned back and pronounced, "Drew, Carla, and Hannah, there is good news and bad news. Let me begin with the good news. First of all, I will take your case and do so on an entirely pro-bono basis."

"God bless you!" Drew exclaimed.

"He already has!" Jerry responded. "That's how I manage to stay in this line of work. Anyway," he continued, "from my point of view, yours is the substantive case I've been looking for that has the potential to boldly challenge and hopefully create a new, more positive precedent. My great hope is that the outcome of all this will be to protect Israeli citizens from the revocation of their citizenship when it is based only on religious grounds. God willing, this may even be an opportunity to weaken the precedent created in *Beresford v. The Minister of Interior* where it was decided that a Jew who believes in Yeshua has changed his religion and is no longer Jewish. However, it is one thing to prevent such a person from immigrating into Israel, and another to revoke his citizenship only because he believes in Yeshua. This is especially so when a person registered himself as a Jew on the immigration application form in good faith, with no intentions of presenting false information. This is my good news. Your good news is that I am confident we will prevail in the end, at least in making sure that you will remain Israeli residents, and that you will not be deported from the country."

"That is all good news, indeed, but what is the bad news?" Drew questioned.

Jerry responded forthrightly. "I am certain that the religious parties and their agents, the Shomrei Israel and the rest, have been looking for a case just like this as well. They will fight this to its bitter end, hoping for a decision that will establish legal precedence they have long sought. Hopefully, this battle we have joined will prevent them from driving most, if not all, of us Jewish believers in Yeshua from the Land, at least those who have immigrated into Israel after they have already believed in Yeshua.

"Now let's get down to specifics," he continued. "As your attorney, I will accompany you to any interview with the police in Afula, if needed. However, I doubt that the police will further investigate this issue, as no one was ever actually convicted in Israel of such a crime, mainly because it is almost impossible to prove criminal thought."

"How do you see this coming down, Jerry?" Carla, who had remained silent for some time, interjected.

"It is much too early to say," he replied thoughtfully, "but if I were a betting man, I would put my money on a no-holds-barred effort by the Ministry of the Interior against you. Unlike a criminal trial, they only need administrative evidence; that is, to prove that you were not only Christians before you immigrated, but that you were also involved in illegal missionary activity (according to Israeli missionary laws) before you immigrated.

"What they are looking for is this great opportunity of their own making to prove, somehow, that you were not Jewish when you immigrated because of your religious beliefs, and that your only incentive for immigrating was to be active missionaries who are out to drink the blood and steal the souls of their children. I ask you," he concluded rhetorically, "how could such monsters like the three of you by any stretch of the imagination be allowed to continue as citizens of Israel?

"Let me say this," Jerry added with particular warmth. "After what you have already been through, it is perfectly understandable that you are extremely on edge and struggling not to come apart at the seams over the real possibility that everything you have worked for and hold dear in this Land of your inheritance is suddenly in jeopardy. OK, you must accept these feelings as perfectly normal, but you must also live every day to its fullest between now and the time the Chief Justice of the Supreme Court bangs his gavel at the conclusion of this matter. I don't think these proceedings will take many months, but I could be wrong. Making you suffer under the yoke of endless delays could be a part of their strategy—their hope in this is that you will simply fold and leave Israel of your own accord if the going gets too rough for you to handle.

"I would like each of you to think of this like the apostle Paul did in his time. Go ahead and accept the fact that you have an unrelenting thorn in your flesh, praise God for it, and rejoice that each day you are growing closer to Him. Then, if I may be so bold, relax in His keeping and let me do my thing. Believe me, your situation will remain in my thoughts constantly, and I can think of nothing that will attract any greater attention than seeing a rightful outcome to this entire affair."

"Thank you, Jerry," Carla replied with great sincerity. "I already feel myself beginning to wind down. Not to change the subject," she continued as she took several steps towards a nearby bookcase that featured a framed portrait of a lovely straw-haired young woman, "is this your wife?"

"Yes" he replied, exuding the love he felt for the one pictured among his law books. "That's my wonderful Maureen. We've been married for twenty-five years."

"Well, I'll tell you what," Carla continued. "We are planning a big traditional Thanksgiving dinner next Thursday. We sort of combine it with the Jewish fall feasts, so admittedly we are a couple of months earlier than the American celebration. Sorry for the very short notice, but if you and Maureen could join us in Tiberias for this very special occasion, we'd be so grateful."

"You've found the way to my heart," Jerry replied. "I'll check with Maureen, just to be sure she has nothing else planned, but as for me, I'm ready for a day of celebrating with new friends."

CHAPTER 20
HANNAH'S STORY
TIBERIAS
(THURSDAY, SEPTEMBER 17, 2009)

HANNAH STOOD LIKE a proud and doting mother next to Drew on the balcony of the Sterlings' penthouse apartment as Drew carefully removed the 14-pound turkey from his Webber kettle cooker and placed it on the large steel-pegged wooden carving board she held out to him.

"This looks and smells absolutely marvelous!" she exclaimed. "You Americans have brought such a lovely tradition with you to the Land!"

"We usually have a house full of dear ones from the congregation, but this year is quite different, to say the least, with all of this intrigue going on and things about to break wide open. We feel so very blessed that you, Jerry, and Maureen are able to join us."

"How many turkeys have you cooked like this, Drew?" Jerry asked with genuine interest as he joined the two of them on the balcony.

"This must be at least number fifty," Drew replied, "but who's counting?"

The holiday feast they had just consumed had lived up to the full promise of the Sterlings' reputation for such productions, to say nothing of the spontaneous praise and admiration that had followed the pumpkin pie dessert—and all the traditional holiday and praise songs sung to the accompaniment of Jerry's well-trained guitar.

"I can't remember when I've enjoyed a Thanksgiving meal so much," exclaimed Maureen, a striking, statuesque blonde of Irish descent who towered over her black-haired, dark-complexioned stereotypical Jewish husband.

"We are so delighted that you could be with us," Drew responded, "but we are not quite finished. You see, it is our tradition at the end of each Thanksgiving meal for each participant to share with everyone the one thing that they are most thankful for that occurred during the past year. Of course, this is entirely voluntary—we certainly don't want to put anyone on the spot. To give you the general idea, I'll go first.

"There are so very many things I could choose from," he began. "But from them all I suppose the single gift from the Lord I am most thankful for is the grace He has given me to continue to shepherd my flock and the great joy I have been afforded to watch it grow and flourish. Praise the Lord."

"Hear! Hear!" Carla raised her German crystal glass filled with Golan Chardonnay. "I propose a toast to the anointed ministry of my beloved husband, Andrew Scott Sterling!"

"Can I be next?" Hannah asked with delight.

"Of course!" Drew responded happily.

"I thank God for His great mercy," she began, "for introducing me to Drew and Carla many years ago, if even for only a moment at that time. Then how He took me out of the depths of loneliness and despair that followed a time of unspeakable horror and loss—how He brought me to Israel and reintroduced me to Drew and Carla, who, by the power of His Holy Spirit, led me to my eternal salvation in Yeshua." She paused to get a grip on her emotions. "He restored my joy and my zest for life. He allowed me to take up my inheritance here in His Land. He gave me Drew and Carla who, as the children of my heart, have become the children of my womb I was rendered unable to bring forth."

"To Hannah Ruth Meyers Silberman," Drew exclaimed as he raised his glass teary-eyed, and the others followed.

"My turn!" Maureen announced, claiming the floor. "This year, as with each of the five years my husband Jeremiah has been the outspoken champion of our fellow Jewish believers, I have come to both admire and love him even more with the passage of time. His selfless devotion, brilliant legal mind, untiring quest for justice, limitless compassion—all of these great attributes are wrapped up in this incredible man I am blessed to call my own." With this she raised her glass, proposing her own tribute: "To Jeremiah Allen Levine, Attorney at Law."

"Hear! Hear!" the others exclaimed in unison.

Being that there were only the two of them remaining, Carla turned to Jerry with a nonverbal invitation to speak next.

"Please go ahead, Carla," he almost whispered. "I would like to be last."

"I am so very thankful for so many things," Carla began. "For my husband, our children and grandchildren, for our many blessed years as citizens of Israel, for our ministry, for our many dear friends. So it is impossible for me to pick out any one of these gifts from all the others. Better for me instead to focus my great love and gratitude on the author of them all, the Lord God of Israel, who has given all of these blessings and so very, very much more."

"To the Lord God of Israel!" Carla exclaimed, raising her glass.

"Hear! Hear!" the others responded in unison.

All eyes now turned to Jerry as he stood and turned suddenly very serious.

"It really is amazing how the Lord works. His sense of timing is genuinely remarkable. Yes, I have something that stands out as the greatest gift that has come my way in the past five years, a time during which I have been working relentlessly to challenge the interpretation of the second amendment to the Israeli Law of Return. Up until now this has been an insidious battle fought on the terms dictated by the government who created this travesty and by the radical religious who have lately gone wild in its enforcement.

"Never, never before," he continued passionately, "have they given those who oppose them more than a tiny sliver of hope upon which to cling. Never, until now, has a major opportunity come forth to fully challenge the current fallacious interpretation of the Law of Return for what it is before the highest court in the Land. Now, by the grace of God, at long last that opportunity has arisen.

"Just last evening," he continued, getting to the heart of what he had to share, "I received a lengthy communication from the Attorney General. It is a copy of a letter he addressed to the State Prosecutor who will represent the government during your response before the Supreme Court. The gist of his message is to underscore the landmark importance of this case and the profound impact it will have, one way or the other, on the long ill-defined matter of human rights in this country and the great gap that remains at the heart of Israeli jurisprudence, especially so because of the unbalanced separation of powers between the three branches of government.

"Make no bones about it," Jerry continued passionately, "the religiously dominated government will spare no effort to win this case. The Ministry of the Interior, in concert with other ministries and extremist political forces, just like us has been looking for a precedent-setting case: ours, that victory will once and for all grant equal human rights to all Jews, regardless of their particular religious worldview and practice; theirs, that victory will open the door to deport many of the believing Jews in the country and close the door to any Aliyah of our kind in the future."

"Dear God!" Carla was the first to speak after a few moments of silence as the enormous potential impact of Jerry's startling summation sunk in. "What are our choices?"

"That's easy to answer," Jerry replied. "You have two clear options. First, you can turn in your passports and ID cards and accept the Interior Ministry's attempt to revoke your citizenship and then, as former citizens, leave Israel forever. Or you can defend yourself before the Supreme Court against the Interior Ministry's request to revoke your citizenship and permanently deport you from Israel. It is as simple as that. There are no other choices.

"If you fold now, without a fight, you will forever lose your chance to challenge this injustice. Someone else along the way, who will be treated the same, will eventually defend himself in court; however, I greatly fear that such a case may not have as strong an argument as yours and therefore result in setting an even greater negative precedent for other believers.

"If you fight this in court and win, it is possible that the second amendment to the Law of Return will eventually be interpreted differently, thus allowing Messianic believers to take up their inheritance in the Land like any other Jew."

"What if we fight and lose?" Hannah interjected.

"Of course, as your attorney, I don't look for this to happen, but should true justice not prevail in your case, your plight and the plight of all believing Jews like us will have been openly displayed before the entire world. You can be sure that the world press will seize upon this opportunity to criticize Israel."

"That's the one thing about this that bothers me," Drew commented thoughtfully. "I love this Land more than I can say, and it pains me to think that we will become instruments for yet more condemnation against it from a mostly anti-Semitic world."

"Drew, please be at peace about this!" Jerry comforted. "You are not coming against Israel! Believe me, I will make it abundantly clear during the proceedings that you are coming against a politically generated law that is diametrically opposed to the very principles upon which the State of Israel was founded, and that you are doing this to reorient the immigration law to conform to these founding principles. While the extremists who created this law in the first place and those who today seek to cast it in cement may balk at what you do, I can't help but believe that the majority—the rest of Jewish Israel—will applaud you for standing up for what is good, fair, and righteous."

"This trial could cost a fortune in legal fees alone," Drew lamented.

"Not to worry!" Jerry replied. "This is the big one we have waited to come along for five years. I have a body of interested parties all over the world who I will ask to support this, and if they are unable or unwilling, then, one way or the other, I will do it on my own."

"So once again we'll be back to trying to figure how we are going to eat and pay the rent," Maureen offered, trying to add a bit of levity to the intensity of the moment.

"You shouldn't worry about money, even for a minute!" Hannah volunteered. "This seems a good time for me to tell you about my darling father, the banker, who put several million dollars worth of diamonds in a vault in Switzerland just about the time Hitler started to annihilate our people. You know, I'm no spring chicken, and I can't take it with me!"

Chapter 21
Hannah's Story
Jerusalem
(Supreme Court of the State of Israel: Sunday, January 10, 2010)

The Trial: First Hearing

Drew, Carla, and Hannah sat behind their attorney in the defense's place on the left side of the lower of two tiers at the front of the courtroom designated as the scene for their imminently forthcoming proceedings.

This was Jeremiah Levine's "moment," and he was exhilarated and raring to challenge Natan Ben Israel, the equally feisty, highly skilled, and well-reputed State Prosecutor, along with members of his formidable staff who were seated just across from the defense on the right side of the lower tier.

Natan Ben Israel, who had been appointed by the Attorney General to represent the state in this landmark proceeding, would have been difficult to pick out in a crowd in any Israeli setting. His well-developed, now somewhat portly medium-height frame had lost what in years past might have seemed to be an athletic distinction. Moreover, the patchwork, stringy, gray beard he carefully cultivated as a hoped-for acceptable compensation for his absolutely hairless, kippah (skull cap) covered pate seemed to underscore his frustrated efforts to rise above the otherwise ordinariness of his outward appearance. However, it is certain that the ordinariness of Natan Ben Israel began and ended with his appearance. To be sure, he had early claimed, and had long remained unchallenged in, his distinction as the enormously respected and greatly feared star advocate of the Office of the State Attorney, the proof of which was the unseemly political fact that he had survived in this position through three successive governments, and there was no end in sight of his adversarial preeminence.

While crucial to the formation and retention of his legendary reputation, his Cambridge law degree and three-year tenure as dean of the University of Haifa Faculty of Law were not his most imposing credentials. It was his brilliance as a trial attorney and as yet unblemished record of success that gave him a long-held aura and well-deserved reputation as the most imposing adversary and champion at the bar of Israel prosecutorial justice.

> Levine *(whispering to his clients)*: There will be five sitting judges on our case. This is a good sign that points to the very high level of interest this case has generated.

Everyone in the court room stood in traditional respect as the Honorable Chief Justice Marcus Bauerstein, the president of the Supreme Court who determined that the case would be heard by five judges, entered, accompanied by four other black-robed magistrates, two male and two female, who now took their places. The chief justice was in the center, flanked by one male and onc fcmale justice on both sides.

> Chief Justice Bauerstein: You may be seated. Good morning, everyone. Since the proceedings we are about to begin are unique, I would like to take a few moments to comment on this uniqueness and why the court has decided that this matter should be heard and the framework and proceedings within which the arguments from both sides should be allowed.
>
> The matter before the court is profoundly important. It goes to the very heart and soul of our nation in that it deals, directly or indirectly, with vital issues that have long been held in contention, some of which have already been addressed by this court and others that have not yet been addressed. The first questions, concerning who is a Jew and who shall be granted Israeli citizenship, have already been addressed by this court. However, additional questions which were not yet addressed, such as under what circumstances, if any, should such citizenship be revoked and by what process, as it relates to the revocation of citizenship to an Israeli, based solely on religious grounds, have not been addressed by this court. As mentioned above, other cases have addressed similar issues. However, because of their sensitivity, we are providing due process for the respondents.
>
> The specific issue before us is about the attempt to revoke the citizenship of three Israeli citizens and subsequently

to deport them. The state has, among other contentions, accused the three respondents of violating the Nationality Law and the Law of Return by obtaining their Israeli citizenship as a result of false information they provided to agents of the ministry.

Before we begin, please understand that it is my intention to afford both sides in this matter a great deal of latitude in the conduct of these proceedings, within reason of course. I will grant both the state and the respondents the opportunity to submit additional affidavits to support their claims, and both sides may cross-examine each witness, based on his affidavit, which is usually uncommon in such cases. This is not a trial, the outcome of which will determine the guilt or innocence of any person or persons. Your purpose is rather to provide the court with as much relevant information as you are able so that we, in turn, can best render our judgment as to the appropriateness or inappropriateness of the actions brought against the respondents regarding the petition of the Minister of Interior in coordination with other agencies of the government. Toward this end, please be assured that the court will allow any action or approach on the parties that it deems to be relevant and that is permitted according to the Supreme Court Procedural Regulations.

The chief justice now made eye contact with Natan Ben Israel, the attorney representing the state, to cue him to begin his opening statement.

Natan immediately stood and, facing the five justices, began to address them.

BEN ISRAEL: May it please the court, my name is Natan Ben Israel, and I will be representing the State of Israel. Your Honors, as you have noted in your opening instructions, there is already abundant precedent established by the court on the interpretation of the Law of Return's clear denial of citizenship to any person who claims to be a Jew but has subsequently changed their religion. Such was the court's finding in *Rufeisen v. The Interior Ministry*, *Hatshins v. the*

Minister of Interior, Dorflinger v. The Minister of Interior, Beresford v. the Minister of Interior, Kendel v. The Minister of Interior, and *David Yochanan v. the Minister of Interior.*

In summary, Your Honors, all court petitions for Israeli citizenship submitted by Jews who have embraced Yeshua as their Messiah have been denied.

Your Honors, the case now before the court is quite a different matter. Under the Law of Return and the Law of Citizenship, the respondents have provided false information and have also been actively involved in illegal missionary work, according to the missionary laws. They decided to immigrate for the sole purpose of converting Jews to Christianity. Therefore, it is quite clear that the respondents intentionally falsified information, and their citizenship should be revoked immediately. This is a case about the integrity of Israel's Law of Return. Indeed, the state has a mandate to ensure that the law is not compromised and to prosecute any violation.

The plain, simple, and indisputable facts concerning the actions and recommendations of the Ministry of the Interior that stand under the desperate challenge of the respondents are as follows:

One, the Minister of Interior is responsible under Israeli law for all matters pertaining to Israeli citizenship.

Two, the Minister of Interior, upon thorough investigation and due consideration, determined that the conduct of the respondents posed a threat to the security of the State of Israel and that the respondents immigrated to Israel in order to conduct missionary activity. Moreover, and most importantly, upon further investigation, the Minister of Interior determined that each of the respondents received Israeli citizenship based in part upon fraudulent claims made in their respective applications.

Finally, the Minister of Interior determined that the nature of the aforesaid grievous actions of the respondents was such that the appropriate remedy thereto was to initiate action that would result in the revocation of the citizenship of said respondents as well as their permanent deportation.

Three, there is only one legitimate basis for a response concerning the actions of the state in this matter. Plain and simple, did the Ministry of the Interior and the State Attorney act responsibly within the limits of their authority under the law? That they did so is irrefutable.

Your Honors, the respondents have consciously deceived the state in their immigration application, and they have as well usurped the authority of the Law of Return. According to administrative evidence, which we have in our possession, the respondents have violated Israeli missionary laws and have actually immigrated to Israel with the sole purpose of proselytizing. This is beyond other substantial evidence that they did not present information in good faith during their immigration application, during which they also falsified information.

Finally, Your Honors, the state will demonstrate that the respondents' response has been from the outset, and remains, irrevocably mute. Your Honors, according to the current definition of a Jew in the Law of Return, a person ceases to be a Jew at the very instant he or she becomes a member of another religion. Each of these three respondents has not only become part of the community of another religion but has also promulgated this different religion to others, including minors, who do not belong to that religion.

The state begs the court to not be unduly moved by the passionate outcry of the respondents but rather by the plain and simple lawful facts and implications of the matter at hand. The state will bring before the court indisputable proof that the respondents, acting both separately and in concert, violated the Israeli Law of Return and the Law of Citizenship. Also, according to administrative evidence which we have in our possession, the respondents have also violated Israeli missionary laws and have actually immigrated to Israel with the sole purpose of propagating their beliefs. In conclusion, the respondents' conduct proves that no mistake was made, but rather the respondents intentionally deceived the state by presenting falsified information.

Natan Ben Israel, whose manner reflected an admixture of his deep inner confidence and outward arrogance, returned to his seat in several unnecessarily slow and deliberate steps.

The chief justice now turned to Jerry and made eye contact, cuing him to present his opening argument. Jerry rose without any notes, fully prepared to present an improvised and dramatic case for his three clients. Keeping with his expertise, this was a tactic of only the most skilled attorneys.

Levine: May it please the court, my name is Jeremiah Levine. I represent the respondents: Andrew and Carla Sterling, and Hannah Silberman. Under the Law of Return and the Law of Citizenship, the respondents did not provide false information. Therefore, all charges should be dismissed, and their citizenship should not be revoked.

Your Honors, this case is about the integrity of Israel's Law of Return and about protecting her citizens from government harassment. On one hand the State of Israel presents itself to the world as the "one true democracy in the Middle East." On the other hand, the power to revoke citizenship for unproven subversive activity or disloyalty usually characterizes entirely non-democratic regimes. The respondents have not violated anything in section 11 of the Law of Citizenship, which defines treason. In the famous words of US Chief Justice Earl Warren, "Citizenship is not a license that expires upon misbehavior.... And deprivation of citizenship is not a weapon that the government may use to express displeasure at a citizen's conduct, however reprehensible that conduct may be."[1]

While this case is a matter of contemporary law, its origins are rooted in biblical exegesis and the ancient history of the Jewish people. It is not the intent of the respondents to directly address such issues, which have been pored over by sages since the time of Abraham. Rather, simply acknowledging that the discussion of "Who is a Jew?" has existed for millennia and continues even today should provide ample support for a defense to the claims of the state.

Your Honors, no respected theologian will dispute the historical Jewishness of Yeshua Ben Yosef, Jesus, son of Joseph, the rabbi who dwelt in Nazareth over two thousand years ago. His followers, these same theologians would, however, readily admit, have been the subject of such debate for centuries.

Rabbinical Judaism and Christianity, as pioneered, respectively, by the rabbis and the church fathers, have paralleled the pages of history. Since the sacking of Jerusalem by the Romans and the loss of Jewish genealogical records, who or who is not a Jew has been defined by Halacha, until the development of the modern Law of Return. Expert witnesses will reinforce these claims.

Let me be very clear on this point, Your Honors. The respondents Andrew Sterling and Hannah Silberman are the Jewish offspring of Jewish mothers, according to Halacha. The respondent Carla Sterling has married Andrew Sterling, a Jew. Andrew Sterling founded a congregation in Tiberias that in every way seeks to meticulously follow the religious understandings and practices of Judaism as, according to respected scholars, it was understood and practiced before the end of the first century by many thousands who were then considered to be Jews according to Halacha.

The respondents do not consider themselves to be either Christian or members of the Christian church. They do, however, have in common with Christians and their Christian church the understanding that the One they know as Yeshua is the Messiah of Israel.

Your Honors, let me underscore my point that there are thousands of Orthodox Jewish citizens of Israel who today have varying beliefs about the Messiah. None of them have been, or are, on trial today because of their beliefs. It is only the respondents who happen to embrace Yeshua as the Messiah, who are crying out to this court today for equal protection under the law along with those countless other Jews who over the years and even today have proclaimed seventy-two others to be the Messiah: those such as Shabbtai Zvi, Jacob Frank, and most recently Menachem Schneerson.

The Declaration of the Establishment of the State of Israel, dated May 14, 1948 states in part: "The State of Israel will be open for Jewish immigration and for the ingathering of the Exiles; it will foster the development of the country for the benefit of all its inhabitants; it will be based on freedom, justice, and peace as envisaged by the prophets of Israel; it will ensure complete equality of social and political rights to all its inhabitants irrespective of religion, race, or sex; it will guarantee freedom of religion, conscience, language, education, and culture; it will safeguard the Holy Places of all religions; and it will be faithful to the principles of the Charter of the United Nations."

Your Honors, international law greatly limits the revocation of citizenship and forbids altogether revoking the citizenship of a person or group of people on racial, ethnic, religious, or political grounds. I quote from United Nations Universal Declaration of Human Rights, which states in part: "Everyone has the right to freedom of thought, conscience, and religion; this right includes freedom to change his religion or belief, and freedom, either alone or in community with others and in public or private, to manifest his religion or belief in teaching, practice, worship, and observance."

The respondents contend that the state's interpretation of the Law of Return as amended in 1970 is not in keeping with the founding principles implicitly guaranteed in the Declaration of the Establishment of the State of Israel nor in those of the United Nations Universal Declaration of Human Rights, upon which the State of Israel was founded with the inherent granting of all such guarantees to all of its citizens.

Finally, even if we are to accept the Law of Return's secular definition that a Jew who believes in Yeshua is no longer Jewish, Halacha would still acknowledge him as a Jew. Therefore, when the respondents stated that they were Jewish in their application forms, they had no intention of falsifying information. Rather, they acted in good faith when honestly stating that they were Jewish. The state must prove that the respondents intentionally falsified information. Otherwise, it has only proven itself to be the entity at fault for not conducting an adequate inquiry during the respondents' immigration application. If the respondents were asked whether they believed in Yeshua when they filed their application forms, they would have clearly and honestly said yes.

Your Honors, the respondents are innocent of the charges the state has brought against them. If Israel is to sustain herself as a beacon of freedom and justice and as a deterrent of tyrannical government tactics, the request to revoke the citizenships of the respondents should be dismissed.

With that, Jerry smiled and bowed ever so slightly in deference to the court and to indicate that he was finished for the moment.

CHIEF JUSTICE BAUERSTEIN: Thank you for your opening statements, gentlemen. The parties are both instructed to present to the court, within thirty days, affidavits of the relevant witnesses that each party desires to examine. The court will now stand in recess until tomorrow morning at nine o'clock when the state may call its first witness.

All rose, according to protocol, as the justices left the room.

Chapter 22
Hannah's Story
Jerusalem
(Supreme Court of the State of Israel: Monday, January 11, 2010)

The Trial: Second Hearing

Jeremiah Levine had many outstanding talents that, working together, had propelled him to the very top of his profession as a defense attorney who specialized in protecting the God-given human rights of his clients. Not the least of these was his innate ability to deeply instill the same confidence that he himself perpetually exuded into those whose causes he passionately represented.

It was thus, filled with both hope and positive expectation, that Jerry led his three clients to their places on the second tier of the courtroom just before nine o'clock on the morning of the second hearing of the proceedings that threatened to forever take from them what they all held most dear—their God-given right to worship His Son, Yeshua, in the Land of their inheritance.

Now, the three respondents, bolstered as it were by the very awesome spirit of their attorney, waited with him for the beginning of the onslaught against them by one who was inarguably the most capable adversary found in Israel to so serve the state.

Chief Justice Bauerstein: Mr. Ben Israel, you are now invited to bring the substance of the state's evidence against the respondents. While this is not a trial, you are instructed to proceed on the same basis as if it were. That is, you may call witnesses, cross-examine the witnesses brought by opposing counsel, and you may submit any and all relevant matters and/or exhibits into evidence. My point is, I want to assure both sides that this court will be extremely flexible in these proceedings so that in the end, no relevant matter will remain unaddressed. You may call your first witness.

BEN ISRAEL: Thank you, Your Honor. The state calls Segal Cohen.

A black-haired, fully figured and radiantly attractive young woman dressed in a close-fitting uniform of an Israeli Defense Force inductee, made her way to the witness stand and was sworn in.

BEN ISRAEL: Segal, would you please tell the court how old you were on May 16, 2009.

COHEN: I was seventeen years old, sir.

BEN ISRAEL: Segal, where were you on Motze Shabbat, May 16, 2009?

COHEN: I was in Tiberias, just south of the city, attending a Christian missionary outreach meeting being held in the auditorium of a local kibbutz.

LEVINE: Objection! Assumes facts not in evidence. The character and purpose of this meeting has not been established.

BEN ISRAEL: Withdrawn. *(He conceded and took a different tack.)* If the person or persons who were conducting this meeting you speak of are in this courtroom today, would you please point to them.

COHEN: He is the one! *(She pointed to Drew accusingly.)*

BEN ISRAEL: Do you recognize anyone else in this courtroom today with whom you spoke at this meeting on May 16, 2009?

COHEN: Yes! *(She pointed to Carla.)* She spoke with me after the meeting. And her *(pointing to Hannah)*. She spoke with me and served me refreshments after the meeting. She told me her name was Hannah.

BEN ISRAEL: Let the record show that the witness identified the respondent Andrew Sterling as the person conducting the meeting in question, the respondent Carla Sterling as one she spoke with after the meeting, and the respondent Hannah Silberman as another who spoke with her and served her refreshments after the meeting.

Now listen to me very carefully, Segal. This is very important. What was the nature of the message you heard Andrew

Sterling speak at this meeting on Motze Shabbat, May 16, 2009?

Cohen: He told us many things about Yeshua, the one the rabbis call 'Yeshu'; how this Yeshua was the Son of God; how He was sacrificed for our sins and how we could have eternal life if we simply confessed our sins and believed in Him.

Ben Israel: Would you say, then, that the purpose of this message was to persuade you to change your religion?

Levine: Objection! The prosecutor is leading the witness and answering his own question.

Chief Justice Bauerstein: Overruled. The witness may answer the question.

Cohen: Yes, that was it, exactly! He was trying to get me to change my religion! *(She suddenly begins to sob.)*

Ben Israel *(after a few moments, when Segal had regained control)*: What did Andrew Sterling do after he concluded his message on the evening in question?

Cohen: He invited anyone who had decided to accept Yeshua to come forward to the front of the room to be prayed for.

Ben Israel: What did you do, Segal?

Cohen: I, ah…ah *(in a nearly inaudible whisper)*, I went forward to the front of the room.

Ben Israel: Why did you do this?

Cohen: Because Andrew Sterling had convinced me that I needed to change my religion, that I needed to stop waiting for the Messiah to arrive, that Yeshua was the Messiah and He had already come. I wanted to pray with him about this.

Ben Israel: Would you say that Andrew Sterling was showing you that you needed to give up being a Jew and become a Christian?

Levine: Objection! The prosecutor is assuming facts not in evidence. Nothing in these proceedings has defined the nature of either Christianity or Judaism, much less the matter of disavowing or embracing either of them!

CHIEF JUSTICE BAUERSTEIN: Sustained! Mr. Ben Israel, please let the witness answer your questions using her own terms of reference.

BEN ISRAEL: Very well, Your Honor. Segal, you testified earlier that you spoke with Carla Sterling after the meeting. Please tell the court what she told you.

COHEN: She told me how happy she was that I had become a believer in Yeshua.

BEN ISRAEL: Did she tell you anything else?

COHEN: Yes, she invited me to join a group of other new believers who were being discipled to get them ready for baptism.

BEN ISRAEL: Segal, you also earlier testified that you spoke with Hannah Silberman after the meeting and that she served you refreshments. What did she say to you?

COHEN: She told me that she too was a new believer and how Yeshua had totally transformed her life. She gave me cookies and punch that we shared together in celebration of the wonderful changes the true Messiah had made in our lives.

BEN ISRAEL *(taking a step back and motioning toward Jerry)*: I have no further questions. Your witness, Mr. Levine.

LEVINE: Good morning, Segal *(gently beginning his cross-examination)*. There are just a few matters I would like to clear up regarding what you have shared with us so far. Let's begin with this. You told us that you were seventeen years old on the date of the meeting led by Andrew Sterling on May 16, 2009. Is that correct?

COHEN: Yes, it is.

LEVINE: How old are you now, Segal?

COHEN: I am eighteen.

LEVINE: When did you become eighteen?

COHEN: On my birthday, May 28.

LEVINE: Let me get this straight *(raising his voice sharply)*. You became eighteen years old just twelve days after the meeting you attended in Tiberias on May 16, right?

COHEN: Yes.

LEVINE: Segal, would you please describe your employment status, if any, on May 16, 2009? Did you receive any payment whatsoever from any services of any kind you may have performed on that date on behalf of any person or agency or any other employer? Remember, Segal, you are under oath.

COHEN: Anna Feinberg and I met and developed a friendship with someone from an organization called Shomrei Israel who occasionally comes to our synagogue. He told us that a group of Christian missionaries in Tiberias were stealing the souls of innocent Jewish children and they needed to be stopped. He offered to pay us each one thousand shekels just to attend one of these meetings so we could see what was going on for ourselves.

LEVINE: Did you have to agree to anything else other than just attending such a meeting?

COHEN: Well, yes *(carefully choosing her words)*, we agreed that we would testify at some future proceeding, such as I am doing today, should the need arise.

LEVINE: Who is this individual who paid each of you two young women for the services you have described, Segal?

COHEN *(without hesitating)*: He is Rabbi Mordecai Ben Shlomi, director of the Tiberias chapter of Shomrei Israel.

LEVINE: Did this Rabbi Mordecai Ben Shlomi coach you on what you were to look for and generally or specifically how you were to testify before this court at this proceeding?

COHEN: Only generally *(somewhat defensively)*. He told us that his goal was to expose these missionaries for what they were so that they could no longer carry on their evil work.

LEVINE: Do you know the meaning of the term 'mole,' Segal?

COHEN: Yes, a mole is a sort of secret agent planted in a group someplace to spy on them.

LEVINE: That's exactly correct. Then, would it be fair to say that you and Anna were both moles in the employment of Shomrei Israel on May 16, 2009, for the purpose of spying on Andrew Sterling and the proceedings of the meeting he was conducting near Tiberias on that date?

COHEN: Yes, that is correct.

LEVINE: Just a few more questions, Segal. Did Rabbi Mordecai Ben Shlomi coach you to go forward when any nonbelievers who were present at the meeting in question were invited to do so?

COHEN: No, he did not *(her voice quavering and beginning to tremble).*

LEVINE: Then why did you go forward?

COHEN: Because something deep inside me told me I should do this *(weeping openly).* It was like the voice of God speaking to me.

LEVINE: There is another matter, Segal. Did Carla Sterling ask you your age at any time during the evening in question?

COHEN: Yes, she did ask.

LEVINE: How did you reply?

COHEN: I told her I was twenty—people tell me that I look old for my age, and I don't like anyone to think of me as a teenager.

LEVINE: Did Carla ask your age before or after you two talked about Yeshua?

COHEN: Before.

LEVINE *(cautioning)*: Segal, I want you to listen very carefully to my next question and to remember you are under oath and subject to prosecution for perjury should it be discovered that you are not telling the truth. Do you understand?

COHEN: Yes-s-s *(brushing away her continuing tears).*

LEVINE: Segal, did anyone in any way instruct you that you should not tell the truth about your age should anyone ask you about this?

COHEN: Yes.

LEVINE: Who instructed you to do this?

COHEN *(unhesitatingly)*: Rabbi Mordecai Ben Shlomi, director of the Tiberias chapter of Shomrei Israel.

LEVINE: Thank you, Segal. I have no further questions.

CHIEF JUSTICE BAUERSTEIN: The witness may step down. Mr. Ben Israel, you may call your next witness.

BEN ISRAEL: The state calls Anna Feinberg.

Anna, a full-figured, deeply tanned brunette, like Segal, looked quite smart in her IDF uniform as she took the witness stand. After Natan had properly identified her for the record and sworn her to be truthful, he began his interrogation with a series of short, crisp questions.

Ben Israel: Anna, where were you on the evening of May 16, 2009?

Feinberg: I was attending a missionary meeting at a kibbutz just south of Tiberias.

Levine: Objection! There has been nothing presented thus far as to the nature of this meeting. The term "missionary" may mean many different things to different people.

Chief Justice Bauerstein: Overruled. Earlier testimony has established that the meeting in question was at least in part conducted for the purpose of encouraging those present to change their religion, which is certainly within the generally understood meaning of "missionary" outreach. You may continue, Mr. Ben Israel.

Levine *(demanding)*: Your Honor, please let the record show that the defense protests your ruling on the grounds that—"

Chief Justice Bauerstein *(slamming down his wooden gavel and scolding professorially)*: Mr. Levine, need I remind you that you are standing before the Supreme Court of the State of Israel and that I am the Chief Justice of said Court who is presiding over these proceedings. Counselor, you will please hereafter note and respect my rulings, bearing in mind that there is no higher court to which they may be appealed. Do you understand?

Levine: Yes, Your Honor. I understand completely.

Ben Israel *(smugly after his adversary's scolding)*: Anna, who was presiding over the meeting you attended on May 16?

Feinberg *(pointing to Drew)*: Andrew Sterling.

Ben Israel: Why do you believe that this meeting was missionary in its nature?

Feinberg: Because Andrew Sterling invited anyone present to come forward and pray with him about changing their religion.

BEN ISRAEL: Anna, what was your age on May 16, 2009?

FEINBERG: I was seventeen.

BEN ISRAEL: Can you be more precise?

FEINBERG: Yes. I was seventeen years, ten months, and six days old on May 16, 2009.

BEN ISRAEL: Did anyone else present in this courtroom today who was also present at the meeting in question say anything to you or in any other way attempt to induce you to change your religion that day?

FEINBERG *(pointing to Carla)*: Yes, Carla Sterling talked to me about gaining eternal life through Yeshu. *(Then pointing to Hannah)* Hannah Silberman gave me some cookies and punch while she spoke to me about how wonderful her own experience had been since she had been saved in this congregation.

BEN ISRAEL: Did you change your religion that day?

FEINBERG: No.

BEN ISRAEL: Thank you, Anna, I have no further questions. Your witness, Mr. Levine.

LEVINE *(immediately on the attack)*: Anna, were you paid by anyone to attend the meeting in question on May 16, 2009, and if so, how much and for what purpose?

FEINBERG: The two of us who attended, Segal and I, were each paid one thousand shekels by Rabbi Mordecai Ben Shlomi, director of the Tiberias chapter of Shomrei Israel. We were instructed to be on the alert for anyone at the meeting who tried to persuade us to change our religion and to report back to him after the meeting.

LEVINE: Did the two of you meet with Rabbi Ben Shlomi after the meeting?

FEINBERG: Yes, we met with him immediately afterwards.

LEVINE: Have you met with him since then?

FEINBERG: Yes.

LEVINE: When was your most recent meeting?

FEINBERG: Segal and I met with him last evening.

LEVINE: For what purpose?

Feinberg: To discuss our appearance here at these proceedings.

Levine: Would it be fair to say that Rabbi Ben Shlomi coached you on how you should testify?

Ben Israel: Objection! Counsel is leading the witness.

Levine: Withdrawn. I will rephrase. Please tell us, Anna, did Rabbi Ben Shlomi give you and Segal any specific suggestions or instructions relative to these proceedings at your meeting last evening?

Feinberg: Yes.

Levine: What were these instructions?

Feinberg: He suggested that we emphasize the missionary nature of the meeting.

Levine: Did you receive any additional payment or other inducements for attending this meeting?

Feinberg: Oh no, nothing more than our regular salaries from Shomrei Israel.

Ben Israel *(shouting)*: Move to strike! The witnesses' employment status is not relative to these proceedings, Your Honor.

Chief Justice Bauerstein: Of course it is, Mr. Ben Israel! You may continue, Mr. Levine.

Levine: How long have you been employed by the Shomrei Israel?

Feinberg: The two of us have been employed by them since May 2009.

Levine: How much are you paid each month?

Feinberg: Two thousand shekels, plus expenses.

Levine: How many hours are you required to work for them each month?

Feinberg: It depends on if they need us to attend any meetings or other information gathering—things like that. Sometimes we don't have to work during any given month at all.

Levine: Would it be fair to say that you are a part-time employee of Shomrei Israel with duties that involve spying on what that organization characterizes to be "missionary" meetings and other such activities?

Feinberg: Yes.

LEVINE: By the way, Anna, at any time during your conversation with Carla and/or Hannah that evening, did either of them ask you your age?

FEINBERG *(evasively)*: What exactly do you mean?

LEVINE: It shouldn't be that difficult, Anna. Did either Carla and/or Hannah ask your age? Did they ask how old you were?

BEN ISRAEL: Objection! Counsel is badgering the witness.

CHIEF JUSTICE BAUERSTEIN: I'll allow the question. The witness is instructed to answer the question.

FEINBERG: Yes, Carla brought up the subject when we were all gathered around the refreshment table.

LEVINE: What answers did you give them?

FEINBERG: We both told them we were twenty.

LEVINE: Did Carla ask your age before or after you two talked about Yeshua?

FEINBERG: Before.

LEVINE: Anna, do you remember if Carla asked you this question regarding your age before or after you began to eat the refreshments offered by Hannah?

FEINBERG: I'm sorry, but I couldn't say for sure. It was probably while we were eating the refreshments; that's when we were talking.

LEVINE *(cautioning)*: Anna, I want you to listen very carefully to my next question and to remember that you are under oath and subject to prosecution for perjury should it be discovered that you are not telling the truth. Do you understand?

FEINBERG: Yes-s-s.

LEVINE: Anna, did anyone instruct you in any way to misrepresent your actual age to anyone who might ask?

FEINBERG: Yes.

LEVINE: Who instructed you to do this?

FEINBERG *(unhesitating)*: Rabbi Mordecai Ben Shlomi, director of the Tiberias chapter of Shomrei Israel.

LEVINE: Thank you, Anna. I have no further questions.

Chief Justice Bauerstein: The witness may step down. The court will now stand in recess for two hours and will reconvene at two o'clock.

Ben Israel *(when the court had reconvened)*: The state calls Rabbi Mordecai Ben Shlomi.

The immaculately attired ultra-Orthodox rabbi took his place in the witness chair, adjusted his very large broad-brimmed black hat to fit squarely on his head, and nervously ran his hands through his full waist-length salt-and-pepper beard.

Ben Israel *(greeting his hoped-for star witness):* Shalom, Rabbi Ben Shlomi. It is good that you were able to find time from your very busy schedule to be with us today.

Ben Shlomi: I have looked forward to this day for a very long time. I wouldn't have missed this for the world.

Ben Israel: Rabbi, how long have you been working with Shomrei Israel?

Ben Shlomi: Shomrei Israel has been at the center of my life since I joined them more than twenty-five years ago.

Ben Israel: Tell us, Rabbi, when did you become the director of the Tiberias branch of this organization?

Ben Shlomi *(pridefully)*: It has been my great honor and duty to serve in this capacity for nearly five years.

Ben Israel: For the record, Rabbi, would you please give the court a brief summary of what you consider to be the principal objectives of your organization?

Ben Shlomi *(professorially)*: There are more than one hundred twenty aggressive Christian missionary cult congregations operating here in Israel. Indeed, every city has at least one such congregation that runs programs and activities aimed at luring Jews. Until recently the three such relatively small soul-stealing congregations in Tiberias have been kept under control by our constant surveillance and pressure. However, Andrew Sterling has formed a new congregation that works very aggressively to defeat our efforts to curtail their conversion activities. The fact is, in the last six months, Sterling's group has increased in size from under fifty lost Jewish souls to over one hundred, and with the help of Satan himself, there seems to be no end in sight to this outrageous increase. The annual budget of the missionaries in Israel is in the millions of dollars, often funded from foreign sources.

Under the guise of assisting the public, they open community centers, as well as drug-treatment facilities, that serve to advance their cause. The missionaries have at their disposal kibbutzim, convention centers, youth hostels, coffeehouses, publishing houses, and much more to spread their poisonous message.

BEN ISRAEL: Can you tell us, Rabbi, who among our people are especially vulnerable to this Christian missionary outreach of which you speak?

BEN SHLOMI *(enjoying every moment)*: Three main groups are especially vulnerable to the influence of these Christian missionaries: those who suffer from economic or emotional distress, underage children and young adults, and new immigrants, especially those who come from countries like those of the former Soviet Union in which they were raised uneducated about their Judaism.

People who are in crisis can be lured easily by offers of assistance. The Christian missionary groups step in and distribute food to the needy or schoolbags to their children. These programs are part of a wider strategy, a way of acquiring the trust of these most vulnerable potential victims who are most needy and struggling to survive.

Moreover, it seems clear that these Christian missionaries are intensifying their efforts among our new immigrants, who are showing an increasing interest in what they have to offer. Many of the immigrants are isolated; they don't understand Hebrew, miss the homes they left behind in their native countries, and yearn for human contact. This, in addition to their difficult financial situation, provides fertile ground for the stealing of their souls.

There is yet another population group that is highly vulnerable: young Israelis, often straight out of the army, who are searching for meaning in their lives. These young people have been failed by the state educational system, which didn't offer them any sense of the beauty of Judaism, and so many have gotten caught up in cults in the Far East or in other mystical pursuits. Even worse than this, many more have been entrapped and lost their souls to Christian missionaries.

Ben Israel: Tell us, Rabbi, how does Shomrei Israel go about combating these missionaries and what you describe as their outrageous satanic outreach?

Ben Shlomi *(militantly)*: We fight these Christian missionaries in a variety of ways, some of which, due to their sensitive nature, can't be described in detail. One of our most important functions is to closely track their missionary activities and respond to them in appropriate ways. Through our agents and enormous number of cooperative contacts, we are updated every time the Christian missionaries schedule a conference, open a new center, or schedule a baptism. To be sure, we have a variety of means to foil them.

When we receive a report of a family that has gotten caught up in a cult congregation, we intervene with tried and tested methods. We establish contact and begin a series of meetings aimed at discovering what caused these Jews to seek assistance from the cults and help them make their way back to the Jewish people. We also offer economic support and counseling for families or people in distress who have been snared by the missionaries in their moment of weakness.

In the fight against missionaries, prevention is as important as intervention, if not more so. We run programs that strengthen awareness of Judaism among new immigrants. These include a growing network of Torah classes around the country, as well as seminars.

We have also been very effective in organizing protests in neighborhoods that have been infiltrated by missionaries. These alert local residents as to the nature of the "innocent" classes being offered at an apartment on their block that has been rented by missionaries. These protests have led to the cancellation of classes, the removal of missionary centers, the prevention of baptisms, and awareness among the general public as to the extent of the problem.

I can tell you here and now, Mr. Prosecutor and the Israeli people, we will not be stopped in our program to stamp out Christian missionary activity in Israel until it has once again vanished from the Land much in the same manner it did at the end of the fifth century when the last remnants of the original so-called "Way" were finally driven into oblivion by our predecessors, the Pharisees of that day, the government, and by the Gentile Christian church to which they gave birth.

BEN ISRAEL: Thank you, Rabbi. Would you now please briefly describe the relationship of the Tiberias chapter of Shomrei Israel to the Ministry of the Interior?

BEN SHLOMI: Shomrei Israel is an entirely independent anti-missionary organization composed of concerned Israeli citizens who are determined to root out and eliminate the cult of so-called "Messianic Judaism" from Israel. Legally speaking, if we have information, it is our duty to inform whoever needs to be informed. If a person commits a felony against the state, since we are citizens of this state, it is our duty to report this person to the proper authorities. We only expose those people who come here to deceive the country. They say they want to convert to Judaism, but let the missionaries in through the back door. Thirty percent of the country's citizens are not Jewish; God forbid the two parts mix, and what will be left? You can be sure, we perform no mischief with the government or the police.

BEN ISRAEL: Rabbi, with respect to the hearing currently before this court, would it be fair to say that your organization has gathered a large amount of data concerning the alleged missionary activities of the respondents and that you voluntarily have provided this data to the Ministry of the Interior as a matter of your perceived civic duty?

BEN SHLOMI *(smugly)*: Yes, Mr. Ben Israel, that is correct.

Ben Israel: Rabbi, would you please now briefly describe the nature of your staff and how you are funded?

Ben Shlomi: Certainly. Since the Tiberias chapter, like all Shomrei Israel, is funded solely by contributions, we must run a very tight ship. What must seem ironic to the missionaries we oppose, much of our funding flows indirectly from evangelical churches in the United States.[1]

Ben Israel *(persisting):* What about the size and composition of your staff?

Ben Shlomi: Like all of our many chapters, my organization maintains a small paid staff who are assisted by a large volunteer corps. Our staffers must combine professionalism with selfless dedication and an ability to operate under pressure. Each department is staffed with professionals who have been trained to deal with its specific area of responsibility. For instance, the staff of the counter-missionary and counter-cult department have delved deeply into the intricacies of many cults and learned about their origins, beliefs, and tactics. They have received special training in how to help Jews who have been brainwashed. Staffers and volunteers must both be on call around the clock.[2]

Ben Israel: Rabbi, getting back to the case at hand, can you tell us what specific information about the alleged missionary activities of the respondents your organization was able to gather and then transfer to the Ministry of the Interior?

Ben Shlomi: I must say it would take many hours for me to share these very complete and very detailed files with the court. Perhaps it would suffice for me to give several poignant examples concerning each of the respondents.

Ben Israel: We can certainly begin there, Rabbi. Please go ahead.

Ben Shlomi *(withdrawing a thick stapled document from a black leather portfolio he had carried with him)*: This file is a record of the respondent Andrew Sterling's phone calls to other missionary organizations within Israel and the United States as well as his so-called pastoral conversations with members of his own congregation.

BEN ISRAEL *(warily)*: How is this data of value to us in the current proceeding, Rabbi?

BEN SHLOMI: It is of great value indeed in that it clearly proves that the respondent is a Christian and not a Jew. Moreover, it inarguably establishes that he is deeply active in all manner of missionary work and therefore that he is clearly a missionary who is out to steal the souls of our innocent, highly vulnerable brother and sister Jews.

BEN ISRAEL: What about the respondent Carla Sterling? Can you tell us something relevant about her activities?

BEN SHLOMI *(drawing another thick stapled file from his portfolio)*: I have here both photographic and documentary evidence that Carla Sterling conducts a children's Torah school for primary-school-age innocent victims each Shabbat morning. I can show you both the names of the children who attended each of these classes for the past year, as well as photographs of several of these sessions.

BEN ISRAEL: Rabbi, what was the general content of these children's Torah school lessons?

BEN SHLOMI *(somewhat exasperated)*: Don't you get it, Mr. Ben Israel? The missionary Carla Sterling has been teaching these innocent children all about the cult God Yeshu—the blasphemy that He is one with God and the savior of their precious young Jewish souls.

BEN ISRAEL: Very well, then, can you tell us something pertinent about the respondent Hannah Silberman?

BEN SHLOMI: Indeed I can *(withdrawing the file from his portfolio)*. I have here a complete file concerning the activities of the respondent during the years immediately following her release from Auschwitz concentration camp. It seems that she regularly attended a Roman Catholic church in Freising, Germany, and that she took pre-baptismal instructions from the clergy of that church. It thus seems clear that this respondent had already become a missionary before she wrongfully made Aliyah to Israel.

BEN ISRAEL: Do you have copies of all these files with you today, Rabbi?

Ben Shlomi: Of course. According to your instructions I made three copies—one for the court, one for you, and one for Mr. Levine.

Ben Israel: Good. Rabbi would you please give me the copies marked for the court and for Mr. Levine. *(He hands copies to their intended recipients.)* Your Honor, the state submits these files to the court marked for the record as State Exhibit One. I have no further questions. Your witness, Mr. Levine.

"I hardly know where to begin," Jerry whispered to himself with delight.

Levine: Good day, Rabbi Ben Shlomi. I have a number of questions concerning parts of your testimony that need clarification.

Ben Shlomi *(defensively)*: I have nothing to hide!

Levine: Excellent! Rabbi, you testified that there are over one hundred twenty aggressive Christian missionary congregations that you characterized as cults operating in Israel, four of which are now located in Tiberias. Moreover, you indicated that your primary concern was with the alleged missionary activities of what you characterized as the cult led by the respondent Andrew Sterling. Is that correct?

Ben Shlomi: Absolutely!

Levine: From your obviously expert, well-studied position, Rabbi, can you tell the court something more about these congregations, or cults of which you speak? First, what is your estimate of the total number of ethnic Jews that, as you say, have had their souls stolen by them?

Ben Shlomi: Many thousands!

Levine: Specifically, how many thousands?

Ben Shlomi: Our estimate falls in line with those of most others. I would say there are around five thousand such Jews in Israel who have fallen victim to the missionaries and converted to Christianity.

Levine: Is it your testimony that there are about five thousand Jews who have embraced whom they call Yeshua in the one hundred twenty congregations that you characterize as cults in Israel?

BEN SHLOMI: Yes, that would be a good estimate.

LEVINE: Do you believe then, Rabbi, that at least some of these five thousand were already believers in Yeshua before they made Aliyah and that they may have formed or joined existing congregations primarily for the purpose of worshiping God in the manner of their own choosing?

BEN SHLOMI: Yes, I suppose that is true. However, don't forget that stealing the souls of other Jews remains very high on their agendas.

LEVINE: Rabbi, to your knowledge is the proselytizing of Israeli citizens who are eighteen years old or older by other Israeli citizens for the purpose of causing them to change their religion specifically prohibited by Israeli law? Please answer simply yes or no.

BEN SHLOMI *(visibly stunned and evasive)*: The rabbis and the Talmud teach us—

LEVINE: Stop right there, Rabbi! What the rabbis and the Talmud or anyone else, or anything else, have to say, other than what is established by the letter of Israeli law, is not relevant to the matter before this court. Please answer my question. Rabbi, is proselytizing of persons eighteen years and older in violation of any Israel statute? Yes or no.

BEN ISRAEL *(making a valiant effort to rescue his cornered star witness)*: Objection! Counsel is badgering the witness.

CHIEF JUSTICE BAUERSTEIN: Your objection is sustained, Mr. Ben Israel. The witness, after all, is a rabbi, not a lawyer. The fact is, it may not be within his sphere of knowledge that Israeli law clearly allows religious proselytizing among adults.

LEVINE *(delighted by having had the chief justice make his point)*: OK, Rabbi, to summarize, is it fair to say that these some five thousand Jews who embrace Yeshua and attend these one hundred twenty or more what you call cult congregations in Israel, however or whenever they came into their faith, constitute a miniscule minority within a minority of less than one-tenth of one percent of the 5.4 million Jews who now reside in Israel?

Ben Shlomi: Yes, that would seem to be mathematically correct.

Levine: Rabbi, you testified earlier that Shomrei Israel fights these so-called Christian missionaries in ways that you can't describe in detail. Is that correct?

Ben Shlomi: Absolutely!

Levine: Are all of these so-called sensitive means you speak of ethical?

Ben Shlomi: Yes! The offense justifies the means.

Levine: Are all of these sensitive means lawful?

Ben Shlomi *(hesitating)*: Ahh, ahh, yes.

Levine: Rabbi, I'm trying to clarify your understanding of a fundamental matter. Do you consider the State of Israel to be a nation founded upon and governed by a variety of laws?

Ben Shlomi *(cautiously)*: Yes-s-s.

Levine: I must say, Rabbi, the huge amount of information your organization has assembled relative to my three clients is most impressive. Tell me; in your understanding, was all of this information obtained by lawful means and then shared lawfully with another agency?

Ben Shlomi *(defiantly)*: All means are justified to counter-missionary activity!

Levine: Would these means you speak of include wiretapping?

Ben Shlomi: As I said, Mr. Levine, all means are justified!

Levine *(turning for help from the bench)*: Your Honor, would you please direct the witness to answer the question before him?

Chief Justice Bauerstein: Rabbi Ben Shlomi, please answer the question.

Ben Shlomi *(feigning ignorance)*: What was the question again?

Levine: Let me rephrase. Rabbi, did Shomrei Israel employ wiretapping as a means to obtain information regarding the affairs of my clients, which in turn was revealed to the Ministry of the Interior?

Ben Israel: Objection! The witness is not on trial here!

Chief Justice Bauerstein: Overruled.

Ben Shlomi: Yes, Mr. Levine, Shomrei Israel has many means available to collect data, including the monitoring of telephone and other communications.

Levine: Rabbi, are you aware of an Israel statute commonly known as the Protection of Privacy Law, a statute that specifically prohibits non-consensual monitoring of telephone communications and that a person's consent for any invasion of privacy must be conscious? Moreover, Rabbi, according to this statute, an injured plaintiff may be awarded statutory damages of up to NIS 50,000. Even further, if the invasion to privacy is found to be the result of a willful act, then the sum of statutory damages may be doubled. Rabbi Ben Shlomi, are you aware of these provisions under the law?

Ben Shlomi: I am aware that the Shomrei Israel has never been held to be in violation of any such law, nor do I believe is it likely to be.

Levine: Upon what do you base this assessment, Rabbi?

Ben Shlomi: Our legal counsel has advised us.

Levine: Rabbi, do you consider stoning to be lawful?

Ben Shlomi: I have never personally been involved with such a tactic, but again, the offense justifies the means.

Levine: Rabbi, I have photographic evidence that the Tiberias chapter of Shomrei Israel, with you present and leading their assault, did in fact, during the recent mikvah in the Jordan River of the respondent Hannah Silberman, cast stones in an attempt to prevent this mikvah.

Ben Israel *(shouting)*: Objection! Rabbi Ben Shlomi is not on trial here. Your Honor, I request that he be instructed not to answer the question before him.

Levine: Your Honor, I agree; the witness is not on trial here today, but he certainly should be at some time in the near future—after all, subordination of perjury and perjury are crimes. I am trying to establish entrapment as the basis of our defense.

Chief Justice Bauerstein: Then you had better find another way to do this, Mr. Levine. The objection is sustained. Please move on.

Levine: OK, Rabbi, let's set aside for now who may or may not have been involved in any specific act of stoning. In your expert opinion, do you consider stoning to be a lawful remedy?

Ben Shlomi *(nervously righting his large hat and stroking his long beard)*: Young man, I suggest that you read your Torah—if you have one. Shomrei Israel did not invent this remedy; it can be found as a common practice written many places in the Holy Scriptures.

Levine: Rabbi, thank you for your most appreciated lesson on biblical practices. May I also ask, do you find using false witnesses to establish an allegation of criminal wrongdoing both ethical and lawful?

Ben Shlomi: I'm not a lawyer, Mr. Levine. I don't understand your question.

Levine: Then let me be more specific. Did you or did you not pay one thousand shekels each to Segal Cohen and Anna Feinberg, two young women in your employ, to attend a meeting conducted by the respondent Andrew Sterling on May 16, 2009?

Ben Shlomi: Yes, that was a part of their regular duties.

Levine: Did you instruct these two young women, who were technically within a few days of reaching the age of eighteen, at that time to misrepresent their age as twenty instead of their actual age of seventeen to anyone at that meeting who might inquire as to their actual ages?

Ben Shlomi: Again, the offense justifies the means.

Levine: That is exactly the point of my question, Rabbi. Please answer simply yes or no. Do you or do you not consider it ethical and lawful that these two young women were instructed by you to lie about their ages to my clients in order to make them believe they were adults rather than still technically minors?

Ben Israel: Objection! Calls for a conclusion! The witness is neither qualified to make such an assessment, nor is he on trial.

Chief Justice Bauerstein: Sustained. Please move on, Mr. Levine. I trust you are almost finished with this witness?

LEVINE: Thank you for your indulgence, Your Honor. I have only one more line of questioning.

CHIEF JUSTICE BAUERSTEIN: You may proceed.

LEVINE: Rabbi, I will be brief. Did you or did you not, in a meeting last evening, specifically instruct the two witnesses, Segal Cohen and Anna Feinberg, as to the specific nature and content of the testimony they were to bring before this court during the proceedings at hand, and did you or did you not induce this testimony by paying them each a bonus of one thousand shekels?

BEN ISRAEL: Objection!

CHIEF JUSTICE BAUERSTEIN: Enough! Mr. Levine, I will not warn you again. The witness is not on trial in these proceedings. The issue we are trying to determine here is whether or not any or all of your three clients violated the laws of Israel as alleged. It is as simple as that! For the last time, do you understand?

LEVINE *(pressing on relentlessly)*: I apologize, Your Honor. Just a few more questions, Rabbi. Have you had and do you currently have information-gathering agents commonly known as "moles" planted within Andrew Sterling's congregation and more specifically within Carla Sterling's children's Torah school?

BEN SHLOMI: I cannot say.

LEVINE: Isn't it rather, Rabbi, that you will not say?

BEN SHLOMI: Mr. Levine, I manage a huge organization and do not have all the details of its many operational activities at my finger tips.

LEVINE *(addressing the bench)*: Your Honor, I—

CHIEF JUSTICE BAUERSTEIN *(slamming down his gavel)*: Mr. Levine, don't you get it? The witness cannot say how Shomrei Israel managed to obtain incredibly detailed information, much less photographs of Mrs. Sterling's Torah school and its students. Your question was asked and answered. Mr. Levine, the witness cannot say.

Levine *(picking up on the chief justice's not even subtle sarcasm)*: I'm certain of it! Your Honor—yes, I do get it! Just one more thing, Rabbi, would you please tell us specifically how your organization managed to obtain information regarding Hannah Silberman's brief investigation of Roman Catholicism, which occurred long ago in Germany, even before Israel became a state?

Ben Shlomi *(sounding sincere)*: I honestly don't know. I can only say that Shomrei Israel has a great number of volunteers, many of whom are located throughout the world. Moreover, when all of these myriad data are entered into our huge database, there is little we cannot recall regarding any citizen or would-be citizen of the State of Israel.

Levine: Rabbi, to your knowledge, does Shomrei Israel have any official document indicating that Hannah Silberman actually converted to Roman Catholicism?

Ben Shlomi: We infer that she changed her religion from the church records in our possession that establish she took a course of instruction preparing her for baptism.

Levine: Let me tell you, Rabbi, you can stop looking. Hannah Silberman only investigated Roman Catholicism. After doing so she was not baptized and did not become a member of that church. Putting it in your terms, she did not, at that time, change her religion.

Ben Shlomi: Let me tell you, Mr. Levine, as long as there is even one Christian missionary like the three respondents remaining in Israel, Shomrei Israel will never stop looking!

Levine: Thank you Rabbi, I have no further questions.

Chief Justice Bauerstein: The witness may step down. The hour grows late. Mr. Ben Israel, you may continue your examination of witnesses tomorrow morning when we reconvene at nine o'clock. We stand adjourned until then.

Chapter 23
Hannah's Story
Jerusalem
(Supreme Court of the State of Israel: Tuesday, January 12, 2010)

The Trial: Third Hearing

Ben Israel: Your Honor, the State calls Emil Lugavitz.

When he had been duly sworn, the witness, a black-suited, grossly overweight, middle-aged, ultra-Orthodox, professional Jewish public servant struggled, with great difficulty, to squeeze himself into the generously sized wooden witness chair.

Ben Israel: Mr. Lugavitz would you please tell the court the nature of your work, your job title, and how long you have held this position?

Lugavitz: I am one of several deputy directors of the Public Administration Division of the Ministry of the Interior. My office is located in Jerusalem. For the past ten years I have been in charge of the investigation and subsequent actions of the ministry relative to unlawful missionary activities such as those attributed to the three respondents who stand before this court today.

Ben Israel: Mr. Lugavitz, will you please be more specific about these duties and the responsibilities of your position?

Lugavitz: Certainly, Mr. Ben Israel. I am the "official of last resort," so to speak. Under the Law of Return and the Law of Citizenship, authority has been delegated to me by the state within the Ministry of the Interior to deal with the many instances that are found out within our system where those who are not eligible for Israeli citizenship nevertheless persist in making their application. Usually, such unqualified applicants are discovered by our clerks during their interview with the applicant, and the applicant is rejected right there on the spot. In other cases, however, a more careful review of the applicant's documents reveal some disqualifying fact that slipped by our clerk in the field, and thus, the applicant is rejected at this higher level. My job is to supervise the team of reviewers at the ministry level and ultimately to make the final determination in each case where there may be a question as to the applicant's qualifications for citizenship, or some other status, such as permanent or temporary residency. My department and I in turn also have the ultimate responsibility for investigating cases where citizenship has previously been granted to those persons who somehow have managed to slip through our system and should not have been granted citizenship in the first place.

BEN ISRAEL: Mr. Lugavitz, is it fair to say that you are among the very top experts in Israel with respect to the Law of Return as amended?

LUGAVITZ: You flatter me, Counsel. I have worked with this law every day for the past ten years, and I suppose I would be considered by some to be an expert on its content, purpose, and application.

BEN ISRAEL: Mr. Lugavitz, would you please tell the court what law or other criteria you use to make such determinations regarding eligibility for an applicant to be granted citizenship and/or for a person who already is a citizen to retain such citizenship or to endure its revocation?

LUGAVITZ: Certainly! While other statutes from time to time may bear upon such cases, our "bible," so to speak, is clearly the Israeli Law of Return as amended in 1970.

BEN ISRAEL: Would the key determining issue here be the question of whether or not the applicant or the citizen in question has changed his religion?

LUGAVITZ: Yes.

BEN ISRAEL: Mr. Lugavitz, did you personally make the final determination that the citizenship of the three respondents who stand before this court today should be revoked?

LUGAVITZ: Yes. I did so on the advice of my staff and after I had thoroughly investigated the files of these respondents.

BEN ISRAEL: Did you make this final determination based entirely on the question of whether or not these citizens had wrongfully gained their citizenship status?

LUGAVITZ: This was the key determinant, but in these three cases there were other factors involved.

BEN ISRAEL: Would you please be more specific, Mr. Lugavitz? What were these other factors?

LUGAVITZ: Our investigation determined that all three respondents are Christian missionaries who have purposefully tried to change the religion of minors in direct contradiction to the law, and that their intention for immigrating into Israel was to intentionally break Israeli missionary laws by converting Jews to Christianity.

BEN ISRAEL: Mr. Lugavitz, to summarize, opposing counsel has done a brilliant job in attempting to create a smokescreen of emotion and half-truths in a vain attempt to mislead this court into thinking that the Ministry of the Interior and those with whom you work to uphold the law and to see to the best interest of all Israelis have somehow been in error concerning your action against the respondents and that said action should be overturned.

Mr. Lugavitz, with respect to the revocation of the citizenship of the three respondents who stand before this court, was there or is there anything whatsoever—any action, consideration or decision that was in any way, however minor—in violation of any current statute of the State of Israel?

LUGAVITZ: No, Mr. Ben Israel. No, absolutely not! The court must reject these responses. Not to do so would be to put the entire system of government at risk. In the end the current coalition would surely collapse with potentially devastating consequences.

BEN ISRAEL: Thank you Mr. Lugavitz. Your witness, Mr. Levine.

The attorney for the respondents managed to suppress his hostility toward this key witness against his clients and smiled, albeit patronizingly, as he began his cross-examination.

Levine: Mr. Lugavitz, in your earlier testimony, you categorized the three respondents as Christian missionaries. Would you now be kind enough to share with us the specific basis upon which you made the determination that the respondents are Christians, much less missionaries?

Lugavitz: Isn't that obvious?

Levine: Not to me it isn't. Two of the respondents were born of Jewish mothers. Both were raised as practicing Jews. Neither were ever members of a Christian church or ever identified themselves as Christians.

Lugavitz *(strenuously objecting)*: Come on now, Mr. Levine, take a closer look at the respondent Andrew Sterling. He attended a Christian seminary, served an entire career as a Christian chaplain in the United States Air Force, and now he is leading a congregation in Israel that is set upon changing the religion of innocent, unsuspecting Jewish minors.

Levine: Mr. Lugavitz, let me ask you this: Are all graduates of Hebrew University adherents to some form of Judaism?

Lugavitz: I would think not.

Levine: Are all graduates of the University of Notre Dame members of the Roman Catholic Church, or for that matter, are they all Christians of one sort or another?

Lugavitz: I can't say for certain, but again, I would think not.

Levine: Isn't it possible then, Mr. Lugavitz, that the three respondents are not Christians? Rather, that they are, as they profess themselves to be, simply practicing, religious, ethnic Jews who have a different understanding from other Jews concerning the identity of the Messiah? Mr. Lugavitz, what I'm getting to here is this: are you able to grasp the concept that an ethnic Jew can embrace Yeshua or any other candidate of their choice as their Messiah without having somehow lost their Jewish ethnicity in the process?

LUGAVITZ: Both the law of the State of Israel and Jewish religious law hold that the moment a Jew embraces this Yeshu—at that very moment they become part of another religion and cease to be Jewish. Period!

LEVINE: Tell us, Mr. Lugavitz, are you aware of the Jewish sect in Israel that holds there is no Messiah, nor will there ever be? Are you also aware of yet another Jewish sect that calls for the destruction of the State of Israel and holds that the Messiah will only appear after the current state no longer exists?

LUGAVITZ: Yes, I am aware of these sects and their views that are not in line with mainstream Judaism.

LEVINE: By mainstream Judaism, Mr. Lugavitz, do you mean modern-day Orthodox and ultra-Orthodox Judaism, the adherents to which together comprise about seventeen percent of the Jewish citizens of Israel?[1]

LUGAVITZ: Yes.

LEVINE: Mr. Lugavitz, would you agree that, in round numbers, there are some six million ethnic Jews in the State of Israel today?

LUGAVITZ: Yes.

LEVINE: Are you also aware that there are likely no more than five thousand ethnic Jews in Israel today who embrace Yeshua as their Messiah? This is about one-tenth of one percent of all six million Israeli Jews.

LUGAVITZ: Yes.

LEVINE: Mr. Lugavitz, would it be fair to say that your personal primary mission during your long tenure with the Ministry of the Interior has been to prevent the granting of citizenship to ethnic Jews who are believers in Yeshua and to otherwise revoke the citizenship of those some twenty-five hundred others who have somehow managed to survive in the Land as a tiny minority?

LUGAVITZ: No! My primary mission is to enforce the Law of Return!

Levine: Mr. Lugavitz, will you please tell us about the relationship of Shomrei Israel and other so-called anti-missionary organizations to your department?

Lugavitz: There is no official connection between my department and these organizations you speak of. Nevertheless, we rely very much upon their very dedicated and professional investigative services.

Levine: To your knowledge, are any of these organizations funded either directly or indirectly by the government of Israel?

Lugavitz: Mr. Levine, Shomrei Israel, as you may know, pursues any person or persons whom they consider to be missionaries. To my knowledge, neither Shomrei Israel nor any other such organization receives financial support from the Israeli government.

Levine: Mr. Lugavitz, considering the very small number of Jews who believe in Yeshua and who are citizens of Israel, it would seem you have done your job very well. Can you tell us, how many ethnically Jewish applicants for citizenship have come before your department and been rejected for the sole reason that they embraced Yeshua as Messiah?

Lugavitz *(sweating profusely and squirming in obvious discomfort in the tight-fitting witness chair)*: Many. I can't give you precise numbers.

Levine: OK, would you say by "many" that you mean less or more than one hundred?

Lugavitz: More.

Levine: More than five hundred?

Lugavitz: Yes.

Levine: More than one thousand?

Lugavitz: Perhaps.

Levine: Mr. Lugavitz, is it your testimony that you personally have reviewed the files of more than one thousand Jewish applicants for citizenship over the past ten years and that you rejected these applications solely on the basis of the applicants' conviction that Yeshua was their Messiah and a member of the Godhead?

BEN ISRAEL: Objection! Asked and answered.

LEVINE: Withdrawn. Mr. Lugavitz, let's return for a moment to the Law of Return as amended in 1970. Isn't it true that this law prohibits granting of Israeli citizenship to any ethnic Jew who has changed his religion?

LUGAVITZ: Yes.

LEVINE: Would this provision apply to Jews who have religiously embraced Buddhism, Hinduism, Islam, New Age, or those thousands who have embraced as their Messiah a Ukrainian rabbi named Schneerson who immigrated to the United States and who died in 1994?

LUGAVITZ: No such cases have come before my department for review.

LEVINE: That isn't what I asked, Mr. Lugavitz. Please answer my question with a simple yes or no. To your expert knowledge, does the provision of the law in question pertain to any or all of these Jews whose religious positions I have cited?

LUGAVITZ: I would not be able to make such a determination until such a case came before me for consideration, and then I would have to consider all other factors that may or may not bear upon that specific case.

LEVINE: OK, Mr. Lugavitz, let me put it this way. If the three respondents were adherents to Buddha or Allah or the Dalai Lama, as opposed to Yeshua, and all other factors remained exactly the same, would you personally have taken action to revoke their citizenship?

LUGAVITZ *(stammering)*: I–I–I cannot say.

LEVINE: Really, Mr. Lugavitz, isn't what you mean rather that you will not say?

BEN ISRAEL: Objection! Counsel is badgering the witness.

CHIEF JUSTICE BAUERSTEIN: Sustained.

The witness, whose once-starched white shirt was now soaked with his perspiration, squirmed in yet another vain attempt to better fit his corpulence into the tight confines of the unyielding wooden witness chair. His face was flushed, and he was breathing heavily.

LEVINE *(taking momentary pity on the object of his grilling)*: Mr. Lugavitz, perhaps you would be more comfortable if you removed your heavy jacket—there really is no need for such formality.

LUGAVITZ: Thank you for your concern, Mr. Levine. I am quite comfortable just as I am.

LEVINE *(patronizingly)*: Very well, then, I will do my best not to keep you here much longer. Mr. Lugavitz, you have testified that your decision to recommend revocation of the three respondents' citizenship and that they be deported was based at least in some part upon the investigative data provided to your department by Shomrei Israel. Do I have this right?

LUGAVITZ: Yes.

LEVINE: Then please tell us to what extent your decision to revoke and deport rested upon this data provided by Shomrei Israel.

LUGAVITZ: Shomrei Israel is critical to our operations and decision-making process, but we do not rely upon them entirely. We have other sources, other unofficial fact-finding organizations that are much smaller than Shomrei Israel but that nevertheless operate generally in the same way and enjoy the same relationship with the ministry as does Shomrei Israel.

LEVINE: To what extent did your department verify the specific data submitted by Shomrei Israel relative to the three respondents that ultimately provided the basis for your decision to revoke and deport?

LUGAVITZ: Mr. Levine, please understand that these mostly volunteer informants are spread throughout much of the world—many thousands of them. It is an enormous challenge for the ministry to sort out and enter the huge volume of their input into our database, much less attempt to verify them.

LEVINE: Would it be fair to say then, Mr. Lugavitz, that you made your recommendation to revoke the citizenship of my clients and deport them based largely upon the unverified input of at least several different volunteer, unsupervised agents who are not officially connected to your ministry or to any other branch of the government?

LUGAVITZ: Yes, but—

LEVINE *(cutting off the witness)*: Thank you, Mr. Lugavitz. Your simple yes is quite sufficient. Let's move on. Please tell us, specifically, how did your department notify my clients of your attempt to revoke their citizenship and deport them? Did this administrative suspicion or decision become known to them at the end of any kind of proceeding or interview?

LUGAVITZ: No. They were notified by registered mail.

LEVINE: Tell us, Mr. Lugavitz, are you aware that international law limits the revocation of citizenship and forbids altogether revoking the citizenship of a person or group of people on racial, ethnic, religious, or political grounds?[2]

LUGAVITZ *(patronizingly)*: Mr. Levine, perhaps you missed my earlier testimony that made it perfectly clear that the revocation and deportation action taken against the respondents was based entirely upon their outright violation of the laws of Israel and not in any way based upon racial, ethnic, religious, or political grounds.

LEVINE *(sarcastically)*: Interesting, Mr. Lugavitz. I stand corrected. But Mr. Lugavitz, perhaps you've forgotten your own earlier testimony before this court that your ministry has denied Israeli citizenship to at least many hundreds of otherwise entirely qualified Jewish applicants based solely upon the basis that you found they embraced Yeshua as their Messiah. In your expert opinion, wouldn't you say that such a belief is religious in nature?

LUGAVITZ *(stammering)*: Yes-s-s.

LEVINE: Mr. Lugavitz, were you aware of the ruling of this Supreme Court in September 2008 that Messianic Jews were entitled to equal treatment under the Law of Return?[3]

LUGAVITZ: I am not a lawyer, Mr. Levine. It is not my calling to be aware of such things.

LEVINE: Very well then, Mr. Lugavitz, perhaps you can tell us, to your best recollection, how many applicants for citizenship have been rejected by the Ministry of the Interior on the sole basis that they were atheists, Hindi, Buddhist, or followers of any other religion other than what you lump together as Christianity?

Ben Israel: Objection! Counsel is badgering the witness!

Chief Justice Bauerstein: Overruled. Please answer the question, Mr. Lugavitz.

Lugavitz *(in a near whisper)*: I cannot recall.

Levine *(ingenuously)*: Perhaps I can help. Can you recall for this court one single case where the Ministry of the Interior rejected the citizenship application of an otherwise qualified applicant based solely upon his adherence to a religion other than the understanding that Yeshua, Jesus Christ, was the Messiah? Just one single case, Mr. Lugavitz. No need to elaborate; a simple yes or no will suffice.

Lugavitz *(in a barely audible whisper)*: None that I can recall, but my memory may be failing me under the pressure of your interrogation.

Levine: Are you saying then, Mr. Lugavitz, that there may be many such cases where Jews were denied citizenship because they were atheists, Buddhists, Hindi, Muslims, or adherents to some other religion or non-religion other than some brand of Christianity?

Ben Israel: Objection! Haven't we heard enough of this? Mr. Levine has made his point! His question has been asked and answered!

Chief Justice Bauerstein: Sustained. Please move on, Mr. Levine.

Levine: Very well then, Mr. Lugavitz, let's turn to the three respondents who stand before this court of last resort seeking justice that so far has evaded them. Mr. Lugavitz, setting aside the obviously flawed accusations against the three respondents that arose from the testimony of planted witnesses who were paid to entrap them, can you tell us of a single instance memorialized within your vast files that convincingly shows that any of the three have ever knowingly violated any law of the State of Israel?

Lugavitz: How can I possibly set aside the clear evidence that establishes that these three Christian missionaries are a menace to the State of Israel, and that they immigrated under false pretenses while deceiving the government regarding their religious affiliation and intentions for living in Israel?

LEVINE: OK, Mr. Lugavitz, let me ask the question differently. Beyond any matter against them that has already been brought before this court, can you recall even one instance where any of the three respondents have purposefully violated Israeli law?

LUGAVITZ: Isn't it enough that the three of them are missionaries?

LEVINE *(pleading for help)*: Your Honor—

CHIEF JUSTICE BAUERSTEIN: Mr. Lugavitz, this isn't a debate. Stop being evasive; answer the question!

LUGAVITZ *(hesitatingly)*: Yes, there are such instances in their files.

LEVINE: And what may these instances be?

LUGAVITZ: As I recall, the missionary Andrew Sterling has had at least three driving violations during his residency in Israel.

The many observers who packed the courtroom broke out in a loud spontaneous laughing response that ended only after the chief justice pounded his gavel to restore order and threatened to clear the court should there be any further such outbursts.

LEVINE: So that's it, Mr. Lugavitz? Andrew Sterling has three driving violations? Do you consider this sufficient grounds for your claim that he intentionally presented false information in order to receive Israeli citizenship—that he is a criminal?

LUGAVITZ: Of course not, Mr. Levine.

LEVINE: Excellent! I'm gratified that we finally agree on something. Now tell us, what of Carla Sterling? Beyond her alleged infractions already brought before this court, what does her criminal record look like? Are you aware of any violations she has committed over her many years as a citizen of Israel?

LUGAVITZ: No.

LEVINE: What of Hannah Silberman? Are you aware of any violations stuffed among the vast reaches of her Ministry of the Interior file?

LUGAVITZ: No.

Levine: Would it be fair to say, then, Mr. Lugavitz, that beyond those ludicrous charges that have already been presented during these proceedings, the three respondents could accurately be described as model, law-abiding citizens of Israel?

Lugavitz *(screaming, out of control)*: Mr. Levine, I would rather go to my grave than declare any such enemies of the State of Israel model citizens, much less citizens at all!

Levine *(with obvious satisfaction)*: I have no further questions.

Chief Justice Bauerstein *(sympathetically)*: Any redirect, Mr. Ben Israel?

Ben Israel: None, Your Honor.

Chief Justice Bauerstein: The witness may step down. Mr. Ben Israel, you may call your next witness.

Ben Israel: Your Honor, the state calls the respondent Andrew Scott Sterling.

Levine: Objection! Your Honor, the state is wrongfully trying to establish a basis that may cause the respondent to incriminate himself. This principle is set forth in section 47 of Evidence Ordinance [New Version], 1971. While this citation pertains to criminal procedures, and our case is administrative, nevertheless, falsifying information before the immigration office is, in fact, a criminal offense as well, according to section 16 of the Law of Citizenship and section 11 article 6.

Chief Justice Bauerstein: I commend you, Counsel, for your correct understanding of the law. However, let me remind you and opposing counsel that our purpose here is to get all pertinent facts on the table to enable this court to make a proper and just decision. Therefore, Mr. Levine, your objection is overruled. However, the court duly notes that the respondent is not obliged to answer a question that may incriminate him.

Jerry had thoroughly briefed his clients on the remote possibility that they might be called as witnesses by the state but had essentially dismissed this possibility as unlikely given its self-incriminatory aspects under the law. Drew therefore struggled to appear calm as he took the stand in a vain attempt to conceal the genuine shock he felt at being so called.

BEN ISRAEL: Andrew Sterling, it seems that over the years you've had many official titles, including the Reverend Sterling, Chaplain Sterling, Colonel Sterling, Doctor Sterling, Rabbi Sterling—are each of these correct? Have I failed to include any other that may be significant with respect to these present proceedings?

STERLING: Actually, I have never been the pastor of a Christian congregation and therefore have never had the title Reverend. I have, over the years, variously had the several other titles you mentioned.

BEN ISRAEL: Which of these many titles are you currently known by?

STERLING: Variously by each of them. My former military associates still address me as Chaplain. In scholarly circles I am called Doctor. Members of my congregation and some others know me as Rabbi, and my retirement checks are sent to me as Colonel.

BEN ISRAEL *(handing the witness an official photograph of himself)*: Tell us, do you recognize this photograph of yourself taken from your publicly available Air Force personnel records?

STERLING: Yes.

BEN ISRAEL: Am I correct in saying that you are depicted in this photograph wearing what is known as a Class A uniform, adorned with all of your authorized awards, decorations, insignia of rank, and Air Force specialty badges?

STERLING: Yes.

BEN ISRAEL: To my understanding, there are four different Air Force chaplain badges, each depicting the respective religion of the chaplain whose uniform they adorn. These are, respectively, Christian, represented by a cross; Jewish, represented by a Star of David; Muslim, represented by a half-moon; and Buddhist, represented by a compass. Is this correct?

STERLING: Yes.

BEN ISRAEL: Please tell us which of the four chaplain badges are you depicted wearing in the official photograph you hold in your hand?

Sterling: A silver cross, denoting that in December 1978, when this photo was taken, I was a Christian chaplain.

Ben Israel: So, Chaplain Sterling, please tell us, what were the principal prerequisites necessary for you to be commissioned as a Christian chaplain in the United States Air Force?

Sterling: The three basic requirements were that I held a master of divinity degree from a recognized degree-granting institution, that I be ordained by a recognized Christian denomination, and then approved and sent by this denomination to represent them.

Ben Israel: Did you fully meet the qualifications you have cited to assume this position as a Christian chaplain; that is, were you educated in an Air Force–approved Christian postgraduate institution, were you ordained by a Christian denomination and then approved by them to represent them as a Christian Air Force chaplain?

Sterling: Yes.

Ben Israel: During your career as an Air Force chaplain, did your duties include those of a missionary?

Sterling: No! Missionaries to my understanding reach outside of their immediate congregations or communities. Military chaplains provide the spiritual needs of those who voluntarily seek them, usually from within the framework of their shared military organization or location.

Ben Israel: As a military chaplain, did you ever purposefully seek to convert Jews to your Christian faith?

Sterling: No.

Ben Israel: Can you tell us the nature and location of your military assignment during December 1978?

Sterling: Yes, I was the United States Air Forces in Europe command chaplain, assigned to Ramstein Air Base in Germany.

Ben Israel: Did your duties as a command chaplain involve conducting religious services in various base chapels throughout Europe?

Sterling: No, but I did make it a personal point to do so about one Sunday each month.

BEN ISRAEL: Chaplain Sterling, do you recall where you were on Sunday, December 3, 1978?

LEVINE: Objection! Relevance? Your Honor, this entire line of questioning seems to have no bearing on the matter at hand. If counsel insists on going fishing, it would be good if he did it elsewhere.

CHIEF JUSTICE BAUERSTEIN: Overruled. But Mr. Ben Israel, I must agree; if you have a point, it would be good if you made it. The witness will answer the question.

STERLING: No, not specifically. Really, Mr. Ben Israel, that was more than thirty years ago.

The state's attorney gleefully handed the witness a copy of what appeared to be a community-like periodical.

BEN ISRAEL: Perhaps this will help your recollection. This a copy of the *Ramstein News*, dated 7 December 1978. Please note that the top page is devoted to a section entitled "USAFE Command Notes." Chaplain Sterling, would you be kind enough to read aloud the headline and first paragraph of the lead story that occupies most of the entire page?

STERLING *(struggling to suppress his rising emotions)*: "USAFE COMMAND CHAPLAIN BAPTIZES RAMSTEIN NCO. As the highlight of the regular eleven o'clock Protestant service in chapel number one this past Sunday morning, TSgt. Chaim Goldfarb of the 751st Security Police Squadron was baptized by USAFE Command Chaplain Col. Andrew S. Sterling in a special immersion service that brought an emotional conclusion to TSgt. Goldfarb's several month-long study of Christianity and his conversion to his new faith."

BEN ISRAEL *(gleefully)*: Now, Chaplain Sterling, would you please read the caption under the accompanying picture that depicts Chaim Goldfarb and you standing together in the baptismal, with Sarah Goldfarb, his wife, and their three children, obviously filled with joy and celebration, standing at its side.

STERLING: "'This is the most wonderful day of my life,' TSgt. Chaim Goldfarb proclaimed after he came up out of the baptismal waters, capping his conversion to Christianity in a special ceremony conducted by USAFE Command Chaplain Col. Andrew S. Sterling. TSgt. Goldfarb continued, 'Sarah and our three children will soon join me in our new faith when they complete their discipling, hopefully, before Christmas.'"

BEN ISRAEL *(handing Drew a copy of a different periodical)*: Chaplain, this is a copy of the April 15, 1979, issue of *Stars and Stripes*, an unofficial newspaper that reports mostly on top level United States military news. Would you please read for us the short story entitled "Former USAFE Command Chaplain Immigrates to Israel"?

STERLING: "Chief of Air Force Chaplains Major General Sheldon Thurman announced today that he has received a letter from recently retired Chaplain Colonel Andrew Sterling and Mrs. Sterling announcing that they have succeeded in becoming dual citizens of Israel and the United States.

"In commenting on the Sterlings' successful immigration to Israel, Chaplain General Thurman said: 'I am delighted that my dear friends, Drew and Carla Sterling, have, by God's grace, managed to become Israeli citizens. I wish them great success and every blessing as they take up their new ministry in the Land of their biblical inheritance. The Air Force's great loss is Israel's great gain.'"

BEN ISRAEL: Andrew Scott Sterling, isn't it true that even before you made Aliyah, you were a Christian missionary whose goal it was to convert Jews to Christianity?

STERLING: No!

BEN ISRAEL: Isn't it true that your primary purpose for making Aliyah was to continue in this same missionary pursuit here in Israel?

STERLING: No!

BEN ISRAEL: Please tell us, Andrew Scott Sterling, isn't it true that you became an Israeli citizen under false pretenses?

STERLING: No! No! Certainly not!

BEN ISRAEL *(gleefully)*: Your witness, Mr. Levine.

LEVINE *(soothingly)*: Drew, have you ever been an official member of a Christian denomination or church?

STERLING: Yes, but only to the extent that I attended a conservative seminary operated by a small very conservative Lutheran synod. It was necessary for me to identify myself with this synod in order for me to represent them as an Air Force chaplain. And no, I have never been a member of a Christian church.

LEVINE: Do you consider yourself to be a Jew?

STERLING: Yes. Both sides of my family were Jewish for at least several generations—as far back as I have been able to trace. Many of my relatives on both sides were murdered by the Nazis.

LEVINE: What do you consider yourself to be religiously—a Jew or a Christian?

STERLING: To give you a simple answer to a very complex matter, I am, both ethnically and religiously Jewish. While I reject the so-called 'Oral Law' of modern-day rabbinical Judaism, I totally embrace the Judaism as it was understood and practiced by the first Jewish believers in Yeshua during the first century. That is to say, I, like them, embrace all of the Tenach—the Word of God, but entirely reject the Talmud, Mishna, Gemara, etc. The only principal difference between my understanding and theirs is my belief that Yeshua was and is the promised Messiah.

LEVINE: Would it then be correct to categorize you as a "Messianic Jew"?

STERLING: Sadly, no. Modern-day Messianic Judaism has become a microcosm of the Gentile Christian church where virtually every theological expression of Gentile Christianity can be found, from the most rigid fundamental conservative positions on one side to the most flamboyantly liberal on the other. Moreover, more than half of those who identify themselves with Messianic Judaism are Gentiles.

LEVINE: Is what you have just described the reason why you did not specifically seek certification as a Messianic Jewish Air Force chaplain?

STERLING: It would have been impossible for me to do so. Messianic Judaism is not a denomination—rather, it is a greatly diverse movement. The Lutheran synod that I represented fully understood my theological position and consequent denominational dilemma and still graciously endorsed, and sent me as an Air Force chaplain.

Levine: Do you now consider yourself to be a Lutheran or in any way officially affiliated with this Lutheran synod that sponsored your Air Force chaplaincy?

Sterling: No.

Levine: When and how did your relationship with this synod change?

Sterling: In January 1979, while I was assigned as the Air Forces Europe Command Chaplain, I was nominated to become the Deputy Chief of Air Force Chaplains and for promotion to brigadier general. While we were preparing to move to the Pentagon, we visited the German extermination camp at Dachau. This was such a spiritually overwhelming experience for me that for the first time in my life I fully understood what it meant to be a Jew. Thus I declined my promotion, retired from the Air Force, and made Aliyah. My affiliation with the sending Lutheran synod ended officially and completely upon my retirement. Again, my relationship with them from its outset was entirely and mutually a matter of convenience that allowed me to become an Air Force chaplain.

Levine: What did you claim to be your religion on your official written Ministry of the Interior application for Israeli citizenship?

Sterling: The simple truth as I understood it then and understand it now: Jewish.

Levine: During your official interview with a representative of the Ministry of the Interior when you applied for Israeli citizenship, were you asked anything further regarding your religion?

Sterling: I was asked if I had changed my religion.

Levine: How did you reply?

Sterling: With what I then believed in good faith and still believe in good faith to be the simple truth—no.

LEVINE: How and where did you and Carla practice your religion after you made Aliyah in early 1979?

STERLING: We investigated several different congregations in Tiberias and Haifa but never became members of any of them. Over the next twenty-nine years, off and on, we held weekly prayer meetings in our home. Then, in November 2008, we felt called to begin Kehilat Emet [Congregation of Truth].

LEVINE: How many people attended the prayer meetings you held in your home during your first twenty-nine years in Israel?

STERLING: Never more than twenty, probably an average of ten or so.

LEVINE: Were any of these attendees Jews whom you were attempting to convert to your faith in Yeshua?

STERLING *(genuinely amused)*: Heavens no! They were all already rock-solid believers, most of them Jewish, who came together to worship and pray.

LEVINE: How many Jews and Gentiles did you baptize during this twenty-nine-year period?

STERLING: No Jews, and only two Gentiles—old friends from the United States who wanted to be re-baptized in the Jordan River.

LEVINE: How many Jews and Gentiles have you baptized since you initiated Kehilat Emet some fourteen months ago?

STERLING: Around three hundred Jews and fewer than ten Gentiles.

LEVINE: To your knowledge, have you ever baptized or in any way sought to change the religion of a minor during your entire thirty-one years as a citizen of Israel?

STERLING: Absolutely not!

LEVINE: Was, as the State contends, your purpose in making Aliyah to convert other Jews to your faith in Yeshua?

STERLING: Absolutely not!

LEVINE: In summary, would you characterize yourself as a Christian missionary?

STERLING: No. In the strictest sense, I am neither a Christian nor a missionary. I do, however, among many other understandings, share with Christians the belief that Yeshua is the Messiah. Moreover, I do not actively seek to convert anyone to the faith I hold in Yeshua. I seek only to preach His gospel to any and all persons who attend the meetings of my congregation and who do so entirely of their own free will.

Levine: I have no further questions. Any re-cross, Mr. Ben Israel?

Ben Israel: No. I believe we have heard quite enough. The state calls the respondent Carla McKenzie Sterling.

Carla had hung on every word of Drew's testimony, knowing that she would be the next to run the State Attorney's tortuous gauntlet. She was therefore genuinely composed and poised to stand strong in sharing what she understood in her heart to be the entire truth as she was sworn and took her place in the witness chair.

Ben Israel: Mrs. Sterling, I will do my best to be as brief as possible. Did you make Aliyah with your husband some thirty-one years ago for the express purpose of converting Jews to your Christian faith?

C. Sterling: Certainly not! As my husband has already testified, we were not at all involved in active ministry for the first twenty-nine years of our residency in Israel.

Ben Israel: Mrs. Sterling, at any time prior to your Aliyah in early 1979 were you the president of the Ramstein Air Base Officers' Wives Club?

C. Sterling: Yes. I was elected to that office in May of 1978 and resigned just before we made Aliyah.

Ben Israel: Are you acquainted with the publication "Ramstein Officers' Wives News"? And more specifically with a column therein entitled Notes From the President?

C. Sterling: Yes, to both of your questions.

Ben Israel: Mrs. Sterling, are you now or were you at any time acquainted with one Patricia Anne Babcock?

C. Sterling: Yes. Pat Babcock followed me as president of the club. She and General Babcock had only been at Ramstein a short time before we left, so I didn't get to know her well.

Ben Israel *(handing Carla what appeared to be a copy of a several-page newsletter)*: Evidently, Mrs. Sterling, Patricia

Babcock knew you a lot better than you may think. I hand over to you a copy of the "Ramstein Officers' Wives Club News" dated April 20, 1979. Please turn to page two and read for us the first paragraph of the column entitled Notes from the President by Patricia Babcock.

C. STERLING *(visibly shocked and dismayed as she read)*: "We have just received exciting and encouraging news concerning our lovely past president, Carla Sterling, who recently shocked us all with her departure and Chaplain Colonel Sterling's retirement to take up their new role in Israel as Christian missionaries. Our sincere best wishes for their bountiful harvest of lost Jewish souls as they boldly take up their new calling on the Israeli mission field."

BEN ISRAEL: Thank you, Mrs. Sterling. Now, let's turn for a few moments to January 1979 when you and Rabbi Sterling applied for citizenship and were interviewed by a representative of the Ministry of the Interior. First, how did you respond to the written question "What is your religion?"

C. STERLING: To the best of my recollection, I responded Christian.

BEN ISRAEL: Did the representative of the Ministry of the Interior ask you any questions pursuant to this written assertion that you were a Christian?

C. STERLING: Yes. She asked me if I had changed my religion. I responded yes, that I practiced Judaism in the same manner as my husband. She then asked if I had converted to Orthodox Judaism, to which I responded no since my husband was not an Orthodox Jew.

BEN ISRAEL: Thank you, Mrs. Sterling. I have no further questions. Your witness, Mr. Levine.

Jerry approached his now visibly shaken client and momentarily placed a comforting hand on one of her shoulders.

LEVINE: Carla, at any time after you made Aliyah, did you communicate with Patricia Babcock or anyone else who might have reported information from or about you for publication in the "Ramstein Officers' Wives News?"

C. Sterling: No, I did not! I have no idea what Pat used as a source for this very false information about our reason for making Aliyah. I can only assume that she was either misinformed or more likely simply made this up when she heard through some unknown source that we had safely arrived in Israel.

Levine: Just one more question, Carla. With respect to your application and associated interview during your application for citizenship, did you in any way conceal the truth regarding your religious convictions at that time, and were the responses you made to the Ministry of the Interior representative of a true and good faith representation of your heartfelt convictions at that time?

C. Sterling: In all candor, Mr. Levine, my religious beliefs at the time of our Aliyah were and still remain identical with those of my husband. I fully subscribe to my husband's Jewish understandings and consider myself in a very real way to be his Ruth. Moreover, I have never been nor will I ever be a Christian missionary seeking to convert Jews to my own religious understandings.

Levine: Nothing further, Your Honor.

Chief Justice Bauerstein: Re-cross, Mr. Ben Israel?

Ben Israel: None, Your Honor.

Chief Justice Bauerstein: You may step down, Mrs. Sterling. Mr. Ben Israel, you may call your next witness.

Ben Israel: The state calls the respondent Hannah Meyers Silberman.

As she was seated and sworn to tell the truth, Hannah was spring-loaded to challenge this person whom, in her mind, she had just witnessed vilify the two remaining people in this world she held most dear, and she made no effort to conceal the deep hostility she felt toward him and the very situation that had brought them to this place.

Ben Israel: Mrs. Silberman, where did you reside during the year 1967?

Silberman: In a small apartment in Freising, Germany.

Ben Israel: Did you live there alone?

SILBERMAN: No, I shared the apartment with a fellow Auschwitz survivor, Rabbi Yakov Cohen. He was very ill.

BEN ISRAEL: What was your relationship with Rabbi Cohen?

SILBERMAN: I took care of him.

BEN ISRAEL *(snidely)*: Hmm, I see.

SILBERMAN *(deeply offended and lashing out)*: What's wrong with you? Have you no respect for the dead? No decency? I prepared his meals; washed his clothes; listened for endless hours while he read to me from the Tenach and the Talmud. He was like a father to me! I had no one else—they were all dead! That's it, period!

BEN ISRAEL: I'll ask the questions here, Mrs. Silberman. You answer them. Do you understand?

LEVINE: Objection! Your Honor, Counsel is on a fishing expedition. He is badgering the witness and looking for ways to demean her character.

CHIEF JUSTICE BAUERSTEIN: Overruled; however, Mr. Ben Israel, you are walking a very thin line here, and I urge you to stay on point. The witness will answer the question.

SILBERMAN: What question?

BEN ISRAEL: Never mind, let's move on. Hannah, may I call you Hannah?

SILBERMAN: No you may not. Only my friends call me Hannah, and others who wish me well. You are obviously neither.

BEN ISRAEL: Very well then, Mrs. Silberman, can you tell us why, as you testified, Rabbi Cohen, although he was extremely worn and ill, saw fit to spend what you characterized as endless hours reading to you from the Tenach and the Talmud?

SILBERMAN: I was brokenhearted, utterly destroyed. He was just trying to give me comfort in the only way he knew.

BEN ISRAEL: What was your religion during this time you were seeing to the needs of Rabbi Cohen?

SILBERMAN: I was born a Jew. I was a Jew in 1967. I still am a Jew, and I will always be a Jew! Nothing or no one can change the fact that God made me what I am—a Jew. Period!

Ben Israel: Tell us, Mrs. Silberman, did your Judaism and the counsel you received from Rabbi Cohen provide you with the comfort you told us you so deeply sought?

Silberman *(sadly, wiping away tears)*: No.

Ben Israel: Mrs. Silberman, was it this failure of your Judaism and Rabbi Cohen's counsel that led you to attend a Roman Catholic church in Freising over a period of several months?

Silberman: Perhaps. I was desperate, searching for God, looking for answers.

Ben Israel: Did you receive several weeks of detailed instruction about Roman Catholicism from a priest during this several months that you attended his church?

Silberman: Yes.

Ben Israel: Did you pray with him, confess your sins to him, and regularly attend mass over a period of several months, immediately before you made Aliyah?

Silberman: Yes.

Ben Israel: Was it during this time, before you made Aliyah, that you changed your religion?

Silberman: I have never changed my religion. I'm a Jew!

Ben Israel: Do you now accept the one who is known to Jews as Yeshu and to Messianic Jews as Yeshua as your personal Savior?

Silberman: Of course I do, and so should you! But I didn't find Him in a Catholic church in Freising Germany. I found Him right here in Israel, many years after I made Aliyah—praise His holy name! He has completely changed my life!

Ben Israel: Mrs. Hannah Meyers Silberman, I am sorry to inform you that according to Supreme Court precedents, you are no longer a Jew. Moreover, I must ask—

Hannah jumped to her feet, cutting off her interrogator and shouting back in a voice that sounded like the screaming protest of a wounded animal.

Silberman: Not a Jew! *Not a Jew!* NO LONGER A JEW! Where were you, Natan Ben Israel, attorney for the Devil? Where were you when they gassed and burned my beloved Michael and my blessed parents? Where were you when they took away my innocence, raped me, sterilized me, then made me a sex slave for their elite SS officers?

NO LONGER A JEW? *(Shouting from the depths of her deeply wounded soul, she defiantly and deliberately rolls up the left sleeve of her dark-colored blouse, revealing the purple tattoo indelibly etched into the flesh of her upper arm.)* NO LONGER A JEW? You poor, ignorant excuse for an agent of the Jewish people! If I am no longer a Jew, would you most kindly remove this brand to the contrary, dot by dot, just the way it was burned into my flesh? Here it is! *(She points with her right hand, just under Natan Ben Israel's nose.)* Take it away one dot at a time, A-2-5-2-3-2!

BEN ISRAEL *(strenuously protesting)*: Your Honor! I implore you to restore order to these proceedings and to compel the witness to take her seat! I have no more questions for her!

The genuinely Honorable Chief Justice Bauerstein, who had instinctively allowed Hannah to have her say, now pounded his gavel.

CHIEF JUSTICE BAUERSTEIN *(gently)*: The respondent will return to the witness chair and remain silent. Mrs. Silberman, the court will not tolerate any further outbursts of this nature. *(Hannah immediately returns to the witness chair.)* Mr. Levine, you may cross-examine this witness.

LEVINE: I believe that this witness has already told the court all that any of us need to hear. I have no further questions for Mrs. Silberman.

CHIEF JUSTICE BAUERSTEIN: You may call your next witness, Mr. Ben Israel.

The state's attorney was visibly shaken and still struggling to regain his composure.

BEN ISRAEL: Your Honor, the state rests.

CHIEF JUSTICE BAUERSTEIN: Very well. The court will stand adjourned until nine o'clock tomorrow morning when we will call on Mr. Levine to present the substance of his clients' response.

Chapter 24
Hannah's Story
Jerusalem
(Supreme Court of the State of Israel: Wednesday, January 13, 2010)

The Trial: Fourth Hearing

Chief Justice Bauerstein seemed especially buoyant as he officially gaveled open the morning's proceedings after he and the other four justices had taken their places.

> Chief Justice Bauerstein: Good morning, everyone! Mr. Levine, you may call your first witness.
>
> Levine: Thank you, Your Honor. The respondents call Rabbi Doctor Yonah Reiner, Rosh Yeshiva [Dean] of Yeshiva Eretz Ha Israel, Jerusalem.

The witness, in both appearance and bearing, looked every bit a caricature of an American Santa Claus, with the notable differences being his obviously expensive hand-tailored black suit, white silk shirt, and broad-brimmed black hat that had replaced the traditional bright red, white-fur-trimmed jumpsuit and stocking cap of the legendary character. It was Rosh Reiner's very full waist-length snow-white beard and genuinely jolly countenance, however, that made the comparison irresistible.

He looked about the courtroom and smiled infectiously at everyone present as he was seated and sworn.

> Levine: Rabbi Reiner. I would like to thank you very much for being with us this morning. It is certainly an honor for us to have a Talmudic scholar of your prominence who is both able and willing to share your expert testimony in this very important matter.
>
> Reiner *(with genuine humility)*: You are far too kind.

LEVINE: I think not. Putting your modesty aside, Rabbi Reiner, isn't it so that you are widely considered one of the world's top five Talmudic scholars? Isn't it also true that you are the highly respected rosh yeshiva of the oldest, largest, and universally respected orthodox yeshiva in Israel?

REINER *(smiling broadly)*: If you insist on putting it that way, I am forced to plead guilty on both counts.

LEVINE: Rabbi Reiner, first, I would like to explore with you the sometimes difficult question of who or what modern-day people are the rightful heirs to Eretz Israel.

REINER: You needn't go any further on this point, Counsel. And for that matter, you certainly don't need a Talmudic scholar to answer such a question that should be on the lips of every Jew who has read the Torah, much less the Talmud. The Torah teaches us specifically that the Land was forever covenanted by our Creator, in turn first to Abram, then to Isaac, and finally to Yakov and all of his successive descendants. While Yakov had twelve sons, one of whom was Judah, who was the first Jew, all of the descendants of Yakov early on came to be known as Jews; hence, all of Yakov's descendants were and are Jews. Moreover, Eretz Israel has eternally been granted by the Lord God of Israel as the inheritance of the Jews. The Land and the Jews who inherited this great gift as an everlasting covenant are inexorably bound together in an inseparable eternal relationship. In a very real sense, the Land of Israel and the Jewish nation are one. What constitutes the Jewish nation—those chosen of God, the Jewish people—all Jews.

LEVINE: Thank you, sir. Now, Rabbi Reiner, would you please tell us by what means Isaac and Yakov became the descendants of Abram, who was renamed Abraham, and by what means each succeeding generation of Jews have in turn been the inheritors of the Land of Israel as it was originally covenanted by the Lord God of Israel to Abram?

REINER *(following a loud Santa-like guffaw)*: By what means? A Talmudic scholar you don't need to answer such a question.

Maybe you should ask a sex education teacher like the one I have on my staff to educate my yeshiva boys in such matters.

Levine *(struggling to suppress his own amusement)*: Let me be more specific. Since Judah was technically the first Jew, how and when did it come to pass that the descendants of his brothers, that is, all the sons of Yakov, were also collectively considered to be Jews?

Reiner: According to the Torah, the tribe of Judah consisted of descendants of Judah, who was the son of Jacob and of Leah; however, it is an historical fact accepted by most Hebrew scholars that after the dissolution of the United Kingdom of Israel in about 930 BCE, all descendants of Yakov became known as Jews.

Levine: Rabbi Reiner, prior to the second century CE, a person's individual identity of Jewishness was passed from father to son; that is, by paternal descent. Is that not correct?

Reiner: Yes, Counselor. You have been doing your homework.

Levine: How is it, then, that around 70 CE the establishment of one's individual Jewish identity suddenly changed from paternal to maternal descent; that is, Jewish identity was henceforth passed on by one's Jewish mother rather than father?

Reiner: Ah, at last we are getting into my area of expertise. I'm sure you know that the Sanhedrin moved from Jerusalem to Yavne soon after the destruction of the Temple in 70. One of the top priorities for those rabbis was this issue of paternal versus maternal descent. Thus, the short answer to your question is that those rabbis decided, for reasons of their own, to change the passing on of Jewish identity from one's father to one's mother. They then memorialized this change in the Mishna, which was finally redacted in 220.

Levine: Bear with me, Rabbi Reiner. All of this begs several more questions. First, from a sectarian perspective, who were these rabbis you speak of: Pharisees, Sadducees, or Essenes?

Reiner: They were Pharisees, of course. The Sadducees became virtually nonexistent after the destruction of the temple. And the Essenes had mostly become members of a new sect known as the Way, who were the progenitors of what we know today as Christianity.

LEVINE: Is it fair to say that modern-day rabbinical Judaism evolved from the understandings of the Pharisees?

REINER: Certainly. But one must also consider that each generation of rabbis in one way or another has made additions and changes to these original Pharisaic understandings. Thus, we have had a number of evolutions of the Talmud along with the other commentaries, which are collectively known as the Oral Torah, or Oral Law.

LEVINE: Rabbi Reiner, is it also fair to say that both the written Torah and the Oral Torah are the basis of halakhah; that is, they are equally the foundation of binding Jewish law?

REINER: Absolutely.

LEVINE: Earlier we showed that the written Torah determined that one's Jewishness was established through paternal descent. Then, in redacting the Oral Torah, the rabbis changed this determination of one's Jewishness from paternal to maternal descent. Is that correct?

REINER: Yes. Rabbi Akiva developed an elaborate system of biblical interpretation based upon relative priorities that established rabbinical authority to make such changes. You must remember, the written Torah was scribed by the hand of God, but the world in which it lives is ever changing. Thus, while the written Torah may not speak directly to contemporary circumstances, the Oral Torah can be made to do so through rabbinical wisdom.

LEVINE: Let me get this right, Rabbi Reiner. Are you saying that the rabbis have the authority to change the written halakhah, that is to say, to change the written word of God?

REINER: In the strictest sense, that is correct, but this subject is not at all simple and deserves much study and discussion. This is one of the reasons why we have yeshivas, and many, like I, spend most of their lives studying the Talmud.

LEVINE: OK, Rabbi Reiner, if I may sum up this point, would you agree that today, one's Jewishness is determined strictly and exclusively by the Jewishness of one's mother?

Reiner: Yes.

Levine: Then, this is a matter of biological inheritance. Jewish ethnicity that flows from one's mother is a virtual physical part of one's being, something that can be pointed to in one's DNA?

Reiner: Yes. But DNA science has only just begun to make this Jewish identity possible. For example, the Cohens have a unique and clearly identifiable characteristic that can be pointed to in the DNA. But this is not yet so with the other tribes. However, two recent genome [chromosome] studies, the most compelling by researchers at New York's Albert Einstein College of Medicine, found that the Jewish people—long called the "People of the Book," the "Chosen People," or, in unkind circles, "those people"—are, indeed, a people after all. At long last science can say with assurance what we Jews have known all along in our hearts: The Jewish people are one people with a common genetic thread that evolved in the second or third century BC.[1]

Levine: Rabbi Reiner, can you tell us, does a Gentile convert to Judaism also become a Jew in this physical, ethnic sense?

Reiner: Of course not, but even so, according to halakhah a convert to Judaism is considered to be religiously just as Jewish as one who was born of a Jewish mother. Moreover, the offspring of such a Jewish convert are then considered in every way to be just as Jewish as the offspring of one who was born of a Jewish mother.

Levine: This leads to my next question. Rabbi Reiner, is there any way such a Jew born of a Jewish or converted Gentile mother can cast off—that is, utterly renounce—their ethnic Jewish identity?

Reiner: Absolutely not. Halakhah unequivocally establishes that there is no way that a Jew, including converts to Judaism, can voluntarily give up their Jewishness or by any other means cease to be Jews. The principle of "once a Jew, always a Jew" is clearly etched in the heart of legalistic Jewish ordinances. *(Referring to a small notebook he had up to now left unopened)* Counselor, I anticipated you would examine me on this point. Let me say that I am in complete agreement with several justices at the highest level of the rabbinic court who have ruled that a conversion to Judaism can never be annulled. According to a decision of Justices Brali, Tzarfati, and Bass:

"In the world of Hebrew jurisprudence there is no force capable of changing a Jew...into a gentile. Even if the Jew were to desire this, and even if every Christian priest in the world were to baptize such Jew into Christianity, he would remain a Jew. Moreover, if a convert to Judaism wishes to deny his Judaism, he will not be able to do so and return to his previous faith. He is and will always remain a Jew, and there is no way in the world to take this away from him."[2]

Moreover, the Talmud established this same truth of "once a Jew, always a Jew." We read in Sanhedrin 44a: "Israel hath sinned. R. Abba b. Zabda said: Even though [the people] have sinned, they are still [called] 'Israel.' R. Abba said: Thus people say, A myrtle, though it stands among reeds, is still a myrtle, and it is so called."

The rabbis are showing us here that nothing can change the physical nature, the very identity of a myrtle tree standing among reeds, anymore than any action of men, self-action, or the action of others can change the Jewish identity of a Jew.

LEVINE: Thank you, Rabbi Reiner, for making it perfectly clear that both the rabbinical courts and the Talmud establish as halakhah the long-understood principle "once a Jew, always a Jew." There is just one thing, however, that makes this understanding something less than clear. Rabbi Reiner, can you tell us briefly, who was Rabbi Moses Maimonides, also known as Rabbi Moshe ben Maimon or Rambam, and what was his importance?

REINER *(chuckling)*: Ah! So that is where you are going with this. OK. As I'm sure most Jews know, Rambam was the preeminent medieval Jewish philosopher. He died in Spain in December 1204. In my view, his greatest contribution was his fourteen-volume Mishneh Torah, a mighty foundational work that even today retains its canonical authority as a codification of all Talmudic law. Of perhaps equal importance are Rambam's "Thirteen Articles of the Jewish Faith," which were formulated in his commentary on the Mishnah. The fact is, Rambam's works and views remain the very cornerstone of Jewish thought and study.

LEVINE: You mention Rambam's thirteen articles, Rabbi Reiner. Can you say if any of these thirteen are what one might call lines in the sand as they might pertain to Christianity in general and the case before this court in particular?

REINER: I would say that two of his articles, the second and the third, relate more to Christianity in general than to this case in particular. Rambam's second article, "God is one and unique," would seem to argue against the possibility of a triune Godhead. His third, "God is incorporeal," would argue against the Christian understanding that Yeshua was both God and man.

LEVINE: Rabbi Reiner, with respect to Rambam's second article, isn't it true that the triune nature of the Godhead was a well-established Jewish understanding that was widely taught during the first temple period and remains one of the foundations of modern-day kabbalistic understanding? And is it not true that kabbalism is generally understood to be a mainstream part of modern-day Orthodox Judaism?

REINER: Yes, on both counts.

LEVINE: Wouldn't Rambam's second article then be in direct contradiction to both ancient and modern-day kabbalistic understanding?

REINER: It would seem so.

LEVINE: Then let's move on just a bit further. Please tell us, Rabbi Reiner, to the best of your knowledge did Rambam have any thoughts relative to the immutability of Jewish identity?

REINER: He certainly did! In his Mishneh Torah, he made it clear that any Jew who embraces Yeshu is no longer a Jew.[3]

LEVINE: Is Rambam alone in maintaining this position that seems to be in conflict with both the Torah and the Talmud?

REINER: Heavens no! Many Jewish authorities embrace Rambam's position, as, of course, does the Minister of Interior, which makes it Rambam's view upon which Israeli law is founded. And there are others; for example, two former chief rabbis of Israel, Rabbi I. M. Lau and Rabbi E. Bakshi-Doron, issued a proclamation in 1998 that said in part:

"There are Christian groups that call themselves 'Messianic Jews' whose faith is totally alien to the Jewish faith, and members of these groups who were born to Jewish parents have a status of apostates who removed themselves from the Jewish Nation. They are Christians in every way—the minute they believe in Jesus—even if they don't officially join another faith."

(Consulting his notes once more) Moreover, Counsel, even Jews for Judaism, an international organization which counters so-called missionaries, states emphatically: "A Jew who believes in Jesus as his/her 'Lord and Savior' has become a Christian. Even if not a formal member of a church group that person is a Christian theologically. The Talmud (Sanhedrin 44a) recognizes the biologic link to the Jewish people as inviolate, but also recognizes that as long as one remains an apostate one is not considered to be part of the Jewish community. A willing convert, whether formally or informally, forfeits his/her legal and social rights, which express a Jew's belonging to the Jewish people."

LEVINE: Thank you, Rabbi Reiner. If I may summarize where we have gone with your most interesting testimony: First, we demonstrated that the Torah, the Word of God, according to Judaism, clearly associates Eretz Israel with the paternal descendants of Yakov. Hence, modern-day Jews who are able to demonstrate their Jewish ethnicity are the rightful heirs of the Land.

Next, we found that during the first century, around the year 70, the rabbis, specifically Rabbi Akiva, changed the determination of who is a Jew and with it the matter of who is entitled to inherit the Land from paternal to maternal descendancy. Perhaps more importantly, Rabbi Akiva and others of the Sanhedrin, concurrently with the foregoing, established the principle that the rabbis have the authority to give precedence to the "Oral Torah" over the "Written Torah" in instances that better meet their own learned understanding. Rambam further developed and codified this qualified precedent of the Oral Torah in his landmark Mishneh Torah, which is the central authority for modern-day Talmudic understanding and study.

Rabbi Reiner, does this provide a correct summary of your testimony here today?

REINER: Yes, Counsel, I would say that it does.

LEVINE: Just one more question before I let you go, Rabbi Reiner. We have seen that there are clear conflicts between the teachings of the Torah and the Talmud, and also that there are contradictions within the Talmud itself; for example I cite Rambam's determination that a Jew who embraces Yeshua is no longer a Jew versus the Talmud Tractate Sanhedrin 44a, which recognizes the biologic link to the Jewish people as inviolate. Rabbi Reiner, I ask you now for your own personal assessment based upon your internationally acknowledged standing as probably the world's leading Talmudic scholar. In such instances where either side can be pointed to by its champions as correct—when we have such a conflict as in fact we frequently encounter—how can we determine which side provides the correct determination?

REINER: This seeming enigma is really simpler to explain than it would first appear *(pausing for a few moments, then seeming to address the entire world of Judaism beyond the courtroom where he stood)*. The fact is, in most cases both sides are correct and acceptable. For example, the Talmud shows us in intricate detail several different ways to properly brew a cup of tea, each of them in conformance with halakhah and each of them written by a different rabbi, each in his own generation. In reality, then, any of these methods are the "correct" way. It is simply a matter, so to speak, of how you like your cup of tea.

And before you interrupt, Counsel, let me answer your next question before you ask it. In my, as you say, learned opinion, a Jew who is born of a Jewish mother is a Jew, and nothing can change this person's Jewishness—not the Minister of Interior, not this court, no one, nor anything. However, before you get too excited about what I have just said, let me also say that Rabbi Akiva, Rambam, and the modern-day Minister of Interior are equally correct when they say that a Jew who embraces Yeshua is no longer religiously Jewish and therefore not entitled to continue as a member of the Jewish community.

If what I have just testified sounds to be on its face a self-contradiction, let me quickly agree that indeed it is such. Let me put it another way: Golda Meir didn't have a strong preference one way or the other how her cup of tea was to be brewed, while her Minister of Interior at the time had a very strong preference indeed. That they were able to sit down together and partake of his selection is a testimony to the continuing survival of the State of Israel.

LEVINE: I have no further questions for this witness. Your witness, Mr. Ben Israel.

BEN ISRAEL: If it please the court, Your Honor, I find that the witness for the respondents is most compelling and interesting, even entertaining, but that his testimony was totally irrelevant to the matter before the court. We are not concerned with the disposition between the Torah and the Talmud. We are concerned with the simple issue of the respondents' violation of the laws of the State of Israel: nothing more, nothing less. I therefore have no questions for this witness.

CHIEF JUSTICE BAUERSTEIN: Very well, the witness may step down. Mr. Levine, do you have another witness?

LEVINE: Indeed, Your Honor. I have only just begun.

CHIEF JUSTICE BAUERSTEIN: So be it. The court will stand in recess for two hours. Mr. Levine, please be ready to proceed at two o'clock, immediately following this recess.

LEVINE: I shall be, Your Honor.

A hush of anticipation that had been present throughout these entire proceedings once again fell over the crowded court room as the five justices returned and took their places on the upper podium following the two-hour recess.

Chief Justice Bauerstein: Mr. Levine, you may call your next witness.

Levine: Thank you, Your Honor. The respondents call Rabbi Irving Berger.

With that the middle-aged, inordinately tall, and unhealthily thin-appearing witness was sworn and took his place in the witness chair, which could have simultaneously accommodated a second person of his same stature.

Levine: Thank you for being with us today, Rabbi Berger. I'm told that congratulations are in order regarding your Aliyah. Just how long have you been a citizen of Israel?

Berger: For all of one week. My wife and our two children and I are so excited about taking up our biblical inheritance we can hardly sleep at night!

Levine: From where did you make Aliyah, Rabbi?

Berger: From Miami. I was the cantor in one of the largest congregations in the city.

Levine: What kind of congregation is this, Rabbi?

Berger: Our former congregation is Chabad-Lubavitch.

Levine: Did you then and/or do you now have a personal position regarding the Lubavitcher "Rebbe," Rabbi Menachem M. Schneerson, who departed this earth in 1994?

Berger: Certainly! I personally hold and teach that "Rebbe," as we call him, is the Messiah of Israel who will one day be resurrected from the dead and return to the earth to take up his holy position among us.

LEVINE: Do you intend to teach this understanding to children under the age of eighteen in your new congregation here in Israel?

BERGER: Of course. This understanding is very central to our entire belief system.

LEVINE: When you made Aliyah, Rabbi, did you have an interview with a clerk from the Israeli Ministry of the Interior?

BERGER: Of course. That is required.

LEVINE: Did the clerk who interviewed you ask you anything about your theological understandings?

BERGER: As a matter of fact, this young woman was very curious about the Lubavitcher movement and was at the time of our interview considering joining it herself. We therefore briefly discussed all of our major understandings.

LEVINE: Did these discussions include your belief that Rebbe, as you call him, is the Messiah who will soon return?

BERGER: Of course; this is what she was so excited about.

LEVINE: Thank you, Rabbi. Your witness, Mr. Ben Israel.

BEN ISRAEL: I have no questions for this witness, Your Honor.

CHIEF JUSTICE BAUERSTEIN: The witness may step down. You may call your next witness, Mr. Levine.

LEVINE: The respondents call Astik Ahluwalia.

The tall, medium-build, brown-skinned witness walked slowly to the front of the courtroom. He was dressed in an expensive, hand-woven dhoti, the traditional Hindu apparel for men that consisted of a long, unstitched cloth wound about the lower part of his body that passed between his legs and was tucked in at the waist. He also wore a large, beautifully made, matching turban. He spoke in impeccable, heavily Indian-accented English.

LEVINE: Thank you so much, Mr. Ahluwalia, for taking the time to be with us here today. I won't keep you long, but I do have some very important questions to ask. First, when did you make Aliyah, and why did you do so?

AHLUWALIA: I am a Jew by birth. I have been able to trace the Jewish roots of my family on both sides for six generations, a heritage we are very proud to share with our Israeli brethren. I made Aliyah with my wife and five children one month ago, and we now live in a community of other Indian-rooted olim in Haifa.

Levine: Did you apply for your Aliyah in India or in Israel?

Ahluwalia: It was much more convenient to do so in New Delhi where we lived. We were interviewed there by a representative of the Israeli Ministry of the Interior.

Levine: Were you clad in the same type Hindi sect clothing at the time you met with this representative?

Ahluwalia: Yes, I was. And, may I respectfully correct you, the clothing I am wearing is worn by the Hindi, but they generally do not wear turbans. Sikhism is another religion which was created out of the Hindu religion. This is my religion, and we always wear turbans.

Levine: Did the representative with whom you met ask you if you had changed your religion?

Ahluwalia: No. He is also Indian, and my adherence to Sikhism would have been obvious to him by the nature of my dress.

Levine: Did you have any problem whatsoever getting Israeli citizenship approved for yourself and for the members of your immediate family?

Ahluwalia: None whatsoever.

Levine: Thank you, Mr. Ahluwalia; I have no further questions. Your witness, Mr. Ben Israel.

Ben Israel: The state has no questions for this witness.

Chief Justice Bauerstein: You may step down, Mr. Ahluwalia. Mr. Levine, you may call your next witness.

Levine: The respondents call Michael Hirschberg.

Michael Hirschberg, in his early thirties, of medium stature, dark complexioned, casually dressed, and wearing thick horn-rimmed glasses, seemed every bit a stereotypical Ashkenazi-rooted Jew as he moved toward the front of the courtroom, was sworn, then took his place in the witness chair. He spoke in heavily New York–accented English.

Levine: Mr. Hirschberg, would you please tell the court from where and when you made Aliyah.

HIRSCHBERG: I began the process eight months ago at the American embassy in Bangkok, Thailand. Then I came to Jerusalem on a tourist visa, where, six months ago, I became a proud dual citizen of Israel and the United States.

LEVINE: How did you happen to be in Thailand, and how long had you resided there before you began your Aliyah process?

HIRSCHBERG: I am the only child of two secular Jewish parents. While I was religiously circumcised on the eighth day of my life, that's as far as my religious training at home went since my parents were trying very hard to be totally assimilated into the Gentile world in which we lived and did not want in any way to advertise our Jewish heritage.

The fact is, as a young teenager I felt very empty spiritually and very quietly began to search for God and how I might best come to know Him personally. To make a long story short, many of my friends were very attracted to Buddhism, and through their witness I became fascinated by the teachings of this religion. Consequently I decided to move to Thailand in 1996 when I was twenty years old. I did this because nearly all Thais are Buddhists.

LEVINE: Did you formally become a practicing Buddhist in Thailand?

HIRSCHBERG: Oh yes! I needed to do this to satisfy my future Thai wife's very religious family. We were married in Bangkok in 1998. The two of us and our now nine-year-old son made Aliyah as a family.

LEVINE: What motivated you to make Aliyah?

HIRSCHBERG: Two things, really. First, I am a recognized expert on some very specialized high-tech devices, and a company in Israel that needed a person with this expertise made me a very attractive offer that I simply couldn't refuse.

Moreover, as I have become more mature spiritually, I now treasure my Jewish heritage as a precious underpinning of my Buddhist faith. I want to live my life within this heritage and raise my son to do the same.

LEVINE: Did any Israeli official question you about your adherence to Buddhism at any point during your Aliyah process?

Hirschberg *(genuinely surprised by the question)*: No, why would they? There are many Jews in Israel who are practicing Buddhists. I find that one of the great charms of this Land of my inheritance is that its citizens have freedom of religion.

Levine: Thank you, Mr. Hirschberg; I have no further questions. Your witness, Mr. Ben Israel.

Ben Israel: Your Honor, I have no questions for this witness.

Chief Justice Bauerstein: You may step down, Mr. Hirschberg. Mr. Levine, you may call your next witness.

Levine: Thank you, Your Honor. The respondents call Berihun Fedadu.

Berihun Fedadu, unlike the previous witness, was, in appearance anything but a stereotypical Jew. From his very tall and thin frame, overly long arms to his medium chocolate-colored skin, the only thing seemingly Jewish about him was the seemingly incongruous white skull cap that covered a good part of his oblong-shaped, tight-curled covered head. Even more glaringly non-Jewish stereotypical were the large tattooed taws (equilateral crosses) that dominated each of his cheeks and several other smaller versions of this very early Jewish Christian symbol that were permanently displayed on both sides of his longish neck. When he spoke, he did so in precise Oxford-accented English.

Levine: Good day, Mr. Fedadu. It is so good to have you with us today. Would you please tell the court briefly your citizenship status, how and why you came to Israel, and how long you have resided here in the Land?

Fedadu: Certainly, Mr. Levine. As you can see by my appearance, I am a Falash Mura Ethiopian. I was privileged to be the son of a prominent family in Addis Ababa who had the means to see to my receiving the finest education. I earned my doctorate at Oxford in 2000 and returned to the University of Addis Ababa, where I became a professor of English.

As I am sure you must be aware, while the State of Israel has been most generous in bringing my fellow Falash Mura to the Land, even so, my people have had an inordinately difficult time becoming integrated into the Israeli society. A number of factors have contributed to their very desperate situation, not the least of which has been racial discrimination accompanied by their general lack of both technical and language skills. Consequently, their unemployment rate remains high, and the wages of those who find employment are relatively low. The result of all of this is that 45 percent of these dear people are unable to afford even the most basic requirements for a normal life and thus continue to be marginally supported by the government.

Mr. Levine, as an Ethiopian Jew with the capability to help alleviate the plight of my people in Israel, I felt compelled to make Aliyah, which I finally concluded in 2005, three years after I initiated the process. I am now teaching English to these hurting new Israelis through several different government-sponsored programs.

LEVINE: Mr.—I should say, Dr. Fedadu, what factor or factors caused you to take such a relatively long time to conclude your Aliyah?

FEDADU: Like all Falash Mura, my ethnic roots are Jewish, but for many generations my family was members of the Ethiopian Orthodox Church. As you may have noticed, my face was tattooed with ancient Christian symbols when I was a young boy in order to mark my religious heritage. Thus, the government of Israel insisted that I undergo a lengthy conversion process to Orthodox Judaism as a part of my Aliyah process.

LEVINE: May I ask a very personal question, Dr. Fedadu, that you may choose not to answer as you may desire—how would you describe your religious convictions today?

FEDADU: Officially I underwent the conversion process, and I am an Orthodox Jew. Spiritually, in my heart, I remain otherwise.

LEVINE: Thank you, Dr. Fedadu, I have no further questions. Your witness, Mr. Ben Israel.

BEN ISRAEL: Yes, Dr. Fedadu, with respect to your present religious convictions, when you just said that they remain "otherwise," did you mean for us to infer that you have remained a Christian?

Fedadu: Mr. Ben Israel, let me respond to your question rhetorically. If you were in my place, being questioned by a representative of the state, how would you respond?

Ben Israel *(turning to the bench for assistance)*: Your Honor, the witness' reply is unresponsive.

Chief Justice Bauerstein: Mr. Ben Israel, may I remind you that the witness is not on trial?

Ben Israel: Of course not, Your Honor, but Mr. Levine opened the door to this line of questioning.

Chief Justice Bauerstein: Indeed he did, Mr. Ben Israel. Dr. Fedadu, you will answer the question.

Fedadu *(toying with the process)*: What question was that?

Ben Israel *(belligerently)*: I'll rephrase! Let me put this to you as simply as I am able. Are you still a Christian?

Fedadu *(delighting in the moment)*: Let me respond as simply as I am able, under the present circumstances. Of course not! How could you ever even think such a thing?

Ben Israel: Nothing further.

Chief Justice Bauerstein: The witness may step down. You may call your next witness, Mr. Levine.

Levine: The respondents call Henry Friedman.

Henry Friedman gave the immediate impression of one at perpetual peace, unsullied, and unbowed by the things of this world. Beyond this, even as he was sworn and took his place in the witness chair, he exuded a sense of deep caring—indeed, his genuine acceptance of every person within his personal reach, anyone whom he might in some way touch.

Levine: Mr. Friedman, would you please tell us your nationality and how you happen to be in Israel at this time?

Friedman: I'm a native born American, Mr. Levine. My wife, Sylvia, our son, Josh, and I just happen to be here for our one-month annual visit to the Land of our inheritance. Your staff was quite efficient in discovering our presence, and of course, I agreed to appear here on behalf of the respondents.

Levine: Mr. Friedman, have you ever applied to make Aliyah?

Friedman: Yes, twice. We were rejected in both instances.

LEVINE: Mr. Friedman, would you please give the court a brief overview of your efforts to make Aliyah, and on what basis you and your family were rejected from achieving this status or any status other than your right to visit Israel as "tourists"?

FRIEDMAN: Quite frankly, Sylvia and I were saved in a Messianic congregation in Maryland in the summer of 2000. Before this life-changing experience, we were members of a very large Reform congregation in Baltimore.

I got a great job with Hughes Aerospace in 1998, right after I graduated from MIT, and my career was really taking off about the time we found the Lord. Anyway, both Sylvia and I can trace our entirely Jewish backgrounds for several generations back to Europe, and the more we relished in who and what we had become in Yeshua, the more we began to feel a deep and persistent supernatural calling to drop everything and make Aliyah.

LEVINE: How did you act upon this compelling, supernatural calling?

FRIEDMAN: It seemed that God acted for us! Right out of the clear blue sky I got a phone call from David Adams, the CEO and president of Megatronics, Ltd. in Haifa, who was recruiting engineers and had somehow gotten my name. Anyway, he made me an offer I couldn't refuse. Then, after Sylvia excitedly agreed, I accepted his offer, and we began the Aliyah process.

LEVINE: Just what did that entail?

FRIEDMAN: Well, it seemed only natural that we should go to the Israeli Consulate in Baltimore and fill out the necessary paperwork, so we did. We were then directed to an in-house representative of the Ministry of the Interior who began, to our surprise, what seemed to be a very aggressive interrogation, as if we had something to hide. This, of course, was after we had presented him with solid proof of our Jewishness on both sides of our two families for several generations.

LEVINE: Were there any obvious sticking points during this interrogation?

Friedman: Yes! There were two. We were asked how I planned to make a living in Israel, and I immediately told him of my attractive offer from Megatronics. That was really the end of it, right then and there! At the time we were too naïve and didn't have a clue that we had just blown any opportunity to make Aliyah, then or ever. This, of course, was only for a moment when our interrogator came right back with the question "Did you know that Megatronics is a Christian company whose many employees are missionaries who use this company as a front—as a means to sustain themselves in Israel?"

Since David Adams had not made any mention of his own Christian faith or that it was shared by most of his employees, I was quite taken aback by this revelation, and I told him that this was the first I had heard of this situation.

In any event, the die was cast at that point when he then flatly accused us both of being missionaries, as evidenced by my intention to work for Megatronics, but also by the testimony of a mole who had been planted in our Messianic congregation and who had reported about our so-called religious conversion.

Levine: Did you give up your aspirations to make Aliyah then and there?

Friedman: Oh no! We figured that there was likely little if any communication between the Baltimore consulate and the Ministry of the Interior in Israel, so we made our way to Tiberias. This lovely little city seemed to be more or less out of the way, so we applied for Aliyah at the local Ministry of the Interior office. I must say, we were greatly surprised and saddened to learn that modern technology had found its way into the operation of matters pertaining to Aliyah, and we were, as we were told, "in the computer" and hence again flatly rejected on the spot.

And so, Mr. Levine, we have had only one way to at least touch our inheritance, and that is by spending one month each year here in the Land as tourists. Moreover, when all of this fell apart, I returned to Hughes Aerospace, who has been most gracious to assign me to two ongoing small contracts we have with the IDF that allow me to make several business trips here each year. This is not by any means an ideal arrangement, but the Ministry of the Interior has been unable to change our hearts. Nothing has changed regarding our calling to take up our inheritance, and every precious minute we can spend here in the Land is to us a great and wonderful blessing.

LEVINE: Thank you, Mr. Friedman. No further questions. Your witness, Mr. Ben Israel.

BEN ISRAEL *(accusingly)*: That was a very touching account, Mr. Friedman, but like any other democracy, Israel is a nation of laws. When obedience or disobedience to such laws becomes a question before this or any court, then emotions, however compelling, must take a backseat to the matter of law. Wouldn't you agree?

FRIEDMAN: Of course. I can assure you, Mr. Ben Israel, it wasn't my intention to bare my emotions before this court but rather to give a factual and objective account of the things my family and I have experienced while attempting to become citizens of Israel—nothing more, nothing less.

BEN ISRAEL: Mr. Friedman, let me get right to the point. Did you or did you not change your religion prior to making application for Aliyah?

FRIEDMAN: No. I have always been a Jew. I simply discovered by divine revelation that Yeshua is the Messiah that my Reform Jewish brothers are still looking for but have not yet found. Absolutely nothing else has changed in my walk with God. We worship the Lord God of Israel, we keep the feasts, we relish in our Jewish traditions, our son will be bar mitzvahed next year in a traditional Jewish ceremony—

NATAN *(cutting off the witness)*: What do you say, Mr. Friedman, to the inarguable fact that the law of Israel holds that you are no longer a Jew?

FRIEDMAN: I hold, without hostility, that the law has nothing to do with Judaism and everything to do with corrupt politics! It is blatantly prejudicial and misguided, and it must be changed! It is sheer nonsense to declare that my Jewish DNA of many generations standing has suddenly ceased to exist simply because of my spiritual understanding that Yeshua is the Messiah.

Ben Israel: No further questions.

Levine *(with resolve)*: Your Honor, the respondents rest.

Chief Justice Bauerstein: Very well, the witness may step down. This court stands adjourned until tomorrow morning at nine o'clock, when we will hear your closing statements.

Chapter 25
Hannah's Story
Jerusalem
(Supreme Court of the State of Israel: Thursday, January 14, 2010)

The Trial: Fifth Hearing

Chief Justice Marcus Bauerstein greeted his packed courtroom after he and the other four justices had once again taken their places.

Chief Justice Bauerstein: Good morning, everyone. The court will now hear the respondents' closing statements. Mr. Levine, are you ready to proceed?

Levine *(exuding confidence)*: I am, Your Honor.

Your Honor, the glaring reality—the very fact that these three devoted, law-abiding citizens of the State of Israel should be standing here before this court of last appeal, pleading for their right to dwell as citizens in the Land of their inheritance in peace, privacy, and under the full and equal protection of the law is indeed a great tragedy. Even more, however, their presence before this court is an undeniable manifestation of the state's long-standing discriminatory denial of the inalienable human rights of some of its Jewish citizens based solely upon their religious worldview.

Today, the government of Israel stands tragically transformed by religious extremism into a myth, a mere shadow of what those who trade on dreams and wishful imaginations blindly perceive to be a genuine Western-style democracy. Your Honor, the State of Israel's place in the world as a democracy in the Middle East is compromised by the imbalance of power between its three branches of government and the vast power of the Minister of Interior.

Moreover, Your Honor, I quote from the current Netanyahu government coalition agreement between the near majority Likud and the Orthodox religious Shas parties under the section entitled "Religion and State," which reads in part: "The government will look into the claims regarding the expansion of the scope of illegal missionary activity in Israel and the steps required to deal with it, to the extent necessary."[1]

Your Honor, you can be certain that the Shas did not hold a narrow legal definition of "missionary" when they signed this coalition agreement giving them carte blanche authority to vigorously pursue Jewish believers in Yeshua. Every Messianic Jew in Israel, for instance, is profiled by Shas' rabbis as "an illegal missionary regardless of their actual vocation or behavior."[2]

Moreover, it is this very coalition agreement that has brought my three clients before this court today to plead with you to reverse the gross injustices that have been perpetrated upon them. Equal treatment for all under the law, the right of privacy, free speech, assembly—all of these presumed basic human rights have been swept away by out-of-control religious extremism.

Your Honor, I thank the court for your indulgence in allowing me to speak my mind concerning how we have come to this moment where my clients are compelled to stand before you. In the end, only you can decide if the action taken against them to revoke their citizenship and deport them from the Land of their inheritance is in keeping with the administration of justice and righteousness, which is indeed the court's sworn duty.

May it please the court, during these entire proceedings not one single shred of credible evidence has come forth to even suggest that any of these three respondents ever violated any Israeli law or statute, save for three minor traffic violations. Instead, the state has devastatingly revoked their citizenship and ordered their deportation based entirely upon hearsay evidence gathered by a massive, secretive, nongovernmental agency.

This agency, Shomrei Israel, has systematically and deliberately manufactured evidence against my clients by unlawfully violating their rights to privacy and assembly. Your Honor, overwhelming credible testimony has been placed before you that the state has taken these actions against my clients based upon the unsubstantiated, highly prejudicial hearsay evidence provided by planted spies, wire tapping, outright intimidation, blatant untruthfulness, and even violence.

Your Honor, let me also point out that you have heard solid evidence that the Law of Return, as amended in 1970, has been wrongfully and repeatedly used with premeditated discrimination by the Ministry of the Interior and their illicit body of informants as an outright weapon against the tiny minority of Jews who have embraced Yeshua as their Messiah.

Moreover, some very great incalculable number of such Jewish believers in Yeshua have, without the benefit of due process, been so persecuted by the Ministry of the Interior. However, although vigorously pursued during these proceedings, the Ministry of the Interior was unable to testify as to even a single instance where this law, as amended in 1970, was used against a Jew who had, presumably, "changed their religion" to any other understanding, such as Buddhism or Hinduism.

Andrew Sterling is a Jew, descended from many generations of Jews. He fervently believes he was called to Israel by God to take up his divine inheritance and to dwell in the Land. During his many years as a citizen of Israel, Andrew Sterling has been a model citizen, a devoted husband, father, and grandfather. His only fault, according to his accusers, is that under the label of "missionary" he has been a faithful shepherd of like-minded Jews who shared his religious understandings.

Your Honor, a missionary, by definition, is a person strongly in favor of a program, set of principles, etc., who attempts to persuade or convert others. Andrew Sterling never, during his many years in Israel, attempted to persuade or convert others to his religious understandings who did not first come to him and ask specific questions regarding these understandings. Moreover, he has meticulously avoided sharing such views, according to the law, with those under the age of eighteen, and he has always inquired as to the age of those who might be legally minors before answering any questions on the subject of religion. Again, Your Honor, there is not one single shred of evidence before this court to the contrary.

Your Honor, in all fairness, it must also be added that the door to Andrew Sterling's congregation remained open to any and all who decided of their own free will to enter. Indeed, Andrew Sterling preached his religious understandings from his pulpit to those who entered and were just as free to leave at any time. Never, during the course of his pulpit presentations, did Andrew Sterling ever single out any one individual or group of individuals in his audience, but rather he consistently shared his views with the entire often changing collective body of attendees. This openness in his approach is how it became possible for Shomrei Israel to plant their informants within his congregation for the express purpose of entrapping him on the trumped-up charges that have, in part, led us to this day.

Most importantly, Your Honor, it is vital that the court understand the nature of Andrew Sterling's religious position and duties during his twenty-eight-year service as a United States Air Force chaplain. Yes, he was sponsored to become an Air Force chaplain by a small conservative denomination with their full understanding that he was not religiously a member of their group, nor necessarily in full agreement with all of their precise theological and doctrinal holdings. The respondent sought this sponsorship and they chose to provide it because the Air Force chaplaincy at that time did not recognize Messianic Judaism as a denomination from which one of its adherents could be sponsored as a chaplain.

Your Honor, Chaplain Andrew Sterling was never a Christian in the sense that he was a member of a Christian denomination who represented the greater Christian church.

He was then and remains now quite simply a Jew who shares with all Christians the understanding that another Jew, Yeshua, was and is the Messiah promised by the Tenach.

Certainly, Your Honor, Chaplain Sterling performed the many nondenominational duties of an Air Force chaplain, but he did so entirely from his religious position as a Messianic Jew, not as a Christian or as a member of the Christian church, neither of which he was then, is now, or ever has been.

Your Honor, Carla Sterling, Andrew's devoted wife of many years, has given her life to serving both the nation and its citizens while faithfully standing by her husband's side. Like Andrew, Carla Sterling has never engaged in any so-called "missionary activities." Again, there is not a shred of evidence before the court showing otherwise. Certainly Carla has been a Torah school teacher of the minor children of members of her husband's congregation who were given to her in trust by their like-minded parents in full agreement with the nature and content of Carla's teaching. Moreover, Carla, like her husband, never shared her religious understandings with anyone who might be a minor without first making an honest inquiry as to the age of that person.

Your Honor, my learned opposing counsel has suggested that an article written by a third party and published in an unofficial women's newsletter, after the Sterlings immigrated, offers proof that they knowingly applied for citizenship under false pretenses. Your Honor, there is no evidence whatsoever before this court that the content of this article is anything more than hearsay or gossip, or that this writing accurately represents any communication from Carla Sterling or her religious beliefs or any of her other positions or understandings.

Finally, Your Honor, I address the most ludicrous of the three cases set before you. Hannah Meyers Silberman is a Holocaust survivor who endured sheer hell at the hands of the Nazis, who murdered her entire family and forced her into a life of such horror and depravity that the details of what she endured cannot be reasonably discussed before this court. Yes, after what she endured, Hannah did seek some better understanding of the God she was unable to fully discover in the Judaism of her youth. Yes, immediately after her release from Auschwitz she did investigate the Roman Catholic Church in Freising, Germany. To her great sadness and further confusion, she was unable to find any comfort from this investigation. Let me be very clear in this, Your Honor, never, not for a single moment did Hannah Meyers Silberman embrace the Roman Catholic Church. She simply investigated, then immediately and entirely rejected what she had never in any way embraced.

Your Honor, it was not until very recently, after she had become a citizen of Israel, that, according to her own testimony, Hannah Meyers Silberman found her way to faith in Yeshua under the teachings of Andrew and Carla Sterling, such teaching she, as an adult, sought voluntarily.

I will conclude by sharing the events surrounding Hannah Meyers Silberman's ceremonial Jewish mikvah known as baptism. Some scholars, including Andrew Sterling, believe this is the very same ceremony practiced by Essene Jews during their entire history as it is recorded in the Dead Sea Scrolls. There she was, standing in the waters of the Jordan River, as Andrew Sterling and others of his congregation witnessed her three self-immersions.

But this, Your Honor, was not to be a moment of entire peace enjoyed by a citizen of Israel who by law was supposedly endowed with the right to be there, doing what she was doing without objection, or certainly without the violent interference of those who did not share her understanding.

No, Your Honor, at this very moment in the life of Hannah Meyers Silberman, a fully enfranchised citizen of Israel, Rabbi Mordecai Ben Shlomi and his followers saw fit to cast stones aimed at her and her fellow believers in an effort to disrupt the ceremony and to attempt physical harm to those who were so peacefully assembled.

Your Honor, such believers in Yeshua as Andrew and Carla

Sterling, Hannah Meyers Silberman, and the other thousands of such believers in some one hundred twenty congregations scattered throughout Israel have been forced to live in constant concern for their physical safety or other so-called anti-missionary action perpetually threatened to be taken against them. There is evidence before this court that such so-called anti-missionary actions have been perpetrated with the knowledge and support of the Ministry of the Interior, which now holds a carte blanche license to do so in exchange for the continued stability of the current governing coalition.

Your Honor, the respondents plead with this court to change the current precedent that holds that a Jew who changes his or her religion is no longer a Jew and is therefore not entitled to become or hold Israeli citizenship.

Furthermore, Your Honor, even if this honorable court will not change the current precedent that a Jew who accepts Yeshua as his Messiah has changed his religion, it is clear that none of the three respondents intentionally falsified information upon immigrating. At most, an administrative mistake occurred on the part of the Interior Ministry. None of the three respondents were ever asked whether they believed in Yeshua or whether they belonged to a Messianic congregation. All they were required to do was to fill in on their application form the relevant religious category they belonged to, and they filled in Jewish, and this was done in good faith. Your Honor, the Interior Ministry cannot expect my clients to be aware of the secular definition of who is a Jew as it is set forth in the Law of Return, as amended in 1970, and as it was interpreted in several subsequent Supreme Court decisions. My clients were each sure they were religiously Jewish and declared in good faith that they were so. If they would have been asked whether they believed in Yeshua, Drew and Carla Sterling would have said yes, while Hannah Silberman would have said no, as she only started believing in Yeshua after she became a citizen. Therefore, the request to revoke Hannah's citizenship is farfetched and has no legal standing whatsoever, as she could not have falsified information. The state has a burden to prove that the respondents Drew and Carla Sterling intentionally falsified information. This is something the government has failed to do.

Your Honor, the evidence before this court leaves no other reasonable alternative but to allow these entirely innocent victims of a religious minority to maintain their rightful status as citizens with full license to live out their lives in the State of Israel, the Land of their inheritance, the place where they believe they have been called by their Creator.

With that, Jeremiah Levine bowed ever so slightly in the direction of the bench and quietly returned to his seat.

CHIEF JUSTICE BAUERSTEIN *(after listening intently)*: Thank you, Mr. Levine. Mr. Ben Israel, are you ready to proceed with the state's closing?

BEN ISRAEL: I am, Your Honor. I feel certain that you, like I, have been deeply touched by Mr. Levine's impassioned words. Having said this, Your Honor, let me once again remind the court that neither Shomrei Israel, the Ministry of the Interior, much less the State of Israel is on trial here, nor are they presenting a response to this court. Instead, those who stand before you, pleading for the reversal of the lawfully invoked actions against them, cry out to you for justice on the basis that the governmental system in which we all must live and operate should somehow be held accountable for their own wantonly committed unlawful acts.

Your Honor, whether the three respondents and their attorney like it or not, the State of Israel operates under a body of laws. As with any democratic national government, each of these laws was duly debated and enacted by the central government and is enforced by and through the appropriate agency or agencies of that government. My point here is that the respondents and their attorney may not like or agree with the Law of Return as amended in 1970 or the other several laws that in one way or another bear upon the matter at hand, but each of these statutes, separately and collectively, make up a portion of the great body of laws by which the

State of Israel is governed. It is just that plain and simple.

With respect, Your Honor, it is not the law that is on trial here today but rather whether or not the respondents were dealt with without prejudice in accordance with this law—nothing more, nothing less.

Your Honor, there are only two questions that the court must decide in this matter. Simply, did the actions of the respondents violate the laws of the State of Israel, and if they did, were the actions in response taken against them both lawful and appropriate? Nothing more, nothing less.

Your Honor, there is clear evidence before this court that Andrew Sterling preached the gospel of Jesus Christ and was a Christian minister before he ever immigrated into Israel. Moreover, there is clear evidence before this court that Andrew Sterling personally baptized Jews in the name of Jesus during his pre-Aliyah service as a United States Air Force Christian chaplain.

Your Honor, it is also clear that these two respondents, Andrew and Carla Sterling, intentionally did not mention their faith and belief in Jesus upon immigrating and that they decided to immigrate for the sole purpose of converting Jews to Christianity, thus intentionally breaking the reasonable missionary laws of our country. Even after these two respondents immigrated, there is evidence that they preached their religion to Jewish minors and then sought to change their religion from Judaism to Christianity. This evidence was evaluated and then acted upon by the Ministry of the Interior. The Ministry of the Interior, like Shomrei Israel, is absolutely dedicated to revoking the citizenship of people who have falsified information and cheated our system in order to receive citizenship.

Your Honor, plain and simple, every Jew who embraces Yeshu as his Messiah has become part of another religion. Rabbis Akiva, Rambam, and others teach us this, as does our beloved Talmud and other commentaries.

In conclusion, Your Honor, it comes down to this. The respondents have violated the laws of the State of Israel in such a way that the Ministry of the Interior and the State Attorney have determined they were a threat to the peace and security of the nation.

I have only one thing left to say, and this really needs no recital since what I have concluded about this entire matter must also be completely obvious to the court. Your Honor, these three have clearly presented false information upon immigrating. This is much clearer with Drew and Carla Sterling, who were already operating and working as missionaries for many years before they immigrated and have done so in order to be involved in missionary activity. But it is also highly probable that Hannah Silberman, as a newly subscribed Roman Catholic, was also involved in Christian activity before immigrating. By her own testimony she persisted in a continuing debate over matters of her faith with a rabbi with whom she resided.

Your Honor, if the respondents would have simply informed the clerks at the Interior Ministry of this obvious information before immigrating, they would have not received citizenship. Therefore, the citizenship of the respondents should be revoked and they should be permanently deported.

Natan Ben Israel looked about the courtroom defiantly, bowed slightly to the five justices, and took his seat.

Chief Justice Bauerstein: The court will stand in recess until nine o'clock in the morning of Thursday, January 28, when we will render our judgment.

Having so spoken, the chief justice sounded his gavel firmly, stood with the rest of the justices, then led them from the courtroom.

Chapter 26
Hannah's Story
Ben Gurion International Airport
(Monday, January 18, 2010)

The three of them—Drew, Carla, and Hannah—waited with growing excitement as the passengers from Continental Flight 92 from Newark began to exit the customs area and enter the spacious arrival area of Terminal 3 of the world-class Ben Gurion International Airport.

"I'm so excited that you brought me along to meet your girls," Hannah exclaimed. "I feel like they are the grandchildren I never had, and I haven't even met them. You are all my beloved family," she added from the depths of her being as she drew the two of them close with her outstretched arms.

"The girls are going to love you, Hannah," Carla replied, "just like we do. You have brought so much deep love to our family."

"What a great way for us to check out the congregation's new Volkswagen van," Drew interjected. "Thank you so much, Hannah. What a wonderful blessing!"

"It is really nothing, Drew," she replied. "Look, it already got me a ride to the airport!"

"There they are!" Carla shouted as she recognized Dory, just turned fifty, Rebekah, forty-eight, and their "baby" Rachel, forty-six, as they pushed their baggage carts through the open doors into the arrival area.

They embraced excitedly all the way around with joyful hugs and kisses of reunion, including Hannah, who was instantly and naturally included in such a way that she genuinely felt she had always known and loved the three of them, even though they had just met.

"Daddy!" Dory exclaimed, when their initial excitement had begun to subside, in her usual spokeswoman role on behalf of herself and her sisters. "We could just shoot the two of you for keeping all of this business quiet! Here you are, about to be thrown out of Israel, and you didn't even bother to tell us until we read about it in the *New York Times*."

"My darling daughters," Drew sought to explain, "the Ministry of the Interior placed a news blackout on the trial that some kind fellow finally leaked. We really didn't want to bother you with this until we knew how it was going to end."

"You bet there was a news leak, Daddy," Bekah chimed in. "This thing is all over the media now—even the notoriously anti-Israel CNN has made your story a major item. It seems that the whole world is watching in great suspense waiting to see how this is all going to come down. The fact that Hannah is a Holocaust survivor and they are trying to throw her out of the country, along with your plight as so-called missionaries, has really caught the hearts and gained the support of a lot of people."

"This isn't all good," Drew responded. "Certainly we would love to see a huge amount of pressure placed upon our government to make some major changes in how they are organized and operate, but we would hate to see this as just one more opportunity for the "international anti-Israel club," which of course takes in almost the entire United Nations, to have just one more excuse to blindly bash Israel and Jews in general simply because this gives them an opportunity to do so. I am praying that at least the beginnings of electoral reform will come from all of this."

"Daddy, you and Mom never cease to amaze me," Rachel exclaimed, shaking her head in disbelief. "Here you are, on the very brink of being banished from the Land forever, and you are most concerned with how the world sees Israel. Shouldn't you be putting first things first?"

"Enough of this political stuff," Carla offered as Drew finished loading the girls' luggage into their spacious new van. "Let's head for home and talk about what we have in mind for a very special outing while you are here."

Thursday, January 21, 2010: The Summit of Mount Nebo, Jordan

"I am so very blessed to have all five of you darlings with me at this moment," Drew declared emotionally. "In all the many years we've been in the Land, I've had a deep yearning to visit this place, but up to now the Lord seems to have put me off for one reason or another."

The six of them—the Sterlings, their daughters, and Hannah—stood huddled together on the large platform at the very summit of Mount

Nebo, seeking protection from the brisk winter wind that swept across the place where they stood ankle-deep in unfamiliar snow. This was the holy place where Moses had stood more than three thousand years before them, hungrily and lovingly taking in every glorious feature revealed by the sweeping panoramic view set before him of the Land that had been divinely covenanted to all Jewish descendants of Abraham, Isaac, and Jacob, a Land from which he had been forbidden to enter by the Lord God Himself.

Drew, when he had regained control of his emotions, opened his Bible to the Book of Deuteronomy and read:

> Then Moses went up from the plains of Moab to Mount Nebo, to the top of Pisgah, which is across from Jericho. And the LORD showed him all the land of Gilead as far as Dan, all Naphtali and the land of Ephraim and Manasseh, all the land of Judah as far as the Western Sea, the South, and the plain of the Valley of Jericho, the city of palm trees, as far as Zoar. Then the LORD said to him, "This is the land of which I swore to give Abraham, Isaac, and Jacob, saying, 'I will give it to your descendants.' I have caused you to see it with your eyes, but you shall not cross over there." So Moses the servant of the LORD died there in the land of Moab, according to the word of the LORD. And He buried him in a valley in the land of Moab, opposite Beth Peor; but no one knows his grave to this day. Moses was one hundred and twenty years old when he died. His eyes were not dim nor his natural vigor diminished. And the children of Israel wept for Moses in the plains of Moab thirty days. So the days of weeping and mourning for Moses ended.
>
> —DEUTERONOMY 34:1–8

When he had finished reading, Drew closed his Bible and began to pray: "Heavenly Father, I praise You for these many wonderful years You have given Carla and me to dwell in this wonderful Land of our inheritance, the Land of Israel that You have now set before us in this glorious view. O Lord, I cry out to You; Your will be done, not our will. Should it be Your will that we and our dear sister Hannah are no longer to dwell here in this Land, then I pray You will greatly bless us with a mighty outpouring of Your wonderful grace. Help us then that we might be able to joyfully accept Your judgment and return to the respective lands of our birth and be allowed to continue to serve You there until the very end of our walk upon this earth. Heavenly Father, I pray You will be with those who now sit in judgment over us. O Lord, supernaturally fill their hearts and minds with a clear understanding of Your mighty will concerning how we are to be dealt with.

We pray blessings on those who stand so blindly against us. Father, out of Your great care for them, teach them the truth and bring them to salvation though Your glorious Son, Yeshua. For we pray these things in His mighty name—Your will be done. Amen."

It was Carla who broke the long, seemingly interminable silence, singing out as all of them, except Hannah who was hearing this form of the doxology for the first time, quickly joined in:

> Praise God from whom all blessings flow.
> Praise Him, all creatures here below.
> Praise Him above, ye heavenly host.
> Praise Father, Son, and Holy Ghost.

After a few more moments of extended silence, Dory spoke out what had long filled her own heart and that of her two sisters.

"You know, Daddy, how very much we all love and respect you, and we want the best for you and Mom. Just maybe it is God's will that you are to stay in the Land serving the Lord, shepherding your congregation and blessing others until your dying day. Only He can make that judgment. But Daddy, you must remember, you and Mom are growing older. Being seventy-six is not the prime of your youth. Somehow you both manage to forget that.

"In this, your three daughters agree," she continued emphatically. "Just maybe the Lord has used this trial to release you from your calling of so many years here in the Land. Just maybe you are going to be called home, to the Land of your birth, to live near the three of us so we can once again be blessed by having you close, seeing you often, and caring for you on a regular basis. Just maybe this is God's glorious way of blessing you and your grandchildren with the wonderful opportunity of getting to truly know and enjoy the nearness of one another. Daddy, what we are trying to say is this: if it is God's will that you lose this response and are forced to leave Israel, such an outcome wouldn't be all that terrible."

"I love you so very much, my precious, darling daughters," was Drew's barely audible reply.

Chapter 27
Hannah's Story
Jerusalem
(Supreme Court of the State of Israel: Thursday, January 28, 2010)

The three respondents and their attorney sat together silently at their assigned table, their emotions wound tight, like those of over-tuned stringed instruments near the point of breaking. At long last their day of judgment had arrived, and the three of them waited, their hearts racing in anticipation of what lay just ahead. Chief Justice Bauerstein wasted no time after he and the other four black-robed magistrates had taken their places.

Chief Justice Bauerstein: When we began these proceedings some weeks ago, I shared with you my opinion that the case before us was a matter of very great importance, the nature of which is often described as landmark because of its significance. Indeed, my anticipation in this regard has in no way been diminished by the evidence and testimony that have been placed before this court, inescapable matters of fact demanding judgment.

First, the court sees fit to commend the two advocates who have stood before us. Both the respondents and the state have been represented with professional excellence seldom equaled in our experience.

Now, as I prepare to share with you the judgment of this court in these foundationally important matters, I speak not to just those three who seek relief but also to our honorable prime minister and to all the ministers, especially to the Minister of the Interior. I speak also to all members of the Knesset.

In rendering the judgment of this Court, I speak not only to you three respondents who seek relief from the revocation of your citizenship and permanent deportation, as initiated by a virtually unchallengeable ministry of this government. I also speak to every man, woman, and child who stand together as the citizenry of this nation. In one way or another, knowingly or unknowingly, we all stand before this court seeking both justice and relief.

Before I read the judgment of this court, the parties are hereby notified that the elaborated verdict will be sent to the parties via registered post.

And so let the conclusion of the judgment of this court now be published. Will the respondents please rise.

With that Drew, Carla, and Hannah held hands as they stood with Jeremiah Levine, after which the chief justice continued.

Chief Justice Bauerstein: To begin with, the court finds that the Ministry of the Interior, in improper collaboration with Shomrei Israel, did deliberately and with malice of forethought manufacture false evidence designed to entrap the three respondents and are, therefore, in the strongest terms, herewith sanctioned by this court for having done so. In seeking to put down the entirely lawful religious activities and practices of the respondents, both the Ministry of the Interior and Shomrei Israel have brought discredit upon themselves through their overzealous efforts to impose their own religious understandings upon the accused and upon the entire State of Israel.

Moreover, the court finds that nothing in the conduct of any of the three respondents rises to the level necessary to determine that they have ever posed a threat to the security of the State of Israel, which is not a legal claim whereby the respondents' citizenship can be revoked in any way under these circumstances.

However, Andrew and Carla Sterling, Hannah Meyers Silberman, the Ministry of the Interior and State Prosecutor have maintained that each of you immigrated to Israel under false pretenses. Specifically, that each of you was actively engaged to varying degrees in Christian missionary activity before you applied for Israeli citizenship.

Moreover, the state has also offered evidence suggesting that, during your application process, each of you withheld the fact that you had changed your religion prior to making such application and, therefore, you were not eligible to become citizens under the provisions of the Law of Return, as amended in 1970.

In the case of Hannah Silberman, the court finds that these accusations are at best tenuous. The evidence before us concerning the religious interface between Hannah Silberman and Rabbi Cohen is highly speculative. Moreover, it seems clear that Hannah did not change her religion until she became a member of Andrew Sterling's congregation, some forty-two years after she had become a citizen of Israel.

In the cases of Andrew and Carla Sterling, however, the court finds that both of these respondents were actively involved in Christian missionary activities long before they immigrated to Israel. Moreover, the court finds the evidence compelling that Andrew Sterling baptized Jews in the name of Jesus. Furthermore, the court finds very troubling the evidence, as published in a regular periodical, implying that Carla Sterling deliberately succeeded in "beating the system" to become a citizen.

In any event, no matter how vigorously he has attempted to characterize the matter to the contrary, it is clear that Andrew Sterling changed his religion many years before he made application for Israeli citizenship.

However, the court also finds it clear that Andrew Sterling had considered himself to be an ethnic Jew who believed in Yeshua as Messiah long before his application for Israeli citizenship and that he made such application in good faith both believing and declaring that his religion was Jewish. Had the Ministry of the Interior asked about his specific Messianic belief at the time of his application, the court finds he would have openly told them of his belief in Yeshua. Hence, the burden was principally upon the ministry in this regard, not the respondent.

The findings of the court with respect to Carla Sterling are tied to the fact that she is a Gentile Christian married to a Jew who sought citizenship on the basis of this relationship. There is no credible evidence before the court that she in any way sought to deceive the state during the immigration process.

Andrew Sterling and Carla Sterling, the Supreme Court of the State of Israel renders its judgment as follows:

Andrew and Carla Sterling, your response to this court that the revocation of your status as citizens of the State of Israel be reversed are denied. The Ministry of the Interior is herewith ordered to revoke their order that each of you be deported from the State of Israel. The Ministry of Interior is further ordered to grant each of you the status of "permanent residency" in the State of Israel without prejudice.

Hannah Meyers Silberman, the Supreme Court of Israel renders its judgment as follows:

Your response to this court that the revocation of your status a citizen of the State of Israel be reversed is granted. Moreover, the court considers it to be a great irony that you were considered eligible to be treated as a Jew by the Nazis during the Holocaust but not Jewish enough by the Ministry of the Interior to meet the citizenship requirements of the Israeli Law of Return as amended in 1970. The Ministry of Interior is herewith ordered to revoke their order that you be deported from the State of Israel. The Ministry of Interior is further ordered to award you the sum of 100,000 new Israeli shekels for legal expenses.

(With great warmth and sincerity) Andrew and Carla Sterling, Hannah Meyers Silberman, the court wishes you many happy and persecution-free years here in the Land of your inheritance, where you are fully permitted and encouraged to worship freely and in the manner of your own choosing.

Finally *(with great emotion)*, I would like to take this opportunity to announce my retirement as a member of this court to be effective the moment I sound this final gavel of my long career of heartfelt service, a career during which I have sought, often with great frustration, to bring justice to you all, my greatly loved and highly esteemed fellow citizens of the State of Israel.

With that, Marcus Bauerstein, a moment away from becoming a regular citizen, rapped his gavel three times with unprecedented force, stood, and then with his head bowed, led the four remaining justices from the courtroom. Most of the others who remained in the packed courtroom were filled with respect as they rose, genuinely stunned by what they had just heard and witnessed.

The Chambers of Chief Justice Marcus Bauerstein (Retired)

"Mr. Levine—Jerry, it was so good of you to come," the just retired Chief Justice exclaimed, smiling broadly as he rose from his huge mahogany desk, his right hand extended to properly welcome his guest. Jerry had instantly responded to the curious summons from this tower of the judiciary, whom he so deeply admired and respected, conveyed by his senior clerk, just as he and his clients were leaving the court building.

"Your Honor," Jerry's mind raced as he tried to fathom his esteemed host's purpose in requesting his appearance as they exchanged firm handshakes. He took the proffered chair facing the huge desk. "I am greatly flattered that you wanted to see me after such a grueling trial and at such a major milestone in your brilliant career. How can I possibly be of service to you, sir?"

"Jerry, I am no longer 'Your Honor' but rather simply just another one of your many admiring colleagues. I would be much more comfortable if you called me Marc, as do my closest friends and associates.

"Jerry," Marc moved on, not giving his guest an opportunity to reply to the sudden personalization of their relationship, "one of the reasons I asked you to stop by was to share my personal feelings with you about this case—and the mechanics of how the court arrived at its judgment. Quite frankly, Jerry, I also called you here in a way to apologize, to explain why I'm not totally satisfied with how things turned out."

"Your Honor—Marc," Jerry replied, nearly overwhelmed by the most unusual revelations his host had begun to unfold. "Your willingness to share these insights, especially with respect to such a landmark case, would be both fascinating and of the greatest professional and personal interest. But Marc," he continued, genuinely dismayed, "I can hardly see how and why you feel that you owe me an apology—surely, most observers would claim that my clients enjoyed a significant victory."

"Jerry," the former chief justice exclaimed, making no attempt to conceal his deep personal and professional frustration, "by the standards of precedent it could be argued that you did in fact make noticeable progress in furthering the worthy cause you so passionately represent. But this wasn't enough, not nearly enough. Let me explain where I'm coming from, counselor.

"Jerry, without meaning to sound too radical or professorial," Marc continued, "the very fact that your three law-abiding clients were forced to stand before the court of last appeal, pleading for the restoration of their God-given rights to dwell as citizens in the Land of their inheritance in peace, privacy, and under the full and equal protection of the law is by itself a great failure. Even more so, however, is the shocking yet undeniable manifestation of the great depths of injustice and unrighteousness, the frequent depravation of inalienable human rights that now characterize our beloved Israel."

"Would it be fair to say, Marc," Jerry interjected, "as I passionately pleaded in my opening statement, that today our government stands tragically transformed by religious extremism into a myth, a mere shadow of what those who trade on dreams and wishful imaginations blindly perceive to be a genuine Western-style democracy?"

"Precisely my thinking, Jerry," Marc replied sadly. "The State of Israel is by no means a democracy, much less a republic governed by three equally empowered branches. The government that rules over us today is by no means in its form or operation the government that was envisioned by David Ben-Gurion and the other founding fathers, a government that would provide checks and balances while obviating any excesses, imbalances, or improprieties of those who were empowered to govern by its citizenry."

"I couldn't agree with you more, Marc," Jerry continued excitedly. "The State of Israel is not now nor has it ever been a democracy or democratic republic, even by the most liberal definition of these tried and true forms of government. The State of Israel is rather effectively ruled over by a tiny minority of religious extremists who, with few interruptions throughout its entire sixty-two year history, has extorted concessions and favoritism from successive ruling government coalitions, along with the license to openly intimidate, harass—even militantly seek to disenfranchise—those of its fellow citizens who held views, religious or otherwise, they might strongly have opposed."

"Jerry," Marc began honing in on the principal reason he had requested this meeting. "Now that I am certain we are like-minded, I pray that you will also understand that I did my very best to secure the most favorable possible outcome for your clients. I can now tell you privately, even before the first gavel sounded, certain major government decision makers made it abundantly clear that they expected a much more stringent outcome. The fact is, they were outright insistent from the outset that your clients be stripped of their citizenship and deported. Anything less than this, they argued, would have chipped away at the rock-solid legal precedent, hard won and long enjoyed by the controlling religious minority, an outcome they were unwilling to tolerate."

"How did you manage to bring off their willingness to accept a much more favorable compromise?" Jerry probed respectfully.

"Politics, my friend!" Marc replied with deep sadness. "Political horse trading of the worst sort that cost me dearly. First off, I cashed in every IOU and silver chip I held from the government—a significant collective clout I had accumulated over the years. Then I did the very same thing with my fellow justices, who were at first solidly reticent to change precedent, even in the slightest. They were, as usual, much more inclined to simply roll over and accede to the demands of those who actually control the government rather than to fight what certainly appeared to be an unwinnable uphill battle that could only end unfavorably while creating enormous ill will.

"In the end, I made it clear to those in the government with whom I was negotiating that if I were forced to acquiesce to their demands and send your clients packing, I would go on a personal vendetta to expose the utter miscarriage of justice that such an action would represent, a vendetta that would surely draw both sweeping national and international attention upon themselves and upon our so-called parliamentary democracy."

"And that was enough to turn the tide?" Jerry asked skeptically, beginning to understand.

"Not entirely," Marc replied, sensing Jerry's great perception. "Like I said earlier, this outcome cost me dearly."

"More than just all your personal markers?" Jerry continued to probe.

"I obviously haven't made an abundance of friends in the controlling political minority—like I said, this cost me dearly—personally—need I say more?"

Marc, having now made his sacrifice clear, stopped short of making a direct admission of what he had been forced to do on behalf of the three respondents, but much more importantly, the depth of his personal cost required to win a significant change in precedent.

"Jerry," he continued with great warmth, "I called you here for two purposes: first, to confirm what I already strongly suspected—that we were like-minded on these major issues. I must say, I am delighted that I was completely correct in this regard.

"Having so confirmed your fundamental views and having long admired your professional skills, relative youth, and enormous potential, my second purpose in speaking with you immediately after my own retirement from the bench was to explore your potential interest in becoming my replacement, so to speak—not the chief, of course, but if selected by the committee that formalizes these nominations and then confirmed by the Knesset, that you would accept appointment as a justice of the Supreme Court."

"Of course I would, Your Honor," Jerry replied, overwhelmed with emotion. "I can think of no greater honor, challenge, or distinction."

"Wonderful, Jerry," Marc responded with obvious deep satisfaction. "Of course, I can't promise you anything, but some of the many chips I've already spent are still on the table awaiting my personal selection, and Jerry, that's you. With God's help, I am confident we can make this happen."

The David Citadel Hotel, Jerusalem: Thursday, January 28, 2010

It was late evening of the day of their great victory. The eight of them—Drew, Carla, and their three daughters; Hannah; and Jerry and Maureen—had gathered together in a small private meeting room just off the hotel's main cocktail lounge to celebrate the victorious outcome of their long battle for justice.

Hannah had ordered an unending supply of the most expensive French champagne, along with an abundant array of the chef's selection of the very best beluga caviar, exotic cheeses, and other delicacies.

"May I propose a toast to the man who made this all possible," Drew raised his hand-cut Belgium crystal glass, as the others joined him. "I give you Jeremiah Levine, a brilliant attorney dedicated to truth, righteousness, and the selfless service of our people. May God richly bless you, Jerry, and may this begin here and now." With that, the others spoke a resounding "Hear! Hear!"

When they had put down their glasses, Hannah stood and began to speak in a loving yet serious voice. "Jeremiah, we all know that you are anything but a financially rich person. How could you be, when you give so much of your precious time defending the rights of our fellow Jewish believers pro bono, simply out of your unselfish love for them and the State of Israel?" With that, she removed an envelope from her purse and handed it to him. "Jerry, I will never have a family of my own flesh, so I decided to bless you, my surrogate son, the lawyer. Open this, Jerry," she gently commanded.

"Wow!" Jerry exclaimed, genuinely shocked. "Pay to the order of Jeremiah Levine," he read unbelievingly, "the sum of one million dollars!"

"Now that's what I call an appropriate attorney's fee," Drew exclaimed as all present applauded excitedly.

"Amen!" Maureen added joyfully. "Solvency has once again returned to our household."

"There is something I would like to share with you all," Jerry spoke, after the immediate celebration on his behalf had settled down. "Marcus Bauerstein invited me to meet with him in his chambers this morning, right after the end of the proceedings, which, of course, I did without delay. Well, it seems that this great man wanted to explore my potential interest in accepting an appointment as a justice of the Supreme Court. I can't tell you how completely off guard this unexpected suggestion caught me and how deeply honored I was and remain by his consideration.

"Now, before you all get too excited about this," Jerry cautioned, "this appointment will be anything but a slam dunk. Ordinarily, the chief justice can only suggest such appointments, which are ultimately decided by a senior executive committee. The fact is that Marcus Bauerstein is well loved and respected, but he is no longer the chief justice. Moreover, who knows what level of opposition I have managed to reap as a result of my performance during this just concluded landmark trial that didn't exactly go the way the government would have desired.

"Chief Justice Bauerstein did, however, say that he would spare no expense of his remaining influence to bring about my appointment and that he was very optimistic he would succeed."

"And so it is my honor to propose another toast," Drew proclaimed joyfully. "To the Honorable Jeremiah Allen Levine, the next justice of the Supreme Court of the State of Israel. May the Lord God of Israel guide your every deliberation and mightily bless your service to the state and its people."

"Hear! Hear!" they all shouted.

After the hour had grown late, Hannah could no longer restrain herself from asking a question that had been brewing deep within her. "Drew," she addressed the dear one she regarded both as her pastor and the son she never would have, "how do you and Carla really feel about losing your Israeli citizenship? If it is too hurtful for you to talk about right now, that's OK; I understand."

"Let me begin answering your very proper question with a question," Drew replied thoughtfully. "Hannah, who gave the Land of Israel to Yakov and all of his descendants as an everlasting inheritance?"

"Yahweh!" she replied without hesitation. "Yahweh, the Lord God of Israel!"

"Exactly!" Drew relied with deep conviction. "Rabbis Akiva and Maimonides, all the great rabbis in between and all the great pharisaic rabbis of today, entertained the heretical notion that they, as mere men, are empowered to change the Word of God when they find it not to their liking.

"Let me tell you, Hannah, they are seriously mistaken in this conclusion. No man can change the Word of God, and the Word of God has spoken that every blood descendant of Yakov is a co-inheritor of the Land of Israel, a land where he is given license to dwell for all the days of his life. No ruling of any rabbi or any government or any court can change the God-given reality that you, Hannah, Jerry and I—all Jews—and Carla, by marriage, are, by His Word, citizens of the Land of Israel.

"And so you ask me, Hannah, 'What are we to do? How do I feel about these words and actions of men?' Let me tell you the one thing we can and must frequently do. We must continue to pray for them and their salvation. Nothing could be more important than this."

"OK, Daddy, as long as you are inclined to answer such deep questions," Dory interjected, "let me dare ask just once more: When are you and Mom going to come home? We are leaving tomorrow evening. I'm sure you could arrange to travel to Phoenix with us, and you could always come back here in a few weeks and settle your affairs."

"Let me answer this one," Carla chimed in. "Our greatly loved and most darling daughters, your father and I reached the conclusion long ago that there will never be a way for you to fully understand our calling to this Land and our unshakable decision, God willing, to remain here all the days of our lives. You ask, 'When are we coming home?' To this I answer, dear ones, we are home, and here at home we will remain for as long as God allows, and it is here at home where we will serve Him to the very best of our ability until finally our strength and breath shall fade and we are no longer able to endure. And then, like the patriarchs of old, we pray that you will have the forbearance, kindness, and understanding to come and bury our bones in some quiet place overlooking our beloved lake in the Galilee where you will rejoice with the angels that at last we have gone to our final home to sit in His glorious presence and worship Him without ceasing."

Chapter 28
Hannah's Story
Lisse, Holland
(April 2010)

Margit and Leo Van Burkleo, distant cousins of Theo de Goede, had fallen heir to the Theo de Goede Tulip Farm soon after the war. They, like the precious ones who had preceded them, were warm and thoroughly gracious host and hostess to Hannah who, seeking closure, had instinctively returned to this place of her many both lovely and terrible memories.

Once again she enjoyed a many-course Dutch farm meal that might just as well have been prepared by her beloved Gerta instead of by Margit, her current hostess. Once again, she was given license to privately wander about the grounds, reliving those moments of her life that had fleetingly been spent in this place.

Nothing about the separate building that had been her home had changed. It seemed that even the luxurious feather beds upon which she had slept were still made up with the same linens that once again were calling out to her to find rest, comfort, and protection.

Finally, it was with the greatest emotional difficulty that she made her way to the special planting beds where Gerta had propagated new tulip cultivars and then waited for a number of years to see what God had determined to bring forth from her efforts. It was here in this very place where Gerta and her beloved Theo had fallen, stuck by the bullets of their Nazi assassin. It was here where Gerta had fallen among the cultivars and poured out her life's blood that flowed around the crushed remains of the amazingly beautiful cultivar she had named "Hannah Ruth Meyers" in honor of the one she had come to love as if she were the daughter of her own flesh.

"You simply must stay the night in our guest cottage," Margit Van Burkleo insisted. "The hour grows late, and you can go on to Keukenhof Gardens in the morning, when the displays will be at their best in the morning light."

"You are too kind." Hannah gratefully accepted her most sincere invitation, very much looking forward to yet another lovely evening of fellowship with these modern-day Dutch saints, spent as in yesteryears before the glowing embers of the huge fireplace in the mansion.

The legendary Kuekenhoff Gardens were only minutes away from what was now the Van Burkleo Tulip Farm, thus, after an early breakfast and fond farewells, allowed only with the promise that she would one day return, Hannah made her way to the still nearly empty parking area of the gardens, where she chose a place very near the entrance for her rented Mercedes.

The beauty of her surroundings was beyond description as her breath was nearly taken away by the sheer wonder of God's handiwork, that His hand had rendered such awesome loveliness in bed after bed of majestic tulips, intermixed with all manner of other related bulb species. The scent of hyacinths was breathtaking, as if it were incense spread by holy censers to captivate all who were so greatly blessed to pass this way.

Yielding to her delicious weariness, after she had walked about this place for more than an hour, she decided to rest for a time on a wooden bench overlooking a glorious bed of yellow and orange tulips of various shades and shapes that were perfectly arranged to maximize both their individual and collective beauty.

"What a precious thing it was for me to revisit the farm," she spoke to herself contemplatively in a near whisper. "I felt like I was somehow stepping back through time—like nothing whatsoever had transpired—that somehow Theo and Gerta would be calling to me at any moment—"

Suddenly, she felt a wave of self-depreciation threatening to overtake her great joy and the sheer wonder of her surroundings. "What," she asked herself almost accusingly, "what have I accomplished with my life since the day I left this place? What have I done to justify Theo and Gerta's precious blood spilled in order to secure my survival? What, if anything, have I left behind for the next generation of other peoples' children that might at least in some small way touch them, benefit them, even remind them, however simply, that once I walked this way—that once I lived here, loved here, suffered here?" Then, nearly overcome, she gave up looking for some hidden deep meaning in all of this.

"Perhaps it's time for me to move on and leave these matters beyond my understanding to the loving God who brought me to this place," she concluded. With that, she stood and once more proceeded along the path that would eventually wind its way back to where it had begun.

Thus, she continued on, marveling at the glory of each heavenly crafted floral display as she moved from one beautifully rendered bed to the next, each one seemingly more lovely than the last.

Suddenly, as she rounded a curve in the pathway, she beheld a most extraordinary sight—a revelation of exquisite loveliness. By now, the rays of the late-morning sun had worked their way through the surrounding heavily leafed trees, providing a thick covering for the astoundingly beautiful beds of tulips, daffodils, and hyacinths that lay under their protection.

The bed before her, she immediately perceived, was planted exclusively with one extraordinary variety of tulip. It was now backlit in such a way that each of the several hundreds of stately tall, perfectly formed, long-stemmed, fluted, brilliantly red and white blossoms appeared as if they had opened for the first time with the rising sun that very morning.

Then, in a miraculous moment she recognized what God had once again brought before her eyes as she recalled and silently repeated the words Theo de Goede had spoken so long ago when he had taken his turn to examine for the first time God's handiwork manifested in the rich soil of the farm he so dearly treasured.

"This really is something special!" he had exclaimed excitedly. "Yes indeed, there is no other red and white tulip anywhere in the world nearly as lovely as this! This is one of those rare miracles we experience that makes our work among these lovely flowers so pleasing and rewarding. One day," he had predicted, "when we have been able to produce enough bulbs for national recognition, this cultivar will take its place among the loveliest tulips in the world."

Now, as Hannah stood before this awesome display, she continued with yet another joyful recollection as she tenderly remembered the great prophetic promise made by her beloved Gerta: "When this glorious flower does become famous in the eyes of the world, they will know it by a perfectly chosen and appropriate name." With that, Gerta had taken a label stake she had been concealing under her full sweater and carefully pushed it into the rich soil immediately in front of the newly flowering cultivar as she proclaimed: "From this day forward the world will know this glorious tulip by the name 'Hannah Ruth Meyers,'" the very same name that now, sixty-five years later, was wrought on the enduring large bronze label stake that marked this singularly, majestic, God-crafted display of these glorious blossoms.

Hannah stood transfixed before this awesome floral tribute that bore her name as she continued to recall Gerta's words: "No other name could be more fitting. The brilliant red of the flower is symbolic of your great courage and strength. Its alabaster white speaks fittingly of your remarkable loveliness and virginal purity. I could go on and on, but to summarize what I see in this incredible tulip: its elegance, beauty, strength, and so very much more are a God-painted portrait of our Hannah. May you and this precious new flower long survive in this world gone mad."

Hannah, still very much alone, overcome with emotion, and wearied by her advancing years sat down to rest for a time on a bench directly facing the awesome display of tulips that bore her name.

As she sat there, her tears flowing freely from the depths of her soul, driven by a poignant blend of joy, sadness, celebration, and sorrow, she conjectured, "How could the single cultivar that was crushed and drowned in Gerta's blood have survived, multiplied, and finally made its way to this place where its glory could be shared by the world?"

So deeply was she lost in the depths of her recollections she soon drifted off into a deep sleep, and she began to dream.

It wasn't long before she noticed that she was no longer sitting there alone. An elderly gentleman who had been sitting on a bench a short distance on the other side of the backlit bed, hidden from her view by the bright sun, had approached and was now standing beside her.

"Beautiful! Beautiful beyond description aren't they?" He spoke in a voice that was somehow distantly familiar.

Momentarily startled by his sudden appearance, she turned toward the man. Then, in an instant of incredulous recognition she cried out, "Michael? Dear God, Michael!"

"Hannah? My precious Hannah!" he exclaimed in joyous response as he reached for her. She stood and fell into his arms, and once again they were joined together after a near lifetime of separation.

"My darling Michael!" she exclaimed, nearly overwhelmed, as she gently ran her fingers through his thick, well-trimmed snow-white beard, seeking affirmation that this long-lost love of her life who had suddenly reappeared was real rather than some self-generated phantasmagoric apparition. "They told me you were dead, murdered along with Mutti and Vatti on our very first day at Auschwitz!"

"I was young and strong," he replied. "They kept me for a few days and then sent me off to Dachau, where I managed to survive until we were liberated by the Americans in late April 1945. I was nearly dead from disease and starvation, so they cared for me for two months until I was well enough to hurry back to Auschwitz to look for you. Of course, you weren't there—and the Russians had kept inadequate records that made no mention of you. So I went back to Bogenhausen, thinking that if you were still alive you might have gone there."

"Oh, Michael," she explained, "by then I had become a recluse—hiding in my sorrows where I mourned for you every day in a small apartment in Freising."

"Never mind!" he replied. "Surely, for reasons we may never fully understand, all of this was somehow God's will. Yeshua taught us how to pray to His Father, trusting and affirming 'Thy will be done!'"

Once again she was taken aback by yet another miraculous revelation—first the inexplicable resurrection of the one person she most loved in this world, and now the wonderful understanding that he too had apparently been saved by the precious blood of the Lamb. "Michael, are you a believer in Yeshua?" she asked with joyful incredulity.

"I am!" he replied excitedly, his countenance lighting up with the presence of the Holy Spirit within him. "I was saved in a small home group in Jerusalem, where I have lived since I made Aliyah in early 1946. Hannah, are you—"

She cut him off before he could complete his question. "I was saved very recently in Rabbi Drew Sterling's congregation in Tiberias," she exclaimed. "I moved there after I had lived for many years in Tel Aviv as a pathetic, faithless recluse."

"Dear God!" he exclaimed. "How absolutely amazing that we could have been so near to one another all of these years and yet so very far apart."

"Even more so," she replied wondrously, "that our dear God saw fit to bring us back together in this very special place. Michael, how is it that you happen to be here today?"

"My darling, ever since these gardens were first opened in 1960, I've come here without fail every year during tulip time. And I've sat near this gorgeous bed for the past ten years, ever since it was planted—every day as long as even one of these flowers bearing your name remained in bloom."

"Oh, Michael," she declared joyfully, "our sweet Yeshua has given us the most seemingly impossible desire of our hearts. Never again will we be apart, and then, my beloved, we will live together with our Lord in heaven forever."

They sat snuggled close together until the late afternoon shadows had grown long on this incredible day of their reunion. They hugged, kissed, touched, and often wept as they took turns pouring out the long-suppressed horrors they had endured since the Angel of Death had set them upon the ultimate horror of their now miraculously ended sixty-five years of separation.

Finally, as a cool afternoon breeze announced the soon coming of evening, Michael gently kissed his beloved bride, took her hands into his own, and helped her to her feet.

Then, in the realm of her consciousness, just as suddenly as Michael had appeared, he began to slip away. She struggled desperately to keep him there by her side, but try as she might, she awoke and once again discovered that she stood alone. But only for a moment.

Deep within her being she heard the same still, silent voice she had heard for the first time on the day she was immersed in the Jordan River.

"Come, My precious daughter," He spoke in a voice sweeter than that of all the angels—the font of all love. "What you saw and heard was not of your imagination. Your Michael abides with Me and I with him. He joyfully awaits the day when you will join him in heaven. But not just yet, My beloved daughter. I am calling you to return for a time to Israel, where you will continue to serve Me well. Come, Hannah. Come home with Me now to Israel, to the Land of your inheritance."

AFTERWORD
A CRY OF HOPE, A CALL TO ACTION

I am for freedom of religion and against all maneuvers to bring about a legal ascendancy of one sect over another.[1]
—THOMAS JEFFERSON

SURELY, MOST OUTSIDE observers would find it genuinely amazing, if not unbelievable, that the tiny 7-percent minority of ultra-Orthodox, Haredi religious extremists, through their political maneuverings, have acquired so much influence in the Israeli government. I have long looked for a way to rationalize the unseemly acquiescence of my fellow Israeli citizens to quietly accept such outrageous and continuing compromising of international law that has, among other things, stripped us all of our basic human rights. I cry out for the plight of my fellow Jews!

Since the founding of the State of Israel in 1948, many, perhaps even thousands, of ethnic Jews have been quietly denied Israeli citizenship and instead have been sent packing back to the place from whence they came, forever banished from receiving their God-given inheritance simply because as Jews, they had dared to embrace Yeshua, Jesus Christ, as their Messiah. All but a relative handful of those thus rejected from taking up their rightful place as citizens of the Land, their sacred biblical promise, have bowed their heads and departed without even a whimper of official protest.

The religious extremists have persuaded the Israeli government to deny countless Jews their God-given right to become citizens of the Land simply because, in their thinking, these inarguably ethnic Jews were somehow no longer Jews.

To strip any Jew of his or her Jewishness in keeping with the unbiblical edict of a long-dead rabbi is to make them no less a eunuch than the Michael Silberman of our story. To banish any Jew from the Land of his or her biblical inheritance is to steal his or her very soul.

I am fully persuaded that nothing of this profound injustice will change until the government of Israel is finally emboldened and persuaded, one way or another, to reverse the untoward influence of an extremist religious minority.

I am further persuaded that such change can only be achieved through sweeping electoral reform that in the end will produce a genuine democratic republic as envisioned by Ben-Gurion and the others. Such a Republic of Israel would be solidly reset upon a foundational constitution that, among other things, would, without any regard to religion, guarantee the basic human rights of all its citizens.

In the end, it seems to me that the hedonistic majority of voting Israelis all too often appears quite content to simply enjoy their "good lives" in the Land while blindly accepting the outrageously over-influential religious minority that has empowered itself to, as it may choose, blatantly ignore the professed guarantees of the state's founding fathers of an entirely free democratic republic where:

> Everyone has the right to freedom of thought, conscience and religion; this right includes freedom to change his religion or belief, and freedom, either alone or in community with others and in public or private, to manifest his religion or belief in teaching, practice, worship and observance.
>
> —Article 18, The Universal Declaration of Human Rights of the United Nations

Where, you may be wondering, can these so persecuted and banished would-be Israeli Jews who embrace Yeshua turn for relief? Can the many who remain American citizens (dual citizens) or certifiably legitimate potential citizens of Israel turn to the current government of the United States for assistance? I think not.

Here are just a few examples of why I have reached this unhappy conclusion:

- The government of the United States remains "officially" aware but is not directly involved with preventing the unceasing religious persecution that has become a way of life for its citizens who hold or seek dual Israeli citizenship while daring to embrace Yeshua, Jesus Christ as their Messiah. The US State Department publishes an annual report on world-wide "religious freedom" entitled "Report on International Religious Freedom" which is broken down into regions. A recent version (2008) of these reports for "Israel and the Occupied Territories" states in part:

> Israel has no Constitution; however, the Basic Law on Human Dignity and Liberty provides for freedom of worship. Government policy continued to support the generally free practice of religion; however, some increases in societal abuses and discrimination contributed to a slight decline in respect for religious freedom during the reporting period. Specifically, societal abuses and discrimination increased against some evangelical Christian groups as well as Messianic Jews (persons who identify as Jews and who believe Jesus was the Messiah).
>
> The Declaration of Independence and the Basic Law on Human Dignity and Liberty describe the country as a "Jewish and democratic state." Most members of the non-Jewish minority were generally free to practice their religious beliefs but were subject to various forms of discrimination, some of which have religious dimensions.[2]

- The US Supreme Court has outlawed school-sponsored prayer. Any kind of prayer, composed by public school districts, even nondenominational prayer, is now deemed unconstitutional government sponsorship of religion.[3]
- The federal government has banned any religious theme ornaments from being displayed on the national Christmas tree (holiday tree).[4]
- The Ten Commandments have been removed by court order from a number of public buildings in a number of states beginning as long ago as 2002.[5]
- A navy chaplain's fifteen-year military career was terminated because he dared to pray in Jesus' name and then later dared to lead prayer in Jesus' name in front of the White House.[6]

Thus, I'm sure many would agree that for those who have come from the United States seeking Israeli citizenship, only to be rejected on the basis of their religious worldviews, to turn to this government of the Land of their birth for relief would likely be an exercise in futility.

Hence, some would reasonably ask, "Since this is an Israeli issue, why not turn directly to the government of Israel?" Let me say simply, for reasons already stated, such a course of action taken by Jewish believers in Yeshua could well be likened instead to their jumping into a den of vipers.

"What then are these dear ones to do?" you may ask, if a direct response for relief from any government has seemingly no possibility of success.

Surely some would respond, "Let them turn to the body of Christ, their brothers and sisters in Jesus; let them call upon the church!"

While at first glance this may seem like a reasonable alternative, please consider the following sad report taken from my earlier work *The Ways of the Way.*[7]

The Pew Forum on Religion & Public Life seeks to promote a deeper understanding of issues at the intersection of religion and public affairs. The forum pursues its mission by conducting surveys and delivering timely, impartial information in four key areas of research, including religion. Most recently, in June 2008, the Pew Forum reported their findings from a "Survey of the United States Religious Landscape." These findings, based on interviews with more than thirty-five thousand American adults, detail the religious makeup, beliefs, and practices of the American public.[8]

I pray that the following summary of the most genuinely shocking results (adapted by the author from the report) will be the basis for a rallying cry from all believers, Jewish and Gentiles alike, crying out for the restoration of the body of Yeshua, the church.

Position Statement: "Many religions (other than Christianity) can lead to eternal life."

Members in agreement:

Mainline churches	83 percent
Evangelical churches	57 percent
Catholics	79 percent
Jews	82 percent

Position Statement: "Scripture (the Bible) is the word of God literally true, word for word."

Members in agreement:

Mainline churches	22 percent
Evangelical churches	59 percent
Catholics	23 percent
Jews (traditional)	10 percent

Position Statement: "Frequency of prayer: daily"

Members reporting:

Mainline churches	53 percent
Evangelical churches	78 percent
Catholics	58 percent
Jews (traditional)	26 percent

Position Statement: "Attend religious service once or more each week" Members reporting:

Mainline churches	34 percent
Evangelical churches	58 percent
Catholics	42 percent
Jews (traditional)	16 percent

These responses from the contemporary church beg the question: How would members of the Way have reacted to this same survey from Mount Zion during the mid-first century?

They were with Yeshua when they heard Him clearly say, "I am the way, the truth, and the life. No one comes to the Father except through Me" (John 14:6). Can we believe that 83 percent of the members of today's mainline churches and 57 percent of evangelicals do not believe Him? Do they think He was lying? God is incapable of lying (Num. 23:19).

The apostle John tells us, "In the beginning was the Word, and the Word was with God, and the Word was God" (John 1:1). Yeshua is at once the "living Word" and God incarnate. Thus, it follows that the written Word as it was originally given by God, through the power of the Holy Spirit, must also be perfect and without error.

The Didache, an early Nazarene text, instructed the early church to pray the Lord's Prayer three times each day. Paul instructed us all to "pray without ceasing" (1 Thess. 5:17). Again, I find it almost inconceivable that only 53 percent of "mainline Christians and 78 percent of evangelicals pray daily.

Members of the Way met each day in their homes and every *Motze Shabbat* (Saturday evening) as a congregation. How can it be that only 34 percent of modern-day mainline church members and 58 percent of evangelicals attend services once each week?

In the face of this devastating report on the condition of the modern-day church, consider this also: during the thirty-five years between 1967 and 2002, some 19.2 million members (25 percent) of the top five mainline church denominations left the rolls of their respective churches.[9]

As painful as the foregoing status of the church may be, it gets even worse, much worse. More than 75 percent of the American body of Christ embrace "replacement theology," the understanding that the church has replaced Israel and that God's promises to the Jews and God's promises to Israel have been abrogated, and now the people of God are the church.[10]

The remaining 25 percent of the body, the evangelicals, mostly reject this "replacement" understanding and remain strong spiritual and material supporters of both the Jews and Israel.[11] It is to these dear brothers and sisters, the only true potential earthly friends of the miniscule body of Yeshua-believing Jews who manage to remain in Israel and those who would follow them, I now turn.

Having read this book and meditated upon the ongoing battle for survival of the born-again Jewish believers of Israel, following are reasonable and responsible actions I believe you, my Christian brothers and sisters, can take that may one day lead to achieving the great hopes I have elaborated in this writing. I pray that you will take this matter to the Lord and then faithfully act upon what He may show you in this regard.

First and foremost, I urge you to pray frequently and faithfully for the survival and increase of the body of Israeli Jewish believers in Israel. Pray that those religious extremists within the Israeli government who persecute and seek to banish those Jews who embrace Yeshua will see the error of their ways, cease all forms of their opposition, and repent.

Pray also that the current government of Israel may, by divine intervention, realize both the urgency and foundational necessity to write and adopt a constitution that will eventually bring about the electoral reform of the state as it is suggested in the preceding pages.

Please, very carefully examine and verify precisely where your financial support intended to bless Israel has been and is currently being distributed. If you should determine that your urgently needed financial contributions, given through your church or larger outreach organization, flow in turn to and through some agency of the Israeli government, then consider the following:

- Some, perhaps a large portion of these funds, may be diverted to some entirely secular purpose(s).
- Some portion may pass into the hands of those who are steeped in various acts and forms of political corruption.

- The "religious" entities that ultimately receive what remains of your support will most likely be Orthodox and/or ultra-Orthodox that may well include the very extremist organizations described in the foregoing pages who directly and aggressively oppose the Yeshua-believing body.[12]

There are some 120-plus Messianic Jewish entities in Israel, most of them very small home groups with twenty or fewer participants. Many of these believers remain well below the poverty level and are struggling to survive in the Land to which they have been called. It is quite obvious that no agency of the government would intentionally pass on even a single shekel to any Messianic believer or group from the many millions of dollars donated to Israel each year by well-meaning Christians.

Several relief funds have been established within the Yeshua-believing community for the purpose, in part, of channeling donations from the church at large to the born-again believers in the Land. Following are two of these. I urge you to review them and seek divine guidance with respect to your financial outreach.

1. The Olim Fund of the Land of Israel (2004)

I am the cofounder of this *Amutah* (Israeli charity) first established as an unofficial entity in 1995 to meet the emergency survival needs of Olim (Jewish immigrants). The very low overhead fund currently has representatives in thirty different Yeshua-believing entities spread throughout the Land. Such things as emergency dental care, payment of rent to avoid eviction, payment of utilities to avoid their termination, coverage of emergency medical expenses not otherwise provided, and many other needs have been met. To date the fund has distributed approximately $1.5 million to more than two thousand hurting families and individuals. Our goal, entirely dependent upon financial support, is to one day soon be able to reach out to all 120-plus Yeshua-believing groups in the Land. The net proceeds I receive from the sale of my books are donated in their entirety to the Olim Fund. The fund, it should also be noted, distributes to Olim irrespective of their religion. See www.olimpublications.com for further details.

2. The Jerusalem Institute of Justice

The Declaration of the State of Israel, signed in 1948, emphasizes freedom of religion, conscience, language, education, and culture. However, many institutions in Israeli society do not support our forefathers' commitment to protecting citizens' rights and are guided instead by a blind devotion to maintaining an intolerant and religiously homogeneous environment. The Jerusalem Institute of Justice holds that a Jewish and democratic state is not a self-contradiction but rather an attainable reality. Rendering its democratic values within the justice system, Israel has the power to reinforce tolerance, truth, ethics, and morality, which serve to strengthen the fiber of the nation. Jerusalem Institute of Justice aims to create a better Israel for all citizens by advancing civil rights, freedom of religion, and social justice. They believe that by strengthening Israel's democracy, they are strengthening the legitimacy of Israel's existence as a Jewish state. For more details see http://www.jij.org.il/goals.php.

There are several other humanitarian funds and other sources of legal assistance dedicated to helping Jewish immigrants to Israel, each with its own unique and worthy focus. Moreover, most of the Messianic Congregations in the Land actively solicit financial assistance to help meet the survival needs of their members. I urge each of our Gentile brothers and sisters who are seeking how specifically God would have them fulfill their biblical call (Isaiah 60:5) to support our Jewish immigrants, to pray for His guidance, and to further search the Internet using, for example, "Messianic Jewish Humanitarian Relief Funds." Again, make certain that your support is not sent through some agency of the Israeli government to avoid the possibility of it being distributed for purposes which you did not intend.

Finally, as I conclude this writing during this time of great challenge and tribulation as we await the soon second coming of our blessed Lord, may we all, Jewish and Gentle believers alike, take much comfort in His wonderful and unbreakable promise to Israel:

> I will make you a great nation;
> I will bless you
> And make your name great;
> And you shall be a blessing.
> I will bless those who bless you,
> And I will curse him who curses you;
> And in you all the families of the earth shall be blessed.
>
> —Genesis 12:2–3

NOTES

Prologue

1. Zvi Zhor, "The Debate Around Conversion," HBI eZINE, http://www.brandeis.edu/hbi/614/archives/Volume%202/VII,%2013/article2a.html (accessed January 15, 2011).

2. "Once a Jew, Always a Jew," Newsletter, Jerusalem Institute of Justice, August 12, 2009, http://jerusaleminstituteofjustice.createsend.com/T/ViewEmail/r/0AD97A73AEDF6D6B (accessed January 15, 2011).

3. Israel Ministry of Foreign Affairs, "The Declaration of the Establishment of the State of Israel, May 14, 1948," http://www.mfa.gov.il/MFA/Peace%20Process/Guide%20to%20the%20Peace%20Process/Declaration%20of%20Establishment%20of%20State%20of%20Israel (accessed January 15, 2011).

4. United Nations, "Universal Declaration of Human Rights," Article 18, http://www.un.org/en/documents/udhr/ (accessed January 15, 2011).

5. Israel Ministry of Foreign Affairs, "Law of Return 5710-1950," including "Law of Return (Amendment No. 2) 5730-1970," http://www.mfa.gov.il/MFA/MFAArchive/1950_1959/Law%20of%20Return%205710-1950 (accessed January 15, 2011).

Introduction

1. *Reinforcement* is a technical term referring to the degree of security basic laws must have to remain in effect, and the size of this required special majority in the Knesset (the size of which depends on the type of basic law being proposed for amendment).

2. William J. Bennet, co-Director of Empower America, statement at an April 15, 2002, Israel Solidarity Rally, Washington DC, quoted in ProCon.org, "Israeli-Palestinian Conflict: Is Israel a Democracy?", http://israelipalestinian.procon.org/viewanswers.asp?questionID=357 (accessed January 15, 2011).

3. *Shomrei Israel* is a fictionalized name of the very real organization described in the following pages.

4. Michael Decker has a BA in law and is a licensed attorney in Israel. Mr. Decker also serves as senior legal advisor to the Jerusalem Institute of Justice.

5. Michael Decker, from the article "Revocation of Citizenship—Urgent Call for Amendment Messianic Legal Analysis; a New Campaign by Israel's Ministry of Interior to Revoke the Citizenship of Believers Highlights an Urgent Need for Reform," *Israel Today*, January 1, 2008.

Chapter 1
Hear O Israel: The Martyrdom of Stephen (circa A.D. 35)

1. Author's adaptation of Psalm 78:67–72.
2. Acts 7:51–53.
3. Acts 8:1–3.
4. Adolf Harnack, *Ausbreitung des Christentums* (Leipzig: n.p., 1902).
5. Colin McEvedy and Richard Jones, *Atlas of World Population History* (n.p:, 1978) and US Census Bureau.
6. Raymond Robert Fischer, *The Ways of the Way* (Lake Mary, FL: Creation House, 2009), 96.

Chapter 2
Hannah's Story

1. Excerpt from speech delivered by Adolf Hitler on German radio, January 30, 1939, http://www.jewishvirtuallibrary.org/jsource/Holocaust/hitjew.html (accessed January 15, 2011).
2. Sarah Ogilvie and Scott Miller, *Refuge Denied: The St. Louis Passengers and the Holocaust* (n.p.: University of Wisconsin Press, 2006), 18.
3. Joseph Goebbels, Hitler's minister of propaganda, had decided to use the S.S. *St. Louis* and her passengers in a master propaganda plan. With agents sent ahead to Havana to stir up anti-Semitism, Nazi propaganda fabricated and hyped the passengers' criminal nature, making them seem even more undesirable. The agents within Cuba stirred anti-Semitism and organized protests. Soon, an additional thousand Jewish refugees entering Cuba was seen as a threat.
4. While the saga of the S.S. *St. Louis* is historically accurate as to matters of essential fact, there are several versions of the motivations and specific activities of the central players and nations that were involved. For example, in his autobiography, Captain Schroeder pictures himself as totally dedicated to the terrible situation of his Jewish refugee passengers and even willing to risk the safety of his ship to land them safely in the United States. On the other hand, the official US government records paint quite a different story, never admitting to the allegations that the S.S. *St. Louis* and its passengers was quite deliberately and forcefully turned away from American waters. The truth probably lies somewhere between these versions. However, the fact is that virtually all of the ship's original passengers, except for those relatively few who were allowed sanctuary in Cuba and England, eventually became victims of Hitler's "Final Solution."

Chapter 3
Hear O Israel: The Martyrdom of James, Brother of Yeshua (Jerusalem, circa 62)

1. As interpreted by the author from the separate accounts provided by the ancient historians Hegesippus and Josephus.

2. Holy Apostles Convent, *The Lives of the Holy Apostles: The Apostle James, the Brother of the Lord*, from *The Menology of St. Dimitri The Great Synaxaristes of the Orthodox Church in Greek* (n.p.: Holy Apostles Convent Pubns, 1997), 271.

3. Jerome, *De Viris Illustribus*, quotes Hegesippus' account of James' holiness from the fifth book of Hegesippus' lost *Commentaries*.

4. Ibid.

5. James D. G. Dunn, *Beginning From Jerusalem* (Grand Rapids, MI: Wm. B. Eerdmans, 2009), 1089.

6. Lee W. Woodard, *First Century Gospels Found* (n.p.: n.d.), 91.

7. Arthur E. Palumbo, *The Dead Sea Scrolls and the Personages of Earliest Christianity* (n.p.: Algora Publishing, 2004), 265–267.

8. Marvin R. Wilson, *Our Father Abraham: Jewish Roots of the Christian Faith* (Grand Rapids, MI: Wm. B. Eerdmans, 1990), 76.

9. Author's adaptation and summary of the events derived from Hegesippus, *Fragments from His Five Books of Commentaries on the Acts of the Church*. Also, Holy Apostles Convent, *The Lives of the Holy Apostles*.

Chapter 4
Hannah's Story: Lisse, Holland (1939–1943)

1. Grant Jeffrey, *The Handwriting of God* (Wheaton, IL: Tyndale House, 1998). The Jewish understanding of the tri-unity of God is well summarized by this author.

2. In the days immediately following the Nazi invasion of their country, panic-stricken Dutch Jews attempted to escape from the country. Some made their way southward through France to eventually find sanctuary in Spain, Portugal, or Switzerland. Two hundred others, including eighty children, were evacuated to England.

3. A German civil administration was quickly installed under SS supervision. At its head was *Reichskommissar* (*Reich* Commissioner) Dr. Arthur Seyss-Inquart.

4. Beginning in January 1942, Jews were removed from the provinces and concentrated in Amsterdam. A camp had been established in 1939 at Westerbork in the northeast of Holland for the detention of illegal immigrants. Now, stateless Jews were interned there. A second camp was established at Vught in the south of the country. By April 1943, Jews had been prohibited from living anywhere in the Netherlands, other than in Amsterdam, Westerbork, or Vught.

5. The account of the Westerbork Transit Camp that follows is entirely historical except for the fictional background and characters in which it is set. Many detailed articles about the camp can be found through a search for "Westerbork" on the Internet, several of which were the source for the following account.

6. Rabbinical Judaism avoids using any direct reference to God's name or any biblical reference to it with the understanding that to do so would be to open up the possibility that this name might be taken in vain. Hence, many substitutions are undertaken, such as: Jehovah (the Hebrew vowel points derived from

YHWH), Adonai, G-D, L-rd, and commonly Ha Shem (meaning literally "the name").

7. In the end, more than 103,000 of Holland's 160,000 Jews were transferred from Westerbork to Auschwitz or Sobibor (another extermination camp in Poland).

Chapter 5
Hear O Israel: Rabbi Akiva and the Emergence of Rabbinical Judaism (The Estate of Kalba Savua, March A.D. 75)

1. The biographical account of Rabbi Akiva in these pages is the author's adaptation taken from Meir Lehmann, *Akiva: The Story of Rabbi Akiva and His Times* (New York: Feldheim Publishers, 2003).

2. *Talmud* (Ned. 50a, Ket. 62b et seq.).

3. Joseph Telushkin, *Jewish Literacy: The Most Important Things to Know About the Jewish Religion, Its People and Its History* (New York: William Morrow and Co., 1991).

4. Ignazio Mancini, Ignazio *Archeologiacal Discoveries (Relative to the Judeo-Christians)* (Jerusalem: Franciscan Printing Press, 1968).

Chapter 6
Hannah's Story: Auschwitz-Birkenau Extermination Camp (Poland: July 1943)

1. The specific events that occurred at Auschwitz as noted in this narrative are, of course, fictional, set in the experiences of fictional characters of my invention. However, each and every atrocity noted is based on historically valid and carefully researched truth. Those horrendous acts attributed to Dr. Mengele and others are well documented and taken from historically accurate sources.

Chapter 7
Hear O Israel: The First Holy Crusade (Claremont, France, November 27, 1095)

1. Dr. E. L. Knox, summary of Pope Urban II's speech, Global Ministries, the United Methodist Church, http://gbgm-umc.org/umw/bible/crusades.stm (accessed January 17, 2011).

2. Larry Domnitch, "Commemorating the Crusader Attack Upon Jerusalem," *Jerusalem Magazine*, August 2003.

Chapter 8
Messianic Synagogue Beth Emeth: Jerusalem (Shabbat, January 15, 1099)

1. Ibid. The Crusaders' barbarous burning of Jews in their synagogues is a well-documented historical fact. The account of their burning this messianic congregation is a product of the author's creation.

Chapter 10
Hear O Israel: Golda Meir and the Law of Return (Jerusalem, 1969–1970)

1. Jonathan Rosen, "Unsettled: So Was It Odd of God?", *New York Times*, December 14, 2003.

Chapter 12
Hannah's Story: Tiberias (May 2009)

1. Orthodox Jews, and some others, often refer to God as *Ha Shem* (literally, "the name") in order to avoid using His actual name *Yahweh* or even the word "God" or "Lord" to avoid the possibility of inadvertently taking His name in vain.

Chapter 13
Hear O Israel: A Compendium of Sorrows

1. Michael Dearington, "Israeli Citizenship," http://st2008.trincoll.edu/~mdearin2/Israeli%20Citizenship.htm (accessed January 19, 2011).
2. Michael Decker, "Messianic Jews and the Law of Return," *Israel Today*, September 24, 2007.
3. Ibid.
4. Justice Netanyahu rejected the other families' appeal for other reasons, which do not pertain to this issue.
5. Jerusalem Institute of Justice, e-newsletter, August 28, 2009.
6. Jerusalem Institute of Justice, e-newsletter, March 29, 2009.
7. Larry Derfner, "Watch Out, Missionaries!", *Jerusalem Post*, July 3, 2009.
8. Telephone conversation with Pastor Howard Bass, June 24, 2009; article in the *Jerusalem Post*; a variety of other news sources; and personal e-mails. For a detailed account of the events of this litigation as they occurred, see Congregation Yeshua's Inheritance website, "Streams in the Negev," www.streamsinthenegev.com.
9. Howard Bass, "Lawsuit Update—Verdict Update," Streams in the Negev, June 3, 2010, http://streamsinthenegev.com/lawsuit/lawsuit-update-verdict/ (accessed January 19, 2011).
10. Chris Mitchell, "Turning Up the 'Heat' on Messianic Jews," CBN News, June 4, 2008, http://www.cbn.com/cbnnews/385992.aspx (accessed January 19, 2011).

11. The principal source of this account is the Oritz Family Homepage, created by Avi's mother to memorialize the events surrounding this savage incident. See: http://www.amiortiz.com.

12. Josh Mitnik, "Israel Moves to Rein In Right-Wing Extremists," *Christian Science Monitor*, November 4, 2009, http://www.csmonitor.com/World/Middle-East/2009/1104/p90s01-wome.html (accessed January 19, 2011).

13. Chaim Levinson, "Jewish Terror Suspect 'Unfit to Stand Trial,'" Haaretz.com, May 4, 2010, http://www.haaretz.com/news/national/jewish-terror-suspect-unfit-to-stand-trial-1.288172 (accessed January 19, 2011).

14. Ben Hartman, "Two Haredi Men Held for Allegedly Torching Messianic Jew's Car in Beit She'an," *Jerusalem Post*, December 3, 2009, as related in Jerusalem Institute of Justice, "Persecution in Beit She'an," http://jij.org.il/blog/?p=3 (accessed January 19, 2011).

Chapter 14
Hannah's Story: On the Jordan River (Shabbat, May 9, 2009)

1. "Yeshu" has been used by Jews who oppose *Yeshua* (Hebrew, "salvation") from the first century, beginning in the first believing community on Mount Zion. It is an acronym for the Hebrew expression *yemach shemo vezichro,* meaning "May his name and memory be obliterated," a term traditionally used for those deemed guilty of enticing Jews to idolatry and used in place of the real names of individuals guilty of such sins who are deemed not worthy of being remembered in history.

2. Dead Sea Scrolls (4Q541 9, 1, 1–6).

3. John 8:12.

Chapter 15
Hannah's Story: Tiberias (Motze Shabbat, May 16, 2009)

1. From "Elegy Written in a Country Church-Yard" by Thomas Gray (1716–1771).

Chapter 21
Hannah's Story: Jerusalem (Supreme Court of the State of Israel: Sunday, January 10, 2010)

1. Chief Justice Earl Warren, *Trop v. Dulles*, 1958.

Chapter 22
Hannah's Story: Jerusalem (Supreme Court of the State of Israel: Monday, January 11, 2010)

1. Jill Nelson, "Men in Black," *World Magazine,* April 5, 2008, http://www.worldmag.com/articles/13892 (accessed January 22, 2011).

2. The data concerning Shomrei Israel was suggested by and inferred from several sources, such as *Ha'aretz* article titled "Unbelievable," October 3, 2009.

Chapter 23
Hannah's Story: Jerusalem (Supreme Court of the State of Israel: Tuesday, January 12, 2010)

1. According to figures from the Israel Central Bureau of Statistics for 2007, the latest year such information was available, 7 percent of the Jewish population is ultra-Orthodox, 10 percent is Orthodox, 39 percent describe themselves as "traditional religious" or "traditional non-religious," and 44 percent describe themselves as "non-religious/secular" Jews, most of whom observe some Jewish traditions. Source: U.S. Department of State, International Religious Freedom 2009 Report.

2. Shai Lavi, "Citizenship Revocation as Punishment: On the Modern Bond of Citizenship and its Criminal Breach," http://www.law.utoronto.ca/documents/conferences2/Constitutionalism09-Lavi.pdf (accessed January 22, 2011).

3. Australian Prayer Network, "Supreme Court Says Messianic Jews Must Receive Equal Treatment Under Law," September 29, 2008, http://www.opentheword.org/index.php?option=com_content&view=article&id=1172:supreme-court-says-messianic-jews-must-receive-equal-treatment-under-law&catid=28:christian-news&Itemid=123 (accessed January 22, 2011).

Chapter 24
Hannah's Story: Jerusalem (Supreme Court of the State of Israel: Wednesday, January 13, 2010)

1. Mayrav Saar, "Genetic Testing Raises an Age-Old Question—Are the Jews a People, or a Religion?", *New York Post*, June 13, 2010, http://www.nypost.com/p/news/opinion/opedcolumnists/genetic_testing_raises_people_religion_JfhLi1jF4WntIkfx46Mi6J (accessed January 23, 2011).

2. *Jerusalem Institute for Justice*, "Once a Jew, Always a Jew?", MessianicDailyNews.com, *September 10, 2009, http://messianicdailynews.com/showarticle.shtml?&file=08132009-1138.html (accessed January 23, 2011).*

3. Mishneh Torah, Avodat Kochavim 2:5. See also Maimonides, Hilchot Mamrim Perek 3, Halacha 1–3.

Chapter 25
Hannah's Story: Jerusalem (Supreme Court of the State of Israel: Wednesday, January 14, 2010)

1. Jerusalem Institute of Justice, "Bibi's 'Mission' Impossible," Enewsletter, March 29, 2009, http://jerusaleminstituteofjustice.cmail1.com/T/ViewEmail/r/41BD0025D9087D7C (accessed January 23, 2011).

2. Ibid.

Afterword
A Cry of Hope, a Call to Action

1. Letter of Thomas Jefferson to Elbridge Gerry, 1799, viewed at Thomas Jefferson Quotes on Christianity and Religious Tolerance, http://www.worldfuturefund.org/wffmaster/Reading/Religion/Jefferson.htm (accessed January 23, 2011).

2. US Department of State, "2008 Report on International Religious Freedom: Israel and the Occupied Territories," http://www.state.gov/g/drl/rls/irf/2008/108484.htm (accessed January 23, 2011).

3. *Engel v. Vitale* 82 S.Ct. 1261 (1962).

4. Free Republic, "Federal Government Bans Religious References on Ornaments for 2009 Capitol Christmas Tree," October 1, 2009, http://www.freerepublic.com/focus/news/2352322/posts (accessed January 23, 2011).

5. Religious Tolerance.org, The Ten Commandments: Legal Developments, 2002, http://www.religioustolerance.org/chr_10cb.htm (accessed January 23, 2011).

6. Baptist Press News, "Navy Chaplain Ousted on Grounds Overturned by Congress," January 17, 2007.

7. Raymond Robert Fischer, *The Ways of the Way* (Lake Mary, FL: Creation House, 2009), 3–4.

8. Pew Forum on Religion and Public Life, *U.S. Religious Landscape Survey*, June 2008, http://religions.pewforum.org/portraits.

9. *Charisma*, "The Decline of the Mainline Church," March 2000, 61; and National Council of Churches, "Membership Statistics for the National Council of Churches Member Communions," http://www.electronic church.org/2002/NCC_members.htm.

10. Pew Research Center Publications, "God's Country? Evangelicals and U.S. Foreign Policy," September 26, 2006, http://pewresearch.org/pubs/73/gods-country (accessed January 23, 2011).

11. Ibid.

12. Nelson, "Men in Black."

About the Author

Raymond Robert "Bob" Fischer, the author of *The Ways of The Way* and five earlier works, has lived in Tiberias, Israel since emigrating in 1992. Bob served the land of his birth in the U.S. Air Force from which he retired in 1984 as a Lieutenant Colonel. His second career with the Boeing Company as an international marketing manager was interrupted after nine years by his Biblical call home to Israel, the Land of his Inheritance. Bob is a born-again Jew and his wife, Donna, is married into the covenant. Bob holds a master's degree and a doctorate of humane letters from Faith Evangelical Seminary. Bob is the director of The Olim Fund of the Land of Israel, an Israeli charity providing emergency survival assistance for Jewish immigrants.

Contact the Author

For more information about the author or the Olim Fund, visit their website:

www.olimpublications.com